927

POLITICAL DISAGRI

The Survival of Diverse Opinions within
Communication Networks

Not only is political disagreement widespread within the communication networks of ordinary citizens, but political diversity within these networks is
entirely consistent with a theory of democratic politics built on the importance of individual interdependence. Contrary to commonly held theoretical
expectations, the persistence of political diversity and disagreement does not
imply that political interdependence is absent among citizens or that political
influence is lacking. This book's analysis makes a number of contributions.
The authors demonstrate the ubiquitous nature of political disagreement, even
within the networks and contexts that comprise the micro-environments of
democratic citizens. They show that communication and influence within
dyads is autoregressive – that the consequences of dyadic interactions depend on the distribution of opinions within larger networks of communication. They argue that the autoregressive nature of political influence serves to
sustain disagreement within patterns of social interaction, as it restores the
broader political relevance of social communication and influence.

Robert Huckfeldt is a Distinguished Professor of Political Science at the University of California at Davis. His interests lie in the areas of elections, public
opinion, political communication, urban politics, and, more generally, in the
relationships among groups and individuals in politics.

Paul E. Johnson is a Professor of Political Science at the University of Kansas.
His work includes applications of game theory, social choice theory, and
complexity theory. He currently has an avid interest in the development of
tools for agent-based modeling and computer simulation in the social sciences,
and he is an active contributor to the development of the Swarm Simulation
System.

Professor John Sprague has written on voting and elections, the history of
socialist voting, voting patterns in the U.S. Supreme Court, lawyers in politics, and crime, including homicide. His academic career has been wholly
at Washington University in St. Louis, where he has served as the Sidney
W. Souers Professor in Political Science, as well as chair of the Department of
Political Science.

CAMBRIDGE STUDIES IN PUBLIC OPINION AND POLITICAL PSYCHOLOGY

Series Editors

Dennis Chong, *Northwestern University*
James H. Kuklinski, *University of Illinois, Urbana-Champaign*

Cambridge Studies in Public Opinion and Political Psychology publishes innovative research from a variety of theoretical and methodological perspectives on the mass public foundations of politics and society. Research in the series focuses on the origins and influence of mass opinion, the dynamics of information and deliberation, and the emotional, normative, and instrumental bases of political choice. In addition to examining psychological processes, the series explores the organization of groups, the association between individual and collective preferences, and the impact of institutions on beliefs and behavior.

Cambridge Studies in Public Opinion and Political Psychology is dedicated to furthering theoretical and empirical research on the relationship between the political system and the attitudes and actions of citizens.

Books in the series are listed on the page following the Index.

POLITICAL DISAGREEMENT

The Survival of Diverse Opinions within Communication Networks

ROBERT HUCKFELDT
University of California, Davis

PAUL E. JOHNSON
University of Kansas

JOHN SPRAGUE
Washington University in St. Louis

CAMBRIDGE
UNIVERSITY PRESS

PUBLISHED BY THE PRESS SYNDICATE OF THE UNIVERSITY OF CAMBRIDGE
The Pitt Building, Trumpington Street, Cambridge, United Kingdom

CAMBRIDGE UNIVERSITY PRESS
The Edinburgh Building, Cambridge, CB2 2RU, UK
40 West 20th Street, New York, NY 10011-4211, USA
477 Williamstown Road, Port Melbourne, VIC 3207, Australia
Ruiz de Alarcón 13, 28014 Madrid, Spain
Dock House, The Waterfront, Cape Town 8001, South Africa

http://www.cambridge.org

First published 2004

Printed in the United States of America

Typeface Sabon 10/12 pt.   *System* LATEX 2_ε [TB]

A catalog record for this book is available from the British Library.

Library of Congress Cataloging in Publication data

Huckfeldt, R. Robert.
Political disagreement : the survival of diverse opinions within communication
networks / Robert Huckfeldt, Paul E. Johnson and John Sprague.
   p.   cm. – (Cambridge studies in political psychology and public opinion)
Includes bibliographical references and index.
ISBN 0-521-83430-9 (hb) – ISBN 0-521-54223-5 (pb)
1. Communication in politics.   2. Political participation.   3. Consensus
(Social sciences)   4. Public opinion.   5. Democracy.   I. Johnson, P. E. (Paul E.)
II. Sprague, John D.   III. Title.   IV. Series.
JA85.H83   2004
320'.01'4–dc22   2003067589

ISBN 0 521 83430 9 hardback
ISBN 0 521 54223 5 paperback

For
Sharon, Carolyn, and Carol

Contents

Contents

Contents

Contents

Figures

xiii

Figures

Tables

Tables

Tables

Acknowledgments

Turning a question on its head sometimes ends up being a productive exercise. Arthur Conan Doyle took advantage of this fact when he led Holmes to wonder why the dog had failed to bark. For us, the original motivating question was, what are the sources and consequences of agreement and homogeneity within political communication networks? We do not apologize for the question. Quite to the contrary, we think it continues to raise important issues and yield fundamental insights regarding the nature of groups and individuals in politics.

At the same time, the structure of any question is self-limiting, as it excludes important observations that do not qualify as answers. By turning the original question on its head, we thus open up a new set of possibilities, asking, if individuals are interdependent, what are the circumstances that make it possible for disagreement to survive? We kept bumping up against this question in various settings: when we encountered empirical evidence pointing to the persistence of disagreement within the context of influential communication processes; when we studied racial polarization in politics – a situation in which political heterogeneity within racial groups *has* come close to disappearing far too often; when we realized the imperfect fit between the classic literature on small group influence and the typical contexts of political persuasion.

The result of this exercise is the recognition that persistent disagreement and diversity within communication networks does not necessarily constitute evidence of individual independence. In some contexts, heterogeneity may indeed be a consequence of individual independence. At the same time, and in other contexts, agreement *and* disagreement may *both* be understood within the context of influential patterns of political communication among citizens.

This book represents a continuing preoccupation for all three of us. We have pursued these themes individually as well as collectively for some time, and none of us has any intention of stopping any time soon.

Acknowledgments

This may be mixed news for the colleagues and friends who so generously put up with our questions and arguments and requests! (But so it goes.) In anticipation, we thank them all, as well as singling out several for special attention: Brady Baybeck, Bob Boynton, Ted Carmines, Mike Craw, Russ Fazio, Ron Francisco, Charles Franklin, Erik Herron, Carol Kohfeld, Ken'ichi Ikeda, Bob Jackman, Ron Lake, Howie Lavine, Jan Leighley, Milton Lodge, Jeff Mondak, Diana Mutz, Franz Pappi, Bob Salisbury, Gina Sapiro, Mark Schneider, Randy Siverson, Paul Sniderman, and Walt Stone.

We are also grateful to the Political Psychology series editors at Cambridge University Press, Jim Kuklinski and Dennis Chong, as well as to the Political Science editor, Lew Bateman. A number of colleagues have provided us with valuable opportunities to present the project on their campuses: Barry Ames, Larry Bartels, Frank Baumgartner, Kevin Corder, Bob Erikson, Susan Herbst, Jan Leighley, Tali Mendelberg, Peter Nardulli, and Alan Zuckerman. Peter Mohler, Rüdiger Schmitt-Beck, and colleagues at the Zentrum für Umfragen, Methoden und Analysen in Mannheim have, over a number of years, provided a particularly fertile environment for many of the ideas in this manuscript to develop. Several collaborators – Jeff Levine, Jeanette Morehouse, and Tracy Osborn – made fundamental contributions to parts of the manuscript.

We are also grateful to several journal publishers and editors, first for publishing our work, and then for giving us the permission to incorporate the work into this book. Cambridge University Press gave permission to employ work in Chapter 4 that was previously published as: R. Huckfeldt, J. Levine, and J. Sprague. 2000. "The Dynamics of Collective Deliberation in the 1996 Election: Campaign Effects on Accessibility, Certainty, and Accuracy." *American Political Science Review* 94 (3): 641–51. An earlier version of Chapter 5 was published by Blackwell Publishing as: R. Huckfeldt, P. E. Johnson, and J. Sprague. 2002. "Political Environments, Political Dynamics, and the Survival of Disagreement," *Journal of Politics* 64: 1–21. And an earlier version of Chapter 8 was published by Blackwell Publishing as: R. Huckfeldt, J. Morehouse Mendez, and T. Osborn. 2004. "Disagreement, Ambivalence, and Engagement: The Political Consequences of Heterogeneous Networks," *Political Psychology* 25: 65–96.

The Center for Survey Research at Indiana University in Bloomington was our collaborator in the Indianapolis–St. Louis Project. We are particularly grateful to the director, John Kennedy, as well as to the assistant directors, Nancy Bannister and Kevin Tharp. When we came up with seemingly bizarre ideas, they never blinked. Indeed, they shared our enthusiasm. Their professionalism, expertise, dedication, and creativity were indispensable to the project.

Acknowledgments

The computer model that we developed for this project was a beneficiary of many useful pieces of advice as well as several improvements in the Swarm libraries themselves. The members of the Swarm Development Group as well as the larger Swarm community supplied valuable help at many stages through the Swarm-support e-mail list. In particular, we received great advice from Marcus Daniels of the Santa Fe Institute, Rick Riolo of the University of Michigan, and Lars Erik Cederman, then at UCLA, now at the Swiss Federal Institute of Technology.

We are also indebted to the National Science Foundation for support provided through grant SBR-9515314 to Huckfeldt and Sprague and grant SBR-9709404 to Johnson.

Finally, we dedicate this effort to our truly significant others – Sharon, Carolyn, and Carol.

I

Communication, Influence, and the Capacity of Citizens to Disagree

There is a limit to the legitimate interference of collective opinion with individual independence; and to find that limit, and maintain it against encroachment, is as indispensable to a good condition of human affairs as protection against political despotism.

John Stuart Mill. 1859 (1984). *On Liberty*. New York: Penguin Classics, p. 63.

Democratic electorates are composed of individually interdependent, politically interconnected decision makers. These individual citizens do not go it alone in democratic politics – they depend on one another for political information and guidance, and hence political communication and persuasion lie at the core of citizenship and democratic politics. At the same time, the vitality of democratic politics also depends on the capacity of citizens to disagree – to reject as well as to accept the viewpoints of others. The questions thus arise, are citizens capable of maintaining durable patterns of both agreement and dissent within their closely held social groups? What are the circumstances that give rise to both agreement and disagreement within the networks that connect citizens in ongoing patterns of political communication?

The capacity of citizens and electorates for tolerating political disagreement constitutes a central issue in democratic politics. The model of a free, open, and democratic society is one in which political issues are fully explored, and political debates are fully aired. In such a society, citizens are open to persuasion but sympathetic to ongoing disagreement, the social boundaries on political viewpoints are fluid and shifting, and individuals encounter the full spectrum of issue positions and political viewpoints.

How does this model correspond to contemporary analyses of citizens, communication, and disagreement in democratic politics? How does it correspond to the empirical reality of political communication among citizens?

We observe numerous examples in which disagreement and dissent are seemingly squeezed out of the political communication process among citizens. In a particularly compelling case, disagreement became quite difficult in the aftermath of the traumatic events that occurred on the morning of September 11, 2001. The horror of jet passenger planes slamming into the World Trade Center and the Pentagon carried profound political consequences, not only for American relations with Afghanistan, the Middle East, and the rest of the world, but also for patterns of communication and the expression of political viewpoints among Americans.

A well documented consequence of national crises is the phenomenon in which presidents receive increased levels of popular support, but another related consequence is the increased difficulty experienced by dissenting voices. Several months after the disaster, the publisher of the *Sacramento Bee* was shouted down and kept from finishing her graduation speech at the Sacramento campus of California State University when she attempted to warn the audience of the danger that the crisis posed for fundamental civil liberties (*Sacramento Bee*, December 21, 2001: p. L6).

Events such as this provide vivid and compelling examples of the difficulties posed by disagreement within the context of strongly held beliefs among citizens. Indeed, the tolerance of dissenting voices represents a state of affairs that is often quite fragile, but at the same time crucial to the vitality of democratic politics. Our primary concern is not with speeches and newspapers and politicians, but rather with citizens and their capacity for tolerating disagreement in their relations with one another. The difficulties and challenges posed by disagreement are certainly not unique to the public sphere. Rather, these problems penetrate closely held patterns of political communication among and between citizens in democratic politics.

THE IMPORTANCE OF DISAGREEMENT
IN DEMOCRATIC POLITICS

Why is political disagreement important? More to the point, why are patterns of disagreement among citizens important? The most direct answer is that the legitimacy of conflict and hence the legitimacy of disagreement lie at the irreducible core of democratic politics. It is perhaps safe to say that a democracy without conflict and disagreement is not a democracy. Democratic institutions are not designed to eliminate conflict and disagreement, but only to manage disagreement in a productive manner. In the words of James Madison, taken from the *Federalist 10*: "The latent causes of faction are thus sown in the nature of man; and we see them everywhere brought into different degrees of activity, according to the different circumstances of civil society."

Hence, a central reason for focusing on disagreement relates to the *"different circumstances of civil society"* that affect the capacity of citizens – both as individuals and as groups – to deal constructively with political disagreement and conflict. There is more than ample justification in the historical record to generate concern regarding the capacity of citizens for constructive disagreement. Americans justifiably take pride in the world's longest surviving democratic constitution, but a candid assessment of our political history recognizes a series of democratic failures related to deeply imbedded patterns of conflict and disagreement. The American Civil War – the bloodiest war in American history and the bloodiest war fought anywhere in the nineteenth century – was motivated by the disintegrating consequences of *internally generated* conflict and disagreement organized on a sectional basis. A long and continuing history of racial and ethnic conflict includes race riots, lynch mobs, and the denial of civil rights. And political violence, in various forms, has been an integral part of our political history as well. Hence, one might say that the unruly and intolerant audience that made it impossible for the *Bee*'s publisher to finish her speech was perhaps notable, but not entirely out of the ordinary.

Several different bodies of scholarship have considered the capacity of citizens for responding to political disagreement in a way that coincides with the requirements of democratic politics. One literature focuses directly on political tolerance – the individual circumstances that give rise to tolerance, its incidence in the population, and the meaning of tolerance in political terms. A breakthrough in this literature came in the recognition by Sullivan, Piereson, and Marcus (1982) that tolerance only takes on meaning in the context of political disagreement – that tolerance is only relevant with respect to groups and causes that an individual finds truly objectionable. Hence, political tolerance among liberal Democrats might be conceived in terms of their willingness to tolerate anti-abortion demonstrations in front of abortion clinics, just as political tolerance among conservative Republicans might be conceived in terms of their willingness to tolerate the exercise of abortion rights.

A second body of scholarship focuses on political deliberation among citizens and its potential for enhancing the quality of democratic politics (for example, Fishkin 1991, 1995; Gutmann and Thompson 1996; Rawls 1996). Whereas definitions of deliberation vary across theorists, Mendelberg (2002) distills several ingredients that are particularly important for empirical investigation: Deliberation often takes place in small groups. It involves the egalitarian and open-minded exchange of viewpoints and positions. And it has the potential to produce higher levels of political engagement, tolerance, and compromise among competing viewpoints.

A crucial insight of the deliberation theorists, particularly relevant to our purposes, is that tolerance, compromise, and engagement are anchored in the personal experience of political diversity. In this way the benefits of deliberation depend on disagreement, where disagreement is defined in terms of interaction among citizens who hold divergent

3

viewpoints and perspectives regarding politics. In summary, both tolerance and deliberation lose meaning absent disagreement, and we are particularly concerned with the experience of disagreement within closely
held networks of political communication.

At the same time, the presence of disagreement and political heterogeneity within communication networks provides no guarantee of either
tolerance or deliberation. In particular, political disagreement may fail to
be communicated effectively – individuals may ignore, avoid, or dismiss
politically disagreeable viewpoints, thereby rendering communication ineffective. In this context, it becomes important to make a primary analytic distinction between the effectiveness and the persuasiveness of communication. The communication that occurs between two individuals is
effective when each individual understands the message being transmitted
by the other individual. The same communication is *persuasive* when one
of the individuals changes her opinion or preference as a consequence. A
primary challenge of this book is to examine the factors that give rise to
effective communication, as well as the factors that give rise to persuasive communication, and to understand the role of *both* effectiveness *and*
persuasiveness with respect to the survival of political disagreement.

Disagreement that persists in the context of fully and effectively communicated viewpoints is not inconsistent with either tolerance or deliberation. Effective communication, as opposed to persuasive communication,
does not imply that disagreement should necessarily disappear – citizens
may agree to disagree based on their own understanding of one another's
viewpoints. To the contrary, the persistence of disagreement in the context of effective communication is evidence of democratic vitality rather
than failure. In contrast, if communication among citizens is rendered ineffective by the presence of disagreement, then the potential for tolerant
citizens to be engaged in a productive process of political deliberation is
rendered problematic. If disagreement is incompatible with the possibility
of effective communication, then deliberative democracy is a contradic-
tion in terms.

Viewed from a different perspective, it is conceivable that tolerant citizens might be well equipped to engage in a productive process of political
deliberation, even though on a day-to-day basis they are imbedded within
politically homogeneous networks of like-minded citizens. This is especially true to the extent that tolerance is a normative commitment made
by particular individuals, rather than a socially learned habit encouraged
by systematic and recurrent processes of social interaction.

In a similar vein, opportunities for political deliberation can be created
through opportunities that are designed to be independent from ongoing, everyday patterns of social interaction and political communication.
Most theorists of political deliberation are less concerned with patterns of

recurrent, informal, face-to-face communication regarding politics than with processes of "public reason" (Rawls 1996: 212 ff.) that occur in "the land of middle democracy" (Gutmann and Thompson 1996: 12). The focus is more generally on public settings that provide the need and opportunity for people to confront fundamental forms of moral disagreement. In this context, Fishkin (1995) has sponsored structured public forums which create opportunities for strangers to come together voluntarily in order to discuss political issues and controversies.

Our own view is that the likelihood of a political system characterized by high levels of tolerance is reduced to the extent that political tolerance depends on individually based normative commitments disembodied from social interaction. As Gibson (1992: 350) demonstrates, "(w)hy people differ in their levels of intolerance – and with what consequences – cannot be well understood by conceptualizing the individual in social isolation." Moreover, he shows that homogeneous peer groups, less tolerant spouses, and less tolerant communities place limits on the freedom perceived by individual citizens. Hence, we expect that normative commitments to tolerance and democratic ideals are likely to be short-lived unless they are reinforced through application in naturally occurring contexts of political communication (Gibson 2001).

Similarly, to the extent that opportunities for political deliberation must be created through town hall meetings and specially designed events that are separate and apart from normally employed networks of political communication, the potential for widespread deliberation is likely to be severely curtailed. This is not to minimize the importance of efforts aimed at providing formally and institutionally based opportunities for collective deliberation. Rather, the success of these efforts is likely to depend on the vitality of political communication closer to home – within naturally occurring communication networks.

Even if our view is incorrect – even if we are on the verge of a democratic renaissance in which the individual commitment to political tolerance becomes widespread and citizens make use of opportunities for discussing politics in open forums with strangers – the study of political disagreement is justifiable on its own terms. Substantial bodies of important theoretical work point toward the politically disabling consequences of disagreement (Lazarsfeld, Berelson, and Gaudet 1948; Berelson, Lazarsfeld, and McPhee 1954; Mutz and Martin 2001; Mutz 2002a; Mutz 2002b). Other bodies of important work point to the problematic capacity of maintaining disagreement within a population as the stable equilibrium outcome of a dynamic communication process (Abelson 1964, 1979; Axelrod 1997a, 1997b). But if disagreement produces a political angst that leads to a withdrawal from civic life on the part of individual citizens, or if political diversity is inevitably eliminated as a consequence of communication among citizens, where are we left with respect to the capacity of citizens for the give-and-take that is so crucial to life in a democracy? The ironic result is that disagreement is always on the verge of being eliminated, and the only individuals who are equipped to take on the full role of a participatory citizen are those imbedded within cozy cocoons of like-minded associates.

Finally, this book is not about tolerance or deliberation more narrowly conceived, but rather about the reality of political diversity and political discussion within the lives of everyday citizens – the patterns of disagreement among citizens who regularly communicate regarding politics. We expect that these patterns of disagreement define the potential for tolerance and deliberation within political systems, but the importance of disagreement to democratic politics extends beyond these matters to include fundamental issues regarding political change and the nature of citizenship. If citizens are incapable of accommodating disagreement and hence adopt agreeable preferences that yield political homogeneity within communication networks, then methodological individualism and the role of individual citizens are fundamentally called into question. Political analysts might be well advised to shift their focus to small self-contained groups of like-minded associates as the primary units of analysis. Alternatively, if citizens no longer encounter disagreement and dissonance-producing information, then the motivating force for individual change becomes problematic. As McPhee, Smith, and Ferguson (1963) argued so persuasively, the dynamic of opinion formation is motivated by disagreement among citizens, and if disagreement does not occur, the engine driving electoral change is absent.

Mendelberg (2002: 152) points out that "(d)eliberation is not merely a utopian ideal; it is practiced already, and may become so more and more widely. It is time we understood what it is expected to do, what it is in reality, and what it could become. Doing so can help us better understand how citizens should, do, and could practice politics in a democracy." In the spirit of her admonition, we address a series of issues and questions: Do citizens possess the capacity to sustain ongoing patterns of communication that are characterized by persistent disagreement? Is disagreement politically disabling? Does disagreement render communication ineffective? These are important questions, and the answers to these questions are directly related to the prognosis regarding the vitality and possibilities of democratic politics.

Within this context, we turn to a series of important explanations for the elimination of disagreement among and between citizens in democratic politics. Taken together, these explanations provide a strong set of expectations regarding the inevitability of political homogeneity within closely held networks of political communication.

POLITICAL DIVERSITY AS A RARE EVENT

How have disagreement and dissent been understood within contemporary analyses of citizens, communication, and disagreement in democratic politics? According to one analytic perspective, citizens employ socially supplied information as a labor saving device. By finding well informed individuals with political biases similar to their own, citizens are able to reduce information costs by relying on individuals who are readily available within their own networks of social contact (Downs 1957). Hence, the likelihood of disagreement is reduced because individuals rely on the guidance of politically compatible experts, and political homogeneity is thus the naturally occurring state of affairs within communication networks.

Other analysts, inspired by a conformity model of social influence (Asch 1956), see a powerful social influence process within small, cohesive groups of interdependent citizens. The psychic discomfort of disagreement causes individuals to reduce dissonance through various means (Festinger 1957). In particular, individuals adopt socially prevalent viewpoints, and they avoid disagreement in the first place by censoring their patterns of social interaction to create politically homogeneous networks of political communication.

Neither of these analyses leads one to expect that disagreement would be able to survive within meaningful patterns of communication and deliberation among citizens. In the model of communication as a labor saving device, disagreement is unlikely to occur due to the purposeful action of individual citizens as they seek out politically sympathetic, like-minded experts. In the conformity model, disagreement is extinguished through powerful mechanisms of conflict avoidance and social influence. Hence, the capacity of democratic electorates to consider and reconcile competing viewpoints through a meaningful process of political communication is rendered problematic.

In summary, personal experience and scholarly analyses converge to suggest that political disagreement and dissent from widely held opinions are frequently unpopular; people often and inadvertently avoid political disagreement through a natural strategy for obtaining information in which they seek out like-minded political experts; and when disagreement is encountered, it is likely to be an unpleasant event that produces psychic and social discomfort. Hence, the political give-and-take that might be hoped to lie at the core of a free and open democratic society would instead appear to be unnatural and socially dysfunctional. People do not enjoy disagreement; it is frequently disturbing and they are unlikely to find it helpful.

This leaves students and friends of democratic politics with a problem: the requirements of democratic politics would appear to conflict with the capacities and realities of the way that citizens lead their lives, both as individuals and within the groups and networks of association where they are located. If people do not encounter disagreement as part of social interaction and political communication, the deliberative efficacy of political communication is seriously compromised. Just as important, the capacity of citizens to render political judgment is fundamentally undermined.

EFFICIENCY AND COST CUTTING AS KEYS TO CIVIC CAPACITY

According to the Downsian argument, cost conscious consumers of political information seek out as informants other individuals who are both expert and politically compatible. In this way cost conscious citizens free ride on the efforts of others – they rely on others to assume the costs of acquiring and processing political information. These costs are very real, particularly for individuals who find no intrinsic joy in reading the newspaper or watching talking heads on television news programs. In such a context, these free riding behaviors produce obviously beneficial outcomes at the individual level by allowing citizens to invest their participatory resources in other endeavors. What are the aggregate consequences?

In a very important way, the Downsian analysis suggests that free riding may enhance the citizenship capacity of citizens, *both* as individuals *and* in the aggregate. Free riding becomes an efficient mechanism for a division of labor that is both individually and socially productive. At the individual level, capacity is enhanced because people are able to acquire useful information. Absent social communication, it is unlikely that individuals would work harder to stay informed, and thus political discussion allows individuals to become better informed than they would otherwise be.

The manner in which social communication and free riding benefit the aggregate capacity of the larger political community is perhaps less direct. At the simplest level, a summation of better informed individuals yields a more capable aggregate, but the aggregate benefits extend beyond these summary advantages, and they relate to the larger division of labor in the production of community participation. Although many of us might, in the abstract, endorse the idea that every citizen should stay informed about politics, most of us also recognize the imperatives of the 24-hour day. To the extent that every citizen spends serious time and effort staying informed about politics – reading the *New York Times* and diligently watching the television news shows – we would expect a serious erosion in the social resources available to coach little league teams, to organize Girl Scout cookie drives, to attend church council meetings, and so on. In short, citizenship activities do not begin and end in the voting booth, or even in the world of partisan politics, elections, and public affairs (Putnam 2000). A primary advantage of citizens who look to their politically expert associates for political advice is that this sort of social interdependence has the potential to produce a division of labor that is not only individually efficient, but socially efficient as well.

The problematic aspects of the Downsian argument arise because the utility of communication is seen as being predicated on agreement regarding fundamental points of political orientation. According to Downs, the cost conscious strategy of obtaining political information only succeeds if one has confidence in the expert from whom the information is obtained. And the best way to gain such confidence in the expert is to select one who shares the political biases of the consumer.

The problem with this selection criterion is that, if citizens only communicate with agreeable experts, they are never forced to consider new, novel, and perhaps uncomfortable political ideas. There is little opportunity for persuasion and hence little opportunity for political change. Rather than a community that responds to compelling arguments and changing circumstances, the community is organized into political groupings surrounded by non-permeable social and political boundaries. The capacity of the citizens to exercise judgment is undermined because they are inexperienced and perhaps incapable of entertaining and understanding the full range of political alternatives.

What does this have to do with an audience that shouts down unpopular ideas offered by a newspaper publisher at a graduation ceremony? Public displays of an unwillingness to tolerate dissent and disagreement are symptomatic of a broader unwillingness to tolerate diverse political communication in the countless informal venues that are an integral part of everyday life. In this way the public life of democratic politics is a manifestation of habits and patterns that are learned and employed in countless informal and less public settings.

In summary, the problem is *not* that citizens engage in free riding by making use of the efforts expended by others in the collection and analysis of political information. The problem is rather the Downsian stipulated criterion that free riders impose on the search for a political expert, looking for someone who shares their particular points of political orientation. Before considering this problem in more detail, we consider the related problem of conflict avoidance.

DISAGREEMENT AND CONFLICT AVOIDANCE

The citizen in the Downsian analysis does not necessarily *avoid* conflict. Rather, the cost conscious citizen simply seeks out an agreeable political informant in order to obtain useful political information. In contrast, arguments anchored in group conformity and cognitive dissonance present an even less optimistic picture regarding the civic potential for communicating disagreement among citizens. According to these arguments, disagreement is socially and psychically painful for the people who experience it, and hence political heterogeneity within networks of communication becomes individually and socially dysfunctional. The effort to avoid conflict becomes an involuntary response to social discomfort rather than a purposeful, strategic action aimed at an efficient search for useful information.

If disagreement is inherently dysfunctional, it is difficult to see how the individual or collective capacity of citizens would be enhanced by exposure to diverse political viewpoints. The social conformity model fails to provide any expectation that citizens would look toward others for political guidance, thereby pooling social resources for purposes of reaching political judgments. Moreover, the individual inability to tolerate disagreement suggests that people are naturally averse to, and perhaps incapable of, the give-and-take of political discussion and disagreement.

Taken out of its intellectual context, the experimental research program of Solomon Asch has (wrongly) become the paradigmatic example of the conformity pressures that are generated by the discomfort that attends disagreement. In the Asch (1963) experiments, an individual subject participates in a small group experiment where all the other members of the small group cooperate in a hoax. Except for this one subject, all the other individuals are instructed to provide wrong answers to an exercise that involves matching the length of various lines. The true subject must confront the fact that other group members (the bogus subjects) are giving answers contrary to the subject's own sensory perception. In this setting, the individuals often (but not always) go along with the group judgment, thereby denying their own sensory judgment.

A cognitive dissonance explanation for such behavior is that individuals act to reduce dissonance (Festinger 1957). Indeed, the reduction of dissonance becomes a first principle and an important predictor of human behavior. Within the context of politics and political opinions, dissonance is reduced in a number of ways (Huckfeldt and Sprague 1993). First and most important, disagreement gives way to persuasion as individuals seek to reduce dissonance by adapting their own beliefs to the beliefs of others. Second, individuals might reduce dissonance by avoiding political discussion and potential discussants who introduce ideas that diverge from their own beliefs. Finally, disagreement might also give rise to misperception, as individuals reinterpret the statements of others to reconcile them with their own viewpoints.

These mechanisms and their variations create the reality of political homogeneity within patterns of social interaction, as well as obscuring the transmission of information in a way that artificially exaggerates perceived levels of agreement. Hence the reality of political homogeneity arises both as a consequence of political persuasion and as a consequence of conflict avoidance. People are more likely to interact with others who are politically similar to themselves if they adopt the views of the people around them, but they are also more likely to be imbedded in politically homogeneous networks if their patterns of social interaction are motivated either by conflict avoidance or as an effort to seek out like-minded informants. In this way, disagreement might be eliminated through censored patterns of social interaction. This censoring occurs whenever people avoid interaction with politically disagreeable associates, *and* whenever they hesitate to express their own political viewpoints to potentially unsympathetic audiences.

Just as important, communication becomes ineffective and obscure both when participants selectively perceive – and hence systematically misperceive – the messages being communicated, and when participants hesitate to express controversial viewpoints in order to avoid political disagreement (MacKuen 1990). Individuals are able to avoid the reality of diverse political views by relying on perceptions that are systematically biased in the direction of agreement. The *perception* of disagreement is reduced because people rewrite the scripts of their own discussions, selectively perceiving agreement with people who in reality hold divergent opinions. This sort of selective misperception requires less effort when discussion partners hesitate to express their own divergent viewpoints in a forceful manner!

Starting from a very different point of departure, based on a very different set of premises, theories of group conformity and cognitive dissonance end up at a place quite similar to Downs' theory regarding cost conscious consumers of political information. In both cases, the theoretical end result is a system that does not readily accommodate ongoing patterns of sustained political disagreement. In summary, these theories suggest that the realities of political homogeneity, as well as the exaggerated perceptions of political agreement, tend to squeeze out the experience of political diversity among and between citizens. Moreover, these expectations coincide with a substantial research tradition based on dynamic models of influence and opinion change.

DYNAMIC MODELS OF OPINION CHANGE

A classic analysis in this tradition is based on Abelson's (1964) mathematical model of dynamic changes in attitude distributions due to social influence processes. Abelson's model assumes that, when two members of a population interact, their attitudes tend to converge. Based on this simple assumption, Abelson shows that universal agreement is the end result for any population with a compact network of interpersonal contacts. The network of relationships for a population is compact if there is at least one individual who is connected, either directly or indirectly, to all other population members. And a diffuse network, in contrast, is characterized by a population that does not possess such an individual. The result of communication and persuasion within a compact network is, in Abelson's words, "a complete loss of 'attitude entropy'" (146).

In later work, Abelson shows (1979) that the end result of this process is agreement within groups and disagreement between groups. Inspired by Coleman's work on community conflict (1957), he provides a dynamic, mathematical account of the logic that underlies political homogeneity within groups, and political polarization among groups. Abelson's compelling argument built on the earlier work of French (1955) and Harary (1959), and it fueled continued development within the field. Other more recent efforts within this tradition include the work of network theorists such as Marsden (1981), Friedkin (1986, 1998), Carley (1993), and others. Many of these efforts are aimed at avoiding the conclusion reached by Abelson and others – a conclusion that is troubling both with respect to democratic prospects and with respect to descriptive adequacy. Not only do politically polarized, internally homogeneous groups pose a difficult challenge for democratic politics, but the historical record makes them appear to be a less than inevitable consequence of democratic competition (Lipset 1981).

In this context, it is worthwhile to return to Abelson's advice regarding productive lines of inquiry with respect to the problem (1964: 154–5).

We have been asking, "What sort of a model with simple assumptions is needed to yield intuitively reasonable consequences?" This is probably the most common style of mathematical modeling. Nevertheless, there is an alternative approach, a process-oriented approach. One may ask instead, "What are the important psychological variables and processes involved, and can one objectively specify their interrelations so that it is possible to carry out a simulation of the total system?"

In these comments, and in his own efforts to map out a simulation approach to the problem, Abelson anticipates developments that would occur much later – developments based on agent-based modeling strategies that make it possible to adopt a process-oriented approach to these issues.

AGENT-BASED EXPLANATIONS FOR HOMOGENEITY

An important development in the analysis of the homogeneity problem is provided in Axelrod's (1997a, 1997b) treatment of cultural diffusion. In this analysis, Axelrod employs an agent-based model in which computer generated "agents" are defined as cells on a grid.[1] Each agent possesses a discrete set of traits. For our purposes these traits might be political attitudes and opinions regarding particular issues, candidate evaluations, or political loyalties and identifications. We might think of these traits as opinions (such as opposition to or support for abortion rights), a choice of partisan identification (such as Democratic, Republican, or independent identifications), a particular vote choice, and so on. Hence the simulation begins with a wholly random distribution of features across the grid without any spatially based pattern of clustering.

The agent's traits (or opinions) are subject to modification based on interaction among the agents, where interaction and opinion change are determined by a simple set of rules.

1. Each agent has direct encounters only with spatially adjacent agents on the grid – one of the four agents with which it shares a boundary.
2. The probability that an encounter leads to an interaction is enhanced by the level of trait or opinion similarity between two agents, with interaction failing to occur if the agents do not share any traits in common. In this way, interaction partners are self-selected as a function of similarity, subject to availability in an adjacent cell.
3. If two agents do interact, the agent initiating interaction automatically adopts the other's view on one randomly selected opinion on which the two disagree.

These rules of interaction are implemented as a computationally intensive simulation, and relative to our focus of concern – the survival of disagreement among interacting agents – the outcome in Axelrod's analysis is always the same. The *experience* of disagreement is always extinguished so that, at equilibrium, none of the agents encounters divergent opinions through interactions with other agents. As Axelrod points out, it is still possible – under some conditions – to preserve diversity, but this diversity is always organized into spatially self-contained groups on the grid with impermeable communication boundaries. That is, the distribution of traits is homogeneous within groups, entirely divergent between groups, and thus interaction never occurs between agents holding different opinions.

We take inspiration from Axelrod's lead in subsequent chapters, but for present purposes it is important to recognize that his analysis produces a

---

[1] Axelrod conceives of these agents as villages possessing traits, with each trait being realized in terms of particular features. The agent-villages are, in fact, unitary actors, and hence with no loss of generality we address these agents in the context of individual citizens and their opinions. At the same time, in order to make it clear that agents are the creations of a computer algorithm, we refer to an individual agent as "it" rather than "she" or "he."

formidable result. Even when agents resist interaction with other agents holding divergent traits, these agents are unable to avoid the homogenizing effects of interaction within their surroundings. In general, the entire population of the grid becomes homogeneous across all traits. In some instances, homogeneous groups of agents become totally segregated within larger populations of agents with which they share nothing in common. Regardless of the particular equilibrium outcome, each of the agents ends up being imbedded within a homogeneous interaction cluster where it never encounters divergent opinions.

Axelrod's result is particularly powerful because it is unplanned. There is no centralized source of control over the agents that guides their behavior. No effort is made to load the dice in favor of homogeneity. Rather, homogeneity is the unintentional and emergent consequence of interdependent, adaptive agents that are locally autonomous and independent from central control. Moreover, and as we will see in subsequent analyses, the Axelrod result is particularly robust and resistant to tinkering with the particular form of the rules that govern interaction among the agents.[2]

THE SURVIVAL OF POLITICAL DISAGREEMENT

In very different ways, these bodies of theory generate the empirical expectation that individuals will seldom experience political disagreement within networks of political communication. The major problem with these expectations is that they frequently fail the test of empirical evaluation – they are at variance with the empirical reality in many (but certainly not all) important contexts.

In this book the empirical focus is primarily on political communication among and between citizens during American presidential election campaigns, and we employ two different studies that support such an undertaking. The first of these studies, the 1996 Indianapolis–St. Louis Study, provides interviews with more than twenty-five hundred registered voters in the St. Louis and Indianapolis metropolitan areas, beginning in March of 1996 and ending in November of 1997. The study also provides interviews with nearly two thousand of these individuals' political discussion partners, and hence it supports a detailed analysis of communication and disagreement. We also employ the 2000 National Election Study (NES), which provides the respondents' assessments of their communication networks, thereby providing a representative national sample for purposes of identifying patterns and consequences of perceived political disagreement within communication networks.

---

[2] For modeling efforts in response to Axelrod's work, see Shibanai, Yasuno, and Ishiguro (2001) and Grieg (2002).

The Survival of Political Disagreement

The authors have benefited from contact with a number of long-time colleagues who have frequently questioned whether this is a worthy focus of inquiry. Is the modern presidential election campaign more a matter of symbolic politics and media spectacle rather than a real-life political problem that must be addressed by citizens who combine their efforts to understand a common set of issues and concerns?

The answer to this question depends on the performance of the political system, and system performance has been variable across time and circumstances. In general, however, the presidential election combines several characteristics that create a productive laboratory for studying political communication and interdependence among citizens. In particular, presidential election campaigns involve a population of individuals who face a common task. Each voter must make up her mind on election day. She must collect and analyze information to assess the available choices. Her decision is highly complex, and it is made under extreme levels of uncertainty. Finally, due in large part to media attention, the decision is highly salient for a great many individuals, thereby fostering high levels of communication among many citizens regarding the choices that they face. Indeed, the natural laboratory provided by the presidential election campaign has been sufficiently compelling to produce a long series of studies of the way in which voters in democratic politics reach their individual and collective decisions. We build on these efforts, beginning with the work of Lazarsfeld and his colleagues from Columbia University in their community-based studies of the 1940 and 1948 presidential elections in Elmira, New York, and Erie County, Ohio.

In these pioneering studies of political communication and influence among citizens, the Columbia sociologists articulated a powerful and influential model of political communication and change during election campaigns (Lazarsfeld et al. 1948; Berelson et al. 1954). They argued that political communication among citizens becomes less frequent during the period of time between election campaigns, when the frequency and intensity of political stimuli decrease and people's concerns shift away from politics to other matters. In these politically quiescent times, rates of political discussion and communication are relatively low, political preferences become less socially visible, and political opinions tend to become individually idiosyncratic. So long as their political preferences are socially invisible, citizens are immune to conformity pressures, and hence their preferences tend to be heterogeneous even within closely held social groups.

These circumstances change in response to the stimulus of a new election campaign, as citizens increasingly confront the issues and controversies that are part of the campaign. Correspondingly, the frequency of political communication among citizens also increases; as citizens increasingly become attentive to politics, they share their concerns with others. As the campaign accelerates, so do the rates of political communication among associates, and individual political preferences are increasingly exposed to social scrutiny. Previously idiosyncratic preferences become socially visible, and individuals are correspondingly brought into conformity with their micro-environmental surroundings. In the vivid imagery of Berelson and colleagues (1954: 149): homogeneity is enhanced within groups as polarization increases between groups.

After the election is over, people become less concerned about political affairs, and hence their conversations turn toward other, less political topics. As the rate and intensity of political stimuli decline, social control is relaxed, and individual preferences once again become idiosyncratic and heterogeneous within social groups.

In the context of a high visibility election campaign, the dynamic logic of group conformity pressures is quite compelling. Carried to its conclusion, the logic of group conformity would seem to suggest that political disagreement should disappear within networks of social relations.[3] Indeed, the dynamic logic outlined by the Columbia scholars was so compelling that Downs does not directly challenge the empirical implications of their argument in his *Economic Theory of Democracy* (1957: 229). Rather, he reconstructs the logic of political communication among citizens within the context of information costs and the needs of citizens to economize – to obtain information on the cheap. In the Downsian logic, it is not that homogeneity is created as a consequence of social communication. Rather, agreement is the condition that drives communication, as citizens seek out like-minded experts upon whom they can rely for trustworthy information and advice. In this way, political communication reinforces homogeneity but does not create it.

CONTRARY EVIDENCE REGARDING DISAGREEMENT

As compelling as group conformity arguments may be, they suffer from at least one major shortcoming – disagreement is *not* typically extinguished within networks of social relations, even at the end of high stimulus presidential election campaigns. The tendency for disagreement to survive within communication networks has been documented by a series of national and community-based election studies (Huckfeldt and Sprague 1995; Huckfeldt, Beck, Dalton, and Levine 1995; Huckfeldt, Sprague,

---

[3] Indeed, although the production of political homogeneity within networks of political communication is a lesson frequently attributed to the Columbia studies, their efforts paid ample attention to the importance of disagreement and the natural limits on conformity pressures within campaign dynamics (Berelson et al. 1954: Chapter 7).

and Levine 2000). In each instance, interviews with discussants identified by the original main respondents showed less than perfect correspondence within discussion dyads. No more than two-thirds of the discussants held a presidential candidate preference that coincided with the main respondent who named them, and these levels of agreement are quite typical of other democratic systems as well (Schmitt-Beck 2003; Ikeda and Huckfeldt 2001; Huckfeldt, Ikeda, and Pappi 2003).

These rates of disagreement become even more important when we recall that they are based on dyads rather than networks. If the probability of dyadic agreement within a network is .7, and if the likelihood of agreement is independent across the dyads within a network, then the probability of agreement across all the relationships within a three-discussant network drops to $.7^3$ or .34. In this setting, *disagreement and heterogeneous preferences become the rule rather than the exception within the micro-environments surrounding individual citizens.* The pervasiveness of disagreement within communication networks forces a reassessment of social conformity as a mechanism of social influence, as well as a reconsideration of the dynamic implications that arise due to politically interdependent citizens.

NETWORKS, GROUPS, AND COMPLEX FORMS OF ORGANIZATION

The implications of individual interdependence are subtly yet dramatically transformed when the micro-environments of political communication are conceived in terms of networks of relationships rather than in terms of self-contained groups. It is perhaps no accident that large parts of the literatures concerning group conformity effects and cognitive dissonance, as well as the early Columbia election studies, were undertaken prior to the advent of the dramatic progress in network studies. Without exaggerating, one might indeed argue that the conceptual displacement of "small group" research by "network" studies has transformed the way that political communication and persuasion have come to be understood.[4]

The conception of a small group as a limited number of individuals who are all known and connected to one another – and whose important social relationships all fall within group boundaries – often provides a poor match to empirical reality. Just as important, it provides a seriously understated model of the complex forms of social organization that underlie

---

[4] Small group work led to a number of important research programs in the postwar era of American social science (Asch 1963; Festinger, Back, Schachter, Kelly, and Thibaut 1950). And field research on the operation of small groups quickly led to early studies of social networks (see Festinger, Schachter, and Back 1950: Chapter 8). For a particularly subtle analysis of formal organization, informal organization, group construction, and patterns of relationships, see Homans (1950).

individual interdependence. The limited utility of the small self-contained group quickly became apparent in applied social and political research. In his post war studies of Jewish neighborhoods, Fuchs (1955) explains the greater heterogeneity of political preferences among men as opposed to women by pointing out that, whereas women stayed at home in the neighborhood during the day, men went off to work and hence were exposed to a more heterogeneous mix of viewpoints. Similarly, Lazarsfeld and colleagues (1948) employ the concept of "cross pressures" to accommodate the fact that individuals did not typically belong to a single group, but rather to multiple groups that often pointed in different political directions.

In this context, the representation of "groups" as networks of relationships served to revolutionize the conceptual apparatus that was available for understanding interdependent patterns of communication and influence (see, for example, White 1970). Although it is meaningful to think of individuals residing within small groups – and we use the language of groups repeatedly in this effort – it might be difficult to think of two individuals who restrict their patterns of social communication to the same small circle of associates. Even spouses and close friends are extremely unlikely to duplicate one another's range of contacts exactly. And this fact – that you and each of your associates do not necessarily share a common set of associates – has profound consequences for communication and the survival of disagreement.

In the language of Granovetter (1973), we are drawing the reader's attention to the importance of weak ties within networks. In the vocabulary of Burt (1992), we are pointing toward the importance of bridges and holes within networks – to the absence as well as the presence of relationships among citizens. The crucial point is: When Fuch's (1955) Jewish husbands went off to work, they expanded their range of social contacts to include co-workers who did not communicate with their wives. When Jewish wives stayed in the neighborhood during the day, they expanded their range of associations to include residents of the neighborhood who did not communicate with their husbands.

In summary, these husbands and wives were not located in the same groups. Their sets of contacts formed overlapping but idiosyncratic networks of communication and influence. In the vocabulary of social networks, the relationship densities within their combined networks of association were relatively low. A great many individuals within the combined networks of husbands and wives were not connected to one another. The thesis of this book, developed over the following chapters, is that political heterogeneity and disagreement are better able to survive in (1) lower density networks where (2) the influence of each associate's viewpoint is weighted by the frequency of that viewpoint among the individual's other associates. This thesis depends on the concept of social networks that are riddled with an absence of connecting ties – a form of social organization that is at variance with the conception of highly cohesive, self-contained social groups. We turn, then, to an overview of our argument.

AN OVERVIEW OF THE ARGUMENT

Political heterogeneity might persist within an electorate even if individual members of the electorate never encounter disagreement. One might easily imagine a politically polarized society in which disagreement disappears within networks of political communication at the same time as diverse preferences persist in the larger population (Axelrod 1997; Huckfeldt and Kohfeld 1989). The vitality of democratic politics depends on the survival of political heterogeneity and disagreement at *both* levels – heterogeneous political preferences within larger populations as well as disagreement experienced directly within networks of political communication. Quite clearly, disagreement within networks cannot exist if the larger population is politically homogeneous, and hence our primary focus is on the experience of disagreement among citizens within their networks of political communication.

A substantial body of evidence has accumulated regarding the distribution of preferences within citizens' networks of political communication. Contrary to expectations, these networks are *not* safe havens from political disagreement. It would appear that disagreement is the modal condition among citizens – most citizens experience disagreement and divergent political preferences within these networks. Moreover, this conclusion is based on the closely held, self-reported relationships of the citizens themselves, and on perhaps the most visible of contemporary political choices – support for a particular presidential candidate. Hence a central question becomes: What is the nature of the dynamic process that sustains disagreement among citizens?

As long as persuasion is the inevitable consequence of interaction within discrete dyads, the elimination of political diversity and disagreement may be a foregone conclusion, at least over the long haul. In contrast, a far different outcome emerges when we treat persuasion within dyads as a problematic and less than automatic consequence of interaction across an individual's entire network of contacts. We conceive of persuasion in probabilistic terms, as a consequence arising from a range of factors at both individual and aggregate levels. Most immediately, persuasion depends on the characteristics of the message carrier and the message receiver. Persuasion is most likely to occur when the message carrier is more persuasive and the message receiver is more susceptible to persuasive communication. Hence, conceived in terms of dyads, the effectiveness and persuasiveness of communication depends on the characteristics of the individuals who occupy relevant roles within the dyad.

At a level of abstraction and analysis that is one level higher than the dyad, the effectiveness and persuasiveness of political messages also depend on the distribution of opinions within larger networks of communication. In an argument crucial to our thesis, we assert in Chapter 2 that communication and influence are *autoregressive*, that the probability of agreement within a dyad depends on the incidence of the relevant opinion within an individual's larger network of relationships. That is, individuals are less likely to be persuaded by opinions that win only limited support among the participants within their communication networks. This feature within our model of persuasion is crucial in maintaining diversity and disagreement both in the short run and over the long term.[5]

In many ways this is a surprising outcome. The model of influence we are describing rewards majority opinion at the same time that it punishes the political minority, but it produces an aggregate outcome in which the minority does not disappear. The potential of this mechanism for maintaining political disagreement is that the influence of majorities and minorities are defined according to the distribution of opinion within closely held micro-environments of political communication. Hence, people are able to resist divergent viewpoints within the network because every opinion they encounter is filtered through every other opinion they encounter.

This model has important non-deterministic implications for the political consequences of social communication among citizens. If election campaigns simply serve to recreate a pre-existing political homogeneity within social groups, then the collective deliberation that occurs among citizens is strangely divorced from the real life gave-and-take of issues, debates, and controversies in democratic politics. In contrast, to the extent that individuals are open to disagreement and persuasion – not only by candidates and media reports but also by one another – then a more genuinely deliberative process takes place within networks of political communication. The systematic patterns of communication that occur within these networks become crucial to the outcomes of democratic

[5] The reader should note that this concept of autoregressive influence serves to extend autoregressive network models of individual behavior. In an autoregressive network model, individual opinions depend directly on the opinions of each other individual to whom an individual is connected (Marsden and Friedkin 1994). In a model of autoregressive influence within dyads, whether or not this first individual is influenced by the opinion of a second individual within the network depends on the distribution of opinions across all the other individuals within the network who are also connected to the first individual. In this way, the opinion of each individual within the network is mediated by the opinions of others within the network.

politics, even though the direction and magnitude of the effects may be highly complex and difficult to predict (Boudon 1986).

Finally, the mechanism we are describing is dependent on the structure of the communication networks within which citizens are imbedded. In particular, the survival of disagreement depends quite profoundly on the low levels of network density that are built into our model (see Granovetter 1973; Burt 1992). Networks are defined as being higher density to the extent that more individuals within the network are connected to one another. As a practical matter, this means that dense networks present a situation in which two associated individuals share the same common set of associates. In other words, if you and your associate are located in a high density network, the friends of your friends will be your friends, too. In a lower density network, by contrast, you are less likely to interact with the friends of your friends

If network densities are high – if networks are wholly self-contained so that all members share the same interaction partners – then disagreement would disappear even though diverse preferences might be sustained in the larger environment. That is, no one would ever encounter diverse preferences because every particular network is wholly self-contained and entirely homogeneous. In contrast, low network densities, combined with influence that is predicated on the incidence of particular opinions within networks, serve to sustain political diversity in the larger environment *as well as the experience of disagreement within citizens' closely held networks of political communication.*

HOW IS DISAGREEMENT SUSTAINED?

Disagreement is neither an accident nor an anomaly. Rather, the survival of disagreement is the systematic consequence of complex social organization. But if disagreement is fostered by the dynamic logic of complex social organization, it must also be introduced and sustained by particular mechanisms. What are the crucial ingredients in this process?

First, as we have argued elsewhere, individuals exercise limited discretion in the selection of informants (Huckfeldt 1983; Huckfeldt and Sprague 1995). Even if we accept the argument that people prefer to discuss politics with people who hold agreeable preferences, this is only one of the goals that they impose on the search for compatible associates. Moreover, the construction of a communication network occurs within pronounced constraints on supply. People reside in neighborhoods, workplaces, and organizations that circumscribe their opportunities for social interaction. Hence, even if you prefer to associate with liberal Democrats, there may be few opportunities to find liberal Democrats at the bank where you work. Moreover, you may also prefer to associate with baseball fans, and if the baseball fans at your workplace tend to be conservative Republicans, your search for someone with whom to eat lunch may be severely and impossibly constrained.

Second, although it is certainly true that disagreement sometimes leads to psychic and social discomfort, it is perhaps premature to suggest that all disagreements lead to severe discomfort among all people. In their review of the Asch experiments, Ross, Bierbrauer, and Hoffman (1976) provide a compelling account of the circumstances that give rise to psychic discomfort in the face of disagreement. An understandable but mistaken conclusion based on the Asch experiments is that, if conformity pressures can make people deny their own sensory perception to say that the shorter line is longer than the longer line, then these conformity pressures can make almost anyone do almost anything. Quite to the contrary, as Ross and colleagues point out, it was the very nature of the Asch experiments that made conformity pressures particularly intense.

When individuals inexplicably adopt a viewpoint that is at variance with your own belief, it puts you in a substantial quandary. You have no reason for dismissing the judgment of individuals who assert that the shorter line is longer. In this context, how can you possibly explain the consensual judgment of your fellow group members, *all of whom* say that the short line is longer?

Contrast this situation with the typical political discussion, where there is a virtually infinite supply of reasons for doubting anyone's view about anything. Your friend's wrongheaded view can be explained by the fact that: He is a right-wing Republican, she is a left-wing Democrat, he is not very well informed, she is naturally cantankerous, and so on. The inherently subjective basis of political opinion and belief may encourage and sustain disagreement by making it entirely explicable. As Asch demonstrates, the presence of a single confederate supporting the subject's opinion empowers the subject to reject the falsely reported opinions of the other (bogus) subjects.

The insight of Ross and his colleagues is particularly important to our understanding of conformity pressures, cognitive dissonance, and political heterogeneity within networks of political communication. By arguing that political disagreement regularly survives within networks of political communication, we are *not* arguing that cognitive dissonance or conformity pressures are irrelevant to the experience of divergent preferences. To the contrary, political disagreement is highly likely to be dissonance producing, but the subjective basis of political judgment frequently makes disagreement explicable, and hence the dissonance produced by disagreement becomes much easier to resolve. In other words, psychic distress, political withdrawal, and individual conversion are not the only responses to political disagreement.

Third, political disagreement typically becomes less tolerable when political passions are more intense. The reason for the intolerance of the passionate flows directly from the explicability criterion. As attitudes grow stronger, it often becomes more difficult for individuals to construct compelling accounts of why someone is likely to hold a disagreeable viewpoint. Hence, we would expect that disagreement is least likely among individuals who hold the strongest and most passionate attitudes regarding politics. In fact, for many people, politics does not hold such an exalted status in their list of life concerns, and thus disagreement may be easier to tolerate for the simple reason that they have less at stake. At the same time, disagreement is less likely to be tolerable for the committed true believer, and as we will see, strong partisanship is virtually coterminous with an absence of disagreement.

Fourth, from the vantage point of strategic action, it may sometimes make sense to obtain information *not* from politically like-minded people, but *rather* from people with whom you expect to disagree (Calvert 1985). So long as you are aware of the motivations that lie behind the advice of a political expert, it may be highly useful to hear out the opinions of your political adversary. It may be equally enlightening to know why Milton Friedman favored a policy as it is to know why Paul Samuelson opposed it, regardless of your opinions regarding Keynes, monetarism, and economics in general.

Finally, for some individuals, political discussion and the collection and processing of political information are intrinsically rewarding activities (Fiorina 1990). Rather than being a costly means to a beneficial end, political information *and even political disagreement* may provide their own rewards. If it were otherwise, the market for Sunday morning news programs would certainly disappear. Although these committed consumers of political information may constitute a minority within the larger political community, the Downsian analysis suggests that their impact may be disproportional to their numbers in the population (Huckfeldt 2001). Just as important, their presence is likely to change the way we think about the survival of disagreement within democratic politics.

THE PLAN FOR THIS BOOK

The strategy of this book is both theoretical and empirical. We consider and evaluate theories of influence as they relate to patterns of communication regarding politics. Our goal is to make a contribututution toward a revised theoretical framework for understanding the nature of political interdependence among citizens in democratic societies. Within this context, we evaluate empirical evidence regarding communication, influence, and the survival of political disagreement among citizens within their naturally occurring patterns of social interaction. The empirical evidence for this undertaking comes from two studies: a study of communication and persuasion in the 1996 election campaign as it occurred in the Indianapolis and St. Louis metropolitan areas, and the 2000 National Election Study.

On the basis of these efforts and analyses, we construct and evaluate a series of dynamic, agent-based models of political persuasion. We use these models to assess the mechanisms that might sustain disagreement among citizens. Throughout this effort, we assume that communication among citizens is politically consequential – that citizens are politically interdependent in the sense that they rely on one another for political information, expertise, and guidance. The primary question thus becomes: *What are the conditions under which diversity of opinion is likely to be sustained within the political communication networks where interdependent citizens depend on one another for information and expertise?*

It is important to state the obvious. Disagreement does not always survive; citizens do not always experience dissenting voices within their closely held circles of acquaintance; and the reality of political life is that, in some circumstances with respect to some issues, homogeneity is the rule. We have already cited the unhappy experience of the *Sacramento Bee* publisher, but there is an abundance of other examples as well. In the contemporary Middle East crisis, Israelis and Palestinians seldom have the opportunity to encounter one another in face-to-face discussions regarding the Israeli–Palestinian conflict. In Mississippi in the 1984 presidential election, more than 85 percent of Mississippi white voters supported Ronald Reagan and more than 90 percent of Mississippi black voters supported Walter Mondale. Within the context of Mississippi social interaction patterns in the 1980s, this meant that Reagan voters (whites) seldom encountered Mondale voters (blacks) – or vice versa – within their closely held networks of political communication.

In summary, we are certainly not arguing that citizens always encounter disagreement, or that disagreement inevitably survives. Rather, we are arguing that political disagreement and heterogeneity constitute the lifeblood of democratic politics. And contrary to many theoretical arguments, disagreement appears to be persistent and resilient in a great many politically important settings. Hence our goal is to demonstrate the circumstances under which disagreement is best able to survive – the circumstances that sustain disagreement and thereby sustain the vitality of democratic politics.

2

New Information, Old Information, and Persistent Disagreement

Citizens confront new information in the context of old information, and they are likely to discount information that is not easily reconciled with the information they have already encountered. In this way, political influence is inherently autoregressive – the influence of any information source depends on the influence of every other source. This discounting of politically divergent information has several consequences. First, attitudes and opinions are resistant, but not invulnerable, to political change. In particular, new information is unlikely to gain acceptance until it is widely communicated from a variety of sources. Second, the autoregressive nature of influence helps to explain the persistence of disagreement among citizens. Two individuals who interact on a regular basis are more likely to demonstrate sustained disagreement if (1) their remaining networks of contacts are non-overlapping and (2) these networks transmit divergent political messages. In this way, the continuing experience of disagreement and political diversity depends on the configuration of the communication networks within which citizens are located, and particularly on low density, asymmetric patterns of communication.

Political interdependence and communication among citizens has little consequence if individuals reside in self-contained, politically homogeneous groups. In settings such as these, new information cannot easily penetrate the social barriers that surround the individual. If you are a liberal Democrat, and all your friends are liberal Democrats, the odds are very high that you will never hear one of your friends make a passionately convincing argument in favor of tax cuts. Conversely, if you are a conservative Republican, and all your friends are conservative Republicans, the odds are similarly high that you will never hear a friend make a passionately convincing case for eliminating restrictions on abortion. When networks of communication are populated by individuals who share the same political viewpoints and orientations, the information that individuals receive will correspond quite closely to the information they already possess, and the information conveyed through one exchange will correspond to the information conveyed through every other exchange.

In contrast, if citizens are located in communication networks characterized by political heterogeneity, the exchange of information is likely to take on heightened political consequence. As McPhee and colleagues (1963) recognized, political disagreement gives rise to opportunities for political change. When individuals encounter preferences that are different from their own, they often find it difficult to ignore the event. Either they construct a counterargument to overcome the disagreement, they discredit the message by dismissing its source, they reconsider their own position in light of the disagreement, or they check their sources again. These sources include mass media outlets and messages, but they also include the opinions and guidance of the other individuals within their networks of political communication. In each of these instances, disagreement forces individuals to engage in a critical re-examination – they think more deeply and attend more carefully to the substance of the political disagreement. Even when citizens reject the disagreeable preference, they are forced to reconsider the justification for their own position, and in this way political change can be seen to occur regardless of the manner in which disagreement is resolved.

This potential for micro-level change carries important macro-level consequences. To the extent that citizens are socially insulated from disagreement, the opportunity for collective deliberation is reduced, as are the opportunity and occasion for political influence. Hence, political change at both the micro- and macro-levels becomes disembodied from communication among citizens. Indeed, absent communication among citizens with diverse viewpoints, it becomes difficult to offer a compelling account of the role played by communication among citizens in the process of political change.

The survival of disagreement within closely held networks of political communication gives rise to a number of important questions. How is political disagreement sustained within a context of persuasion and interdependence? In what ways does disagreement affect the flow of information and influence? How is disagreement resolved within these networks, if it is resolved at all? In order to address these questions, we construct a set of arguments regarding the manner in which disagreement within dyads is filtered through larger networks of association. These questions and our arguments are evaluated against evidence taken from the 2000 National Election Study.

NETWORK THEORIES OF POLITICAL INFLUENCE

Any effort to address informational interdependence among citizens in democratic politics necessarily builds on the foundational work of the Columbia sociologists – work that began with Paul Lazarsfeld's arrival in New York City in the 1930s. In particular, the 1940 election study conducted in Elmira by Lazarsfeld and colleagues (1944), as well as the

1948 study conducted in Erie County, Ohio, by Berelson and colleagues (1954) serve as defining moments in the study of political influence and electoral politics. These efforts were extended and elaborated on in the work of Katz and Lazarsfeld (1955), Katz (1957), McPhee and colleagues (1963), and many others.

A primary and enduring message of these studies is that people do not act as isolated individuals when they confront the complex tasks of citizenship. Quite the opposite. The Columbia sociologists demonstrate that politics is a social experience in which individuals share information and viewpoints in arriving at individual decisions, and hence the individual voter is usefully seen within a particular social setting. This framework produces a compelling account of the dynamic implications that arise due to election campaigns. Berelson and colleagues (1954: Chapter 7) argue that political preferences are likely to become individually idiosyncratic as political communication among citizens becomes less frequent during the period of time between election campaigns. In response to the stimulus of the election, the frequency of political communication increases, idiosyncratic preferences become socially visible, and hence individuals are brought into conformity with micro-environmental surroundings (Huckfeldt and Sprague 1995).

Carried to its extreme, the logic of group conformity might seem to suggest that political disagreement should disappear within networks of social relations. Pressures toward conformity should drive out disagreement in several ways (Festinger 1957; Huckfeldt and Sprague 1995). The discomfort of disagreement might encourage people to modify their patterns of social relations so as to exclude people with whom they disagree. People might avoid political discussion with those associates who hold politically divergent preferences, or they might engage in self-censorship to avoid political disagreement (MacKuen 1990). Partially as a consequence of discussion avoidance, people might incorrectly perceive agreement among those with whom they actually disagree. Finally, and perhaps most important, individuals might bring their own preferences into correspondence with the preferences that they encounter within their networks of social relations.

The Columbia studies never suggested that disagreement would disappear, and a major part of their effort was directed toward understanding the consequences of disagreement and cross pressures. Taken together, these analyses constitute an explicit recognition that the dynamic underlying political influence is frequently self-limiting (see McPhee et al. 1963), in part due to the complex webs of association that lie behind the two-step-flow of communication (Katz 1957). The irony is that, among many political scientists, the work has been taken to suggest that citizens reside in homogeneous social settings, that they select their associates to avoid disagreement, and hence the information they obtain is a direct reflection of their own political biases. Such a view has strong appeal among those who would argue that cognitive dissonance serves to extinguish disagreement. It is also in keeping with Downs' (1957) argument that, in order to minimize information costs, rational individuals obtain information from other individuals who share their own political viewpoints.

As compelling as these various arguments regarding group conformity may be, they suffer from a major empirical weakness: Campaigns do *not* extinguish disagreement within networks of social relations. A substantial accumulation of evidence shows that disagreement is a common and enduring experience among citizens in democratic politics, not only in the United States but in other democracies as well (Huckfeldt and Sprague 1995; Huckfeldt et al. 1995; Huckfeldt, Sprague, and Levine 2000; Ikeda and Huckfeldt 2001; Schmitt-Beck 2003). The frequency of disagreement found repeatedly within communication networks stimulates a reassessment of the implications that arise due to patterns of agreement and disagreement. The advances of the early Columbia school occurred before the development of network concepts, and one of the important disjunctures between traditional efforts at small group research and social network studies is the problematic nature of links within networks (Burt 1992; Granovetter 1973; White 1970). In particular, an individual's political communication network may or may not constitute a self-contained small group, and whether or not it does is a direct consequence of network construction. The construction of these networks occurs at the juncture of choice and social circumstance. Some discussion partners are consciously chosen, whereas others are dictated by the circumstances of life – work, play, church, family.

Two important differences arise in the conceptions of groups and networks that are particularly important to our effort. First, the density of relations within networks is variable, and hence two friends may never encounter the friends of *their* friends. Even though Nancy and Tom may frequently engage in political discussions, Nancy may also engage in frequent discussions with individuals who are unknown to Tom (Fuchs 1955). The work of Granovetter (1973) and Burt (1992) demonstrates the importance of network density for the flow of information within and between networks, and it is relevant for the survival of disagreement as well (Huckfeldt, Johnson, and Sprague 2002). Second, relationships in communication networks may be asymmetric and nonreciprocal. Nancy may be a source of information for Tom, but that does not mean that Tom is a source of information for Nancy (see Huckfeldt and Sprague 1995). Both of these factors – low density networks and asymmetric relationships – are crucial to the persistence of political heterogeneity within political communication networks. They create situations in which the particular structure of networks may sustain rather than eliminate political disagreement among citizens.

POLITICAL INFLUENCE IN HETEROGENEOUS ENVIRONMENTS

The importance of asymmetrical relationships and low density networks to the survival of political disagreement leads to a series of questions. How are these networks created? How is a traditional focus on spatially defined groups and contexts different from a focus on individuals who are imbedded within idiosyncratic networks of political communication? What is the relationship between the influence of particular information sources within a communication network and the influence of the network as a whole? In order to address these questions, we informally characterize the manner in which social interaction and political communication occur through time. Several arguments are crucial to this characterization.

First, citizens do not experience their social setting as a whole. They do not consume their diet of information in a single bite, or even at a single meal. Rather, to pursue the metaphor, they consume socially supplied political information through a series of snacks and meals. In this way they obtain the information in a serial, cumulative fashion as a collection of responses, unsolicited opinions, offhand comments, and occasional heated arguments. In short, the process of social communication regarding politics constitutes a virtually endless series of discrete encounters between individuals and the associates with whom they share a social space.

This means, in turn, that citizens never experience the central tendency of their political micro-environment in a direct manner. Rather, they experience the environment in bits and pieces that accumulate into something that may or may not resemble a central tendency. It only *resembles* a central tendency because the citizens are not in the business of producing representative random samples. Rather, their goal is to make sense out of politics – to employ the information at their disposal to construct a meaningful version of political events that will guide them in making political choices (Sniderman, Brody, and Tetlock, 1991). As a consequence, they inevitably take some pieces of information more seriously than others. Hence, even if social interaction is random within a defined social space, some interactions will be weighted more heavily than others.

What are the factors that go into these weights? As Downs (1957) has led us to expect, one set of factors is related to the perceived expertise of the information source. People pay more attention to individuals whom they perceive to be politically expert. Moreover, their judgments regarding political expertise are not lost in a cloud of misperception – they are fully capable of taking into account the objectively defined expertise of others (Huckfeldt 2001). As a consequence, asymmetry is built into the process of political communication.

Another set of factors is even more directly related to the characteristics of the discussant who serves as the potential source of information. Some discussants spend a great deal of time talking about politics, whereas others talk more frequently about fly fishing and the Chicago Bears. Some discussants are strong partisans with unambiguous preferences that are unambiguously articulated. Other discussants are ambivalent in their political preferences and hesitant in their political judgments. In other words, it is important to emphasize the importance of the *messenger* in determining the efficacy of the message. In keeping with an earlier focus on opinion leaders (Lazarsfeld et al. 1948; Berelson et al. 1954; Katz 1957), it becomes clear that the characteristics of the individuals who transmit political messages play particularly important roles in affecting the flow of information (Huckfeldt, Beck, Dalton, Levine, and Morgan 1998a). In this particular way we might even say that the preferences of discussants are self-weighting.

One interpretation of political expertise and its consequences suggests that political communication is asymmetric due to the quality conscious consumer of political information. That is, the Downsian rational actor purposefully selects a political discussant based on bias and expertise. She selects an information source who reflects her own political orientation in a politically knowledgeable manner. In contrast, an agent-based model of individually adaptive behavior suggests that communication is asymmetric because expertise is weighted as the inevitable consequence of limited air time in personal conversation. People become experts – in the broadest sense of the term – because they invest more heavily in acquiring political information. The typical motivation for such individual investment is that our expert-in-the-making finds politics to be compelling or interesting or enjoyable. But the same impulse to invest more heavily in political information also encourages the expert to spend more time focusing on politics in individual conversation.

These experts – the people who invest more resources in acquiring and processing political information – tend to occupy more influential roles in the communication of political information. For present purposes, the outcome is the same regardless of whether we view citizens as purposefully cost-conscious consumers of political information (Downs 1957; Calvert 1985) or as adaptive agents responding to circumstance (Axelrod 1997a, 1997b; Huckfeldt 2001). The process of political communication is inherently asymmetric, and the political expert is more likely than the political novice to play a prominent political role in patterns of political communication.

In short, the central political tendency of a particular setting is never experienced directly, but rather it is reconstructed on the basis of fragmented experiences that are differentially weighted in ways that are idiosyncratic to both the recipient and the source of the information. This view marks an extension and perhaps a departure from a rich tradition of contextual studies in which individuals are seen as responding, more or less directly, to the political climate within which they reside (Lazarsfeld, et al. 1948; Berelson et al. 1954; Miller 1956; Putnam 1966; Huckfeldt 1986).

The asymmetrical nature of communication has important consequences for the structure of networks. If Nancy is a political junky who frequently bombards Tom with political information, she may serve as a primary source of information for Tom, but Tom may not serve as a primary information source for Nancy. In short, communication asymmetries produce patterns of communication that are more likely to include one-way information flows, thereby increasing the complexity of communication and its consequences. Even if two individuals are similarly located within the same communication network, the consequences of communication within the network – as well as the consequences of disagreement within the dyad – may be quite different for each of them.

Second, each information exchange is imbedded within the cumulative (but decaying) effect of every other information exchange. Citizens do not obtain information in a vacuum. Rather, they judge each new piece of information within the context of the information they have previously obtained. This is another way of saying that political influence is spatially autoregressive (Anselin 1988). Within a social space that is defined relative to a particular citizen, the impact of every social encounter depends on the cumulative social impact of all other social encounters. Hence, if we predict individual behavior on the basis of any single encounter or piece of information, our average error in prediction is likely to be correlated with the other sources of information that an individual employs in the given social space.

At the same time, working memory is finite. Any individual is only capable of simultaneously considering a small set of informational elements at any given moment. Hence, information is stored in long term memory and accessed through an activation process that depends on the strength of association among memory elements (Fazio 1995). Lodge and Taber (2000) offer a provocative view of political judgment in which people form summary judgments based on particular political objects that are being continually updated as new information becomes available. This on-line tally is readily accessible from long term memory even though the information on which the judgments are based is not. In short, people form opinions that serve as summary judgments based on a continuing series of incoming information. Hence, these summary judgments are continually being updated as new information becomes available, but the new information is not viewed in a neutral fashion. Rather, it is understood and evaluated within the context of the existing summary judgment (Lodge and Taber 2000).

What are the implications for judgments based on political information that is obtained through social interaction? Individuals who encounter a friend wearing a BUSH FOR PRESIDENT lapel pin may have quite different responses depending on their past history of interactions. If the lapel pin episode is the first time that our individual has ever encountered a positive sentiment regarding Bush, we would expect that the information received through the interaction would be discounted. On the other hand, if our individual has repeated encounters with individuals who are favorably disposed toward Bush, the cumulative impact of the combined messages may be quite dramatic.

In short, the viewpoints of discussants are not only weighted (or self-weighted) by the expertise and interest of the discussants, but these viewpoints are also weighted by the degree to which they resonate with other information that an individual is receiving with respect to a particular political object. Information is not evaluated in an objective fashion. Rather, it is evaluated in a political context with respect to the information that is dominant within the setting.

The important point is that individuals do not simply formulate judgments based on the last piece of information they obtain. Because the veracity of information and information sources is judged relative to stored information, individuals are quite capable of resisting the information that is supplied in any particular informational exchange. Hence, it is not uncommon to find persistent disagreement within networks of political information. Indeed, the autoregressive influence of social communication makes it possible for individuals to *resist* socially supplied information with which they disagree.

For dramatic evidence in support of this assertion, we turn once again to the work of Solomon Asch (1963). In his famous series of experiments, each of eight individuals in a small group was asked to identify which of three comparison lines was the same length as a given standard line. All these individuals except one – the subject – were provided with a predetermined script of responses, and in some cases they were instructed to identify the wrong line. Hence, in these particular instances the uninformed subjects were confronted with situations in which socially supplied information – the other group members' judgments – conflicted with their own sensory perceptions.

Several features of the Asch experiments are especially noteworthy for present purposes. Although he did not intend to suggest that individuals are mindless automata (Ross 1990), Asch demonstrated that the majority is capable of producing important distortion effects on individual judgments. Nearly three-fourths of the subjects denied their own sensory perceptions in at least one instance, adjusting their own judgments to agree with incorrect majority judgments. About one-fourth of the subjects never compromised their own individual judgments, and approximately one-fourth compromised their judgments in at least half of the instances involving mistaken majority judgments. Overall, the subjects embraced majority opinion in about one-third of the instances involving a mistaken majority judgment.

Just as important for present purposes, if only *one other member of the group* was instructed to diverge from the group's mistaken judgment by consistently providing a correct report, the effect of majority opinion was effectively nullified. Hence, in this particular instance, an individual judgment based on sensory evidence consistently survives the challenge of majority disagreement if one other individual supports the subject's judgment. In summary, the influence of particular information sources must be judged not only relative to the individual's own viewpoint, but also relative to the distribution of viewpoints provided by other alternative information sources.

Third, social space is separate from any particular physical location, even though it is constructed on the basis of social proximity. How should we conceive the relevant social space? In another departure from the tradition of contextual analysis, we do not define social space as being coincidental with geographical boundaries. This is not to say that geography is irrelevant, and indeed geographical location goes a long way in helping to explain the particular configuration of the social space that is relevant to a particular citizen (Baybeck and Huckfeldt 2002). Social space is an overlay on physical, geographically defined location, but it is idiosyncratic to the geographical locales of particular individuals.

For example, an individual who resides in south St. Louis County may work at a bank in the central business district of the city. His cubicle may be next to another individual who resides in west St. Louis County, and their homes may be more than 20 miles apart. Our south county citizen may also play racquet ball at a sports club on his way home from work with an individual who commutes from the Illinois side of the river.

What is the relevant social space for this individual? Such a space must be defined in an idiosyncratic manner, relative to the particular construction of his network of social contacts. Is geography relevant to the construction of this network? The answer is quite obvious. It would be impossible to understand the construction of his network without reference to the spatial dimension of social engagement. At the same time, his social setting is not coincidental with any particular spatial setting, and the configuration of his network of contacts is most easily understood with respect to the multiple spatial settings in which he interacts.

The end result is that social space is defined in terms of the communication network within which an individual is imbedded. Although geography and physical location play a central role in the creation of the network, social space is not the same thing as physical space. Individuals who live next door to one another may share the same geographically defined neighborhood, but they may also be imbedded within networks without a single overlapping node. They share the same physical space, but their social spaces may be independent. And such independence may only become apparent during an election campaign, when yard signs pop up on their front lawns.

Perhaps more important, even spouses and close friends are frequently imbedded in communication networks that do not fully coincide. Hence, the idiosyncratic nature of network construction gives rise to low density networks – situations in which the range of contacts for any single individual in a network is less likely to coincide with the range of contacts experienced by other individuals in the network.

OBSERVATIONAL REQUIREMENTS AND DATA SETS

What are the observational implications of the explanation we have constructed? That is, what are the observational imperatives that are dictated by our theory?

First, we need to observe individuals within the contexts of their communication networks. Indeed, we propose to observe all three – individuals, networks, *and* contexts – where contexts are defined relative to the composition of the network as a whole. The first element of this observational triad is the most straightforward. Our argument is anchored in methodological individualism, and hence we employ measures of individual attitudes, predispositions, preferences, choices, attentiveness, engagement, and so on. At the end of the day, democratic politics is about individual citizens, but these citizens demonstrate complex forms of interdependence which require a multi-layered observational strategy.

Hence, in addition to these individual level measures, the argument also requires that individual citizens be located within their networks of political communication. At a minimum, this means that individuals must identify the other individuals who are located within their communication networks, as well as providing information regarding these other individuals. This network information is useful at several different levels of observation. For some purposes, the analytic focus will be on individuals within particular informational settings, and for other purposes the level of analysis will be the dyadic communication connections that occur between individuals. Moreover, pursuant to our conception of autoregressive influence, particular communication connections within the network must be assessed with respect to the network as a whole. Hence, we see individual citizens connected to other citizens in an informational context that is defined relative to the residual network – relative to the remainder of the network absent the particular dyad being considered.

Second, political communication among citizens is imbedded within a dynamic political process. The agenda of political communication is exogenous to individual citizens. These individuals have no control over the timing of political events, the issues being addressed in the media, and so on. Rather, political communication among citizens is a dynamic process that is endogenous to a dynamic political calendar. And our goal is to understand the dynamics that drive political communication, which means that we must observe communication in time.

Third, for some issues and some questions, it is important that information be collected from both sides of the communication dyad – from *both* the individual *and* her discussant. (Recall that we do not assume symmetry in these relationships: Nancy may be an important source of information for Tom, but that does not mean that Tom is an important source for Nancy.) This is particularly crucial when the analytic focus is on factors that enhance and impede the effectiveness of political communication. In colloquial terms, we want to understand who are the good talkers and who are the good listeners in democratic politics. This means that we wish to understand the circumstances of individuals and relationships that give rise to more effective communication, as well as the circumstances that attenuate the transmission of political messages. Such an undertaking is impossible absent interviews from both sides of the dyad.

Fourth, for other purposes, it is important to obtain nationally representative data. One part of our argument is descriptive in nature – we argue that the level and extent of disagreement among citizens have been seriously underestimated in the larger population. Hence, in order to address this issue, it becomes particularly important to provide representative estimates of political heterogeneity and disagreement for communication networks within the larger population.

No single data set provides all the necessary information, but we are fortunate in being able to employ two separate data sets that, in combination, provide an empirical basis for the study we are undertaking. The first data set is the Indianapolis–St. Louis Study that we introduced in Chapter 1. This study provides most of our study's empirical requirements, but it does not provide a national sample. Individuals were interviewed over the course of the 1996 election campaign, as well as nearly a year after the campaign was over, thereby providing a post hoc baseline from which to understand activation effects on communication. The study also provides interviews with both a main sample of individual citizens as well as the discussants who are located within these individuals' networks of communication. Finally, the study includes instrumentation designed for the measurement of effectiveness and persuasiveness of political communication.

The second data set is the 2000 National Election Study. The 2000 NES includes a short battery of questions designed to provide social network measures for respondents. These network data are based entirely on the perceptions of the main respondents. They do not include interviews with the members of the networks identified by the main respondents. Hence, they are not particularly useful for examining communication effectiveness, but they are extraordinarily helpful for a range of other purposes. We employ these network data in Chapter 8 to undertake an analysis of disagreement and political ambivalence. More immediately, we turn to the 2000 Study to consider the extensiveness of political disagreement among citizens in American politics.

HETEROGENEITY AND INFLUENCE WITHIN NETWORKS

The political influence that arises due to patterns of communication among citizens is a fact of life in democratic politics. Citizens depend on one another for information and guidance, and this interdependence gives rise to persuasion and shared political preferences. Evidence in support of this assertion is readily available, and we document the circumstances that inhibit and enhance influence in the pages that follow. But the reality of interdependence and influence, coupled with the persistence of disagreement, gives rise to a number of questions. What are the factors that sustain political heterogeneity in the face of influence and interdependence among citizens? What keeps citizens from ending up in cozy groups of like-minded associates – the sorts of cozy groups that many political scientists have generally assumed to surround most citizens?

We address these issues among respondents to the 2000 National Election Study by examining the distribution of political preferences within the respondents' networks of political communication. Each respondent to the postelection survey of the National Election Study was asked to provide the first names of the people with whom they discussed government, elections, and politics. In a subsequent battery of questions, they were asked to make a judgment regarding the presidential candidates for whom each of these discussants voted. Seventy-four percent of the postelection respondents were able to provide at least one name, and Table 2.1 is based on these respondents.

Parts A and B of Table 2.1 show the distributions of presidential vote choice within the respondents' political discussion networks, based on

Table 2.1. *Level of diversity within political communication networks for the respondents to the 2000 National Election Study. Weighted data.*

A. Percent of network voting for Gore by respondent's vote (unweighted N = 1147)

	Gore	Neither	Bush
None (0%)	14.2%	58.2	64.3
Some	44.3	29.3	28.5
All (100%)	41.5	12.5	7.2
Weighted N =	436	268	399

B. Percent of network voting for Bush by respondent's vote (unweighted N = 1147)

	Gore	Neither	Bush
None (0%)	63.2%	46.7	12.6
Some	32.3	36.2	39.9
All (100%)	4.5	17.0	47.5
Weighted N =	436	268	399

Source: 2000 National Election Study; unit of analysis is respondent; weighted data.

respondent perceptions regarding each of the individually named discussants. These distributions are contingent on the respondents' self-reported vote choices, and hence we are able to consider the level of political heterogeneity experienced by the respondents within their own closely held communication networks. Both parts of the table show clear evidence of political clustering among the respondents – only 14.2 percent of Gore supporters but 64.3 percent of the Bush supporters report that none of their discussants supported Gore. Similarly, only 12.6 percent of the Bush supporters but 63.2 percent of the Gore supporters report that none of their discussants supported Bush.

At the same time, neither part of Table 2.1 offers evidence of overwhelming homogeneity within the discussion networks. Only 41.5 percent of the Gore supporters report that all their discussants supported Gore, and only 47.5 percent of the Bush supporters report that all their discussants supported Bush. This means that, among the respondents who report voting for either Gore or Bush, less than half perceive that all their discussants voted in the same manner. Similarly, whereas 64.3 percent of the Bush voters and 63.2 percent of the Gore voters report that none of their discussants supported the opposite party's candidate, this means that more than one-third of the two-party voters report at least one discussant who voted for the opposite party's candidate.

Hence, Table 2.1 presents a tale of glasses that are *both* half empty *and* half full. On the one hand, the vote choices of respondents are clearly interdependent with the partisan distributions within networks. We do not bother to calculate chi-square measures for the various parts of

37

Table 2.1, but each of them would confirm that we can safely reject the null hypothesis of independence among the columns in each section of the table. At the same time, these patterns of interdependence are far from complete. Indeed the evidence of disagreement is as noteworthy as the evidence of agreement.

Moreover, Table 2.1 inevitably includes modest biases that underestimate levels of diversity. The 2000 National Election Study did not include interviews with the discussants of the main respondents, but a number of other studies have incorporated snowball designs that pursue interviews with members of the networks named by the respondents (Huckfeldt and Sprague 1987; Huckfeldt et al. 1998a; Huckfeldt, Sprague, and Levine 2000). These other studies use the discussant's self-reported vote as the base line criterion against which to judge the presence of systematic biases in the respondent's perception of political preferences in the network. In general, these studies show that respondents are reasonably accurate in their perceptions of discussant preferences. On the other hand, they also demonstrate a number of factors that enhance and attenuate the accuracy of discussant preferences.

Most notably for present purposes, respondents are less likely to recognize the preferences of discussants with whom they disagree. One interpretation of these results is that disagreement produces cognitive dissonance, and respondents avoid dissonance by selectively misperceiving the signals and messages that are thus conveyed. The problem with such an interpretation is that, as Table 2.1 makes abundantly clear, a great many respondents are perfectly able to recognize the existence of disagreement within their networks of political communication! Other explanations point in different directions in accounting for these patterns of perceptual bias (see Chapter 4), but most point toward a tendency for individuals to underestimate the extent of disagreement. This means, in turn, that Table 2.1 probably underestimates the extent to which individuals disagree with others in their communication networks.

Levels of disagreement inevitably depend on the particular construction of specific communication networks (Granovetter 1974; Burt 1992). For example, Part A of Table 2.2 shows that the level of political homogeneity within networks declines rapidly as a function of increased network size. This follows quite directly as a stochastic consequence of the odds underlying dyadic agreement. Returning to our earlier discussion, if the odds of disagreement are independent across dyads, then the probability of unanimity within a network is a declining exponential sequence, with the size of the network serving as the exponent. As it turns out, such an expectation provides a reasonable set of estimates for the levels of agreement among Bush and Gore voters in Table 2.2A. Regardless of sociometric order biases present in the naming of discussants (Burt 1986) – respondents

Heterogeneity and Influence within Networks

Table 2.2. *Patterns of agreement within networks. Weighted data.*

A. Percent of networks in which all discussants are perceived to hold the same presidential vote preference as the respondent, by size of network, for Gore and Bush voters (unweighted N = 1116)

	Network Size: Number of Discussants			
	1	2	3	4
Gore voter	65.8%	50.2	28.2	23.6
	(weighted n = 96)	(127)	(85)	(129)
Bush voter	66.6	64.4	38.6	26.6
	(92)	(99)	(75)	(132)

B. Percent of dyads in which the discussant is perceived to hold the same presidential vote preference as the respondent, by order in which discussant is named, for Gore and Bush voters (unweighted N = 2363)

	Order in which Discussant is Named			
	First	Second	Third	Fourth
Gore voter	66.2%	61.9	58.3	49.4
	(weighted n = 438)	(341)	(215)	(129)
Bush voter	72.9	65.7	65.0	69.2
	(401)	(307)	(208)	(132)

Source: 2000 National Election Study; unit of analysis in Part A is the respondent; unit of analysis in Part B is the dyad; weighted data.

tend to name their closest discussants earlier in the list – Part B of Table 2.2 shows only modest and inconsistent effects on agreement that arise due to the order in which discussants are named. Hence, Table 2.2 points to the importance of a network characteristic (size), rather than to a characteristic of particular discussants (order of mention), as the important explanatory factor predicting disagreement within particular networks.

In summary, it becomes quite clear that political preferences are interdependent within communication networks, that the probability of agreement is higher between individuals who reside within the same network than between individuals who reside in different networks. At the same time, it is equally clear that high levels of political heterogeneity persist within communication networks. How should we account for these patterns of agreement and disagreement within networks?

One explanation is that, whereas citizens are interdependent in the formulation of political choices, they are not individually powerless in the face of social influence. They do not simply go along with whatever a particular discussant happens to suggest. Hence we are simply seeing the limits of social influence. In the end, independence frequently trumps interdependence, resulting in modest clustering effects that do not even come close to producing political homogeneity within networks.

We embrace much of this explanation. Individuals are *not* social automata who simply go along with whatever viewpoints their discussants happen to put forward. At the same time, we reject the idea that disagreement is necessarily evidence of individual independence. Our goal is to construct an explanation for social interaction that takes account of both agreement and disagreement as the potentially systematic outcomes of social influence. We begin by considering the factors that might lead to disagreement before turning to an explanation that might account for both agreement and disagreement within communication networks.

POINTS OF INTERSECTION BETWEEN INDIVIDUALS AND AGGREGATES

When individuals are confronted with political choices, they use the various devices at their disposal to serve as sources of political guidance. Some of these devices are based on individual predispositions and attitudes. The heuristic utility of political attitudes is that they serve to summarize an individual's political experience, as well as the lessons drawn from that experience. In this way, when individuals confront a choice, they are guided by attitudes and orientations that possess an experiential base. Hence, the experience of the Great Depression and the New Deal convinced several generations of Americans to develop positive attitudes and orientations toward the Democratic Party, and these attitudes and orientations served as the bases for subsequent political choices. In a similar manner, the Civil Rights movement reinforced those positive orientations among some, as it led to an erosion of those orientations among others, leading many individuals to reconsider their positive assessments (Carmines and Stimson 1989). In summary, political attitudes and points of political orientation are anchored in information gained through political experience.

The precise manner in which these attitudes and orientations change and respond to experience is a matter of fundamental theoretical concern, and we have come to understand that process more completely in the context of serially occurring events and individual judgments regarding those events (Fiorina 1981; Lodge 1995). Political economists and political psychologists agree that attitudes are not immune to experience, but rather that they evolve in response to individuals' evaluations of political events and objects. In short, individual attitudes and orientations regarding politics are inherently dynamic, formulated at the point of intersection between individual citizens and their experience of the events and dramas of politics.

Intersection between Individuals and Aggregates

In this way, attitudes and orientations serve to inform political choice by bringing a catalog of experience to bear on political alternatives. But attitudes and orientations are not the only points of intersection between an individual and her experience of political events. Individuals also obtain information through channels and networks of social communication. And as we have seen, the political content of messages conveyed through these networks does not simply replicate the political attitudes and orientations of the individuals who populate the networks. These networks of political communication are frequently characterized by high levels of political heterogeneity, and hence individuals often find themselves in situations where their own points of political orientation point in one direction, while the messages received from others point in opposite directions. How do citizens respond to politically diverse messages?

The three panels of Table 2.3 characterize the relationships among individual partisanship, network partisanship, and vote choice among the respondents to the 2000 National Election Study. First, notice that the vast majority of strong partisans are located either in homogeneously partisan networks that support their own partisan orientations or in heterogeneous networks. Only 12 out of 212 strong Democrats are located in networks that are unanimous in support of Bush, and only 7 out of 173 strong Republicans are located in networks that are unanimous in their support of Gore. A somewhat less pronounced pattern occurs among the weak partisans – very few weak Democrats are located in homogeneous Bush networks and very few weak Republicans are located in homogeneous Gore networks. Similarly, the independent partisans – self-proclaimed independents who lean toward one of the major parties – are also quite unlikely to be located in networks that unanimously support the opposite party's presidential candidate.

Hence, although individually based partisan orientations are outstanding predictors of vote choice, it is often quite difficult to separate individual partisan orientations from the political composition of the surrounding communication network. Partisans may associate with others who are politically sympathetic, or strong partisanship may be unable to survive in a politically hostile micro-environment, or there may be some combination of both processes at work. In any event, we do not typically see Democratic sympathizers in a network full of Bush supporters, or Republican sympathizers in a network full of Gore supporters.

At the same time, nearly half of the strong partisans are located in politically heterogeneous networks, and clear majorities of the weak partisans are located in politically heterogeneous networks. What difference does this make? Among the strong partisans, it would appear to make very little difference. Strong Democrats are likely to vote for Gore and strong

New Information and Old Information

Table 2.3. *Respondent vote by aggregate characteristics of network for the respondents to the 2000 National Election Study. Weighted data.*

A. Respondent vote by respondent partisanship in homogeneous Gore networks (unweighted N = 255)

	SD	WD	ID	I	IR	WR	SR
Gore	89.4%	82.2	72.8	44.5	49.8	46.2	0.0
Neither	10.6	9.8	17.8	43.2	7.8	17.6	15.4
Bush	0.0	8.0	9.4	12.3	42.4	36.3	84.6
Weighted N =	95	53	43	13	17	15	7

B. Respondent vote by respondent partisanship in networks that are *not* unanimously in support of either major candidate (unweighted N = 616)

	SD	WD	ID	I	IR	WR	SR
Gore	82.3%	69.6	49.2	23.5	6.6	14.8	0.5
Neither	15.6	22.3	39.9	59.1	40.8	27.9	12.7
Bush	2.1	8.1	10.9	17.4	52.6	57.3	86.8
Weighted N =	105	94	110	60	96	64	72

C. Respondent vote by respondent partisanship in homogeneous Bush networks (unweighted N = 265)

	SD	WD	ID	I	IR	WR	SR
Gore	52.7%	32.9	27.7	10.9	2.7	3.2	0.4
Neither	7.2	46.4	25.3	48.0	22.6	17.7	5.0
Bush	40.1	20.7	47.0	41.2	74.8	79.1	94.6
Weighted N =	12	13	16	15	48	56	94

SD = strong Democrat; WD = not strong (weak) Democrat; ID = independent leaning toward Democrat; I = independent; IR = independent leaning toward Republican; WR = not strong (weak) Republican; SR = strong Republican.
Source: 2000 National Election Study; unit of analysis is respondent; weighted data.

Republicans for Bush, regardless of whether they reside in heterogeneous networks or in networks that unanimously support their own political orientation. A very different pattern exists among the weak and independent partisans: They are substantially more likely to support their party's candidate if they are located in a network characterized by homogeneous support for that candidate, and their support declines in politically heterogeneous networks.

Perhaps not surprisingly, the most pronounced pattern of association occurs among the independents. A clear majority of independents is located in heterogeneous networks – networks that are not unanimous in support of either candidate. In these networks, a clear majority fails to support either of the major party candidates – 23.5 percent support Gore and 17.4 percent support Bush. In contrast, 44.5 percent report supporting

Gore if they are located in networks that unanimously support Gore. In networks that unanimously support Bush, 41.2 percent of the independents report voting for Bush.

In summary, the socially heroic partisan is a rare event in democratic politics. Very few party loyalists reside in communication networks that are unanimously oriented in the opposite partisan direction. In contrast, a great many partisans are located in politically heterogeneous networks. Strong, weak, and independent partisans frequently find themselves in communication networks where their own points of political orientation are not held by everyone they encounter. The central theoretical issues are thus related to the flow of information and influence in politically heterogeneous environments.

SUMMARY AND CONCLUSION

How are we to account for the altered view we are presenting – a view that sees disagreement and political heterogeneity rather than agreement and political homogeneity as the modal conditions within citizens' networks of political communication? Part of the answer to this question is a matter of emphasis. As we have seen in Table 2.1, the evidence on agreement and disagreement within networks shows clear evidence of clustering alongside clear evidence of sustained political disagreement. If one's goal is to demonstrate that citizens are not isolated and independent – that they are interdependent in arriving at political choices – then the resulting analysis is likely to focus on clustering. We certainly do not take issue with such an analysis. We embrace a view of politics that is built on the interdependent nature of citizenship (Huckfeldt and Sprague 1995; Huckfeldt, Johnson, and Sprague 2002).

At the same time, networks of communication among interdependent citizens are capable of creating and sustaining *dis*agreement as well as agreement – divergence as well as convergence in the distributions of opinion among individuals who are engaged in sustained patterns of social interaction. In this way, we are not making an argument that is aimed at qualifying the importance of communication and persuasion, but rather a view that extends the explanatory reach provided by theories of political interdependence. In short, the structure of communication networks might account either for patterns of agreement or for patterns of disagreement among individuals.

This leads to an additional reason for the altered view we are presenting – the development of improved conceptual tools for studying patterns of political communication. If communication and persuasion are conceived in terms of small, cohesive, self-contained groups, it is quite difficult to accommodate disagreement as well as agreement within

43

an explanation based on communication and influence among citizens. Alternatively, when political communication and persuasion are conceived in terms of complex patterns of social interaction within networks, we gain additional analytic leverage on the problem. In this way, our analysis benefits quite profoundly due to the rapid advances in social network theory that have occurred in the past 50 years.

Finally, it is important to recognize that the world is quite different now from what it was at the time of the Erie County and Elmira studies. Processes of social differentiation have continued to unfold, leading to increased levels of political diversity within social groups. When Lazarsfeld and his colleagues were writing, being Catholic often meant being Democratic. Hence, if Catholics interacted with other Catholics, they were much more likely to be imbedded within homogeneous networks of political communication. Today, many of these traditional social groups are no longer as politically reliable and predictable as they once were, either for the politician or for the analyst.

A number of analyses have pointed toward the decreased explanatory power of social group membership in explaining political behavior and political preference (Levine, Carmines, and Huckfeldt 1997). This pattern of diminished effects is not unique to the United States, and it is intimately connected to cross-national patterns of political dealignment in which political party coalitions have seen their bases of support within social groups erode over time (Dalton, Flanagan, and Beck 1984). An alternative way to understand these patterns of dealignment is in terms of increased political heterogeneity within social groups. Hence, self-contained patterns of social interaction within traditional social groups – to the extent that these patterns continue to exist – are less likely to result in politically homogeneous networks of social interaction.

Unfortunately, we have very little reliable evidence over time regarding the social and political content of social interaction, but an important exception is provided in the work of Franz Pappi (2001: 615). Using German social network data collected from 1972 through 1990, Pappi demonstrates that the relationship between political preference and the social composition of networks declined precipitously over the period – that is, the social composition of networks became less predictive of their political composition.

Hence levels of political disagreement within networks may very well be higher at the turn of the century than they were 50 years earlier. To repeat our earlier argument, the political composition of communication networks is not simply or solely a reflection of individual political preference. Rather, the political composition of communication networks is, in large part, a stochastic reflection of the relevant underlying populations from which network members are drawn (Huckfeldt 1983; Huckfeldt and

Sprague 1995: Chapter 8). To the extent that the political composition of these underlying populations has grown more diverse, we would expect this diversity to be reflected in higher levels of disagreement within communication networks. Thus contemporary citizens may experience disagreement more frequently than citizens of 50 years prior, and if this is the case, it would provide an important ingredient to explanations of electoral change.

In this chapter we make several arguments regarding the nature of social influence in politics, and ways in which networks of political communication might sustain agreement as well as disagreement among citizens. In the next chapter we employ these arguments to analyze the distribution of agreement within the communication networks during the election campaign.

3

Dyads, Networks, and Autoregressive Influence

If political influence among citizens is autoregressive – if the political consequences of dyadic encounters depend on the distribution of preferences of citizens across the network – then we should expect to see distinctive patterns of agreement and disagreement. This chapter develops the autoregressive model of influence within a larger literature on the political consequences that arise due to networks and contexts. We then employ this general model to examine variations in patterns of disagreement and agreement within the self-defined communication networks of the respondents to the 2000 National Election Study.

Political influence is autoregressive within networks of communication if the influence due to a particular discussant's viewpoint depends on the distribution of political viewpoints among discussants in the remainder of the network. Hence, in an autoregressive model of influence, each of an individual's dyadic relationships is understood as being contingent on all the individual's other dyadic relationships. Autoregressive patterns of political influence produce distinctive patterns of agreement and disagreement within networks, and this makes it possible to evaluate whether influence is autoregressive by analyzing the distribution of agreement and disagreement within communication networks.

In the chapters that follow, we examine two separate mechanisms that generate these autoregressive patterns – the effects of preference distributions within networks on both the *effectiveness* as well as the *persuasiveness* of communication. Effectiveness is defined with respect to the clarity and accuracy of communication: Effectively communicated messages provide the recipients with clear, accurate, and unambiguous understandings of the senders' preferences and opinions. In contrast, persuasiveness is defined with respect to preference and opinion change: A message is persuasive when the recipient changes an opinion or preference as a consequence of its communication. Network effects operating on effectiveness and persuasiveness produce reinforcing consequences for the larger autoregressive pattern of opinion distributions.

46

Contexts, Networks, and Autoregressive Influence

In the present chapter we focus on the immediate descriptive consequences of autoregressive influence for patterns of agreement and disagreement, and in later chapters we turn to a detailed consideration of
these separate mechanisms underlying autoregressive patterns of opinion
change.

This focus on descriptive consequences produces several significant benefits. Most important, it provides additional insight into the state of affairs
within the communication networks of citizens, a particularly important
advantage given the general dearth of knowledge and data regarding the
distributional properties of agreement and disagreement across citizen
networks. Moreover, it provides an opportunity to make further use of a
data set that is particularly valuable in this regard – the battery of network
questions included within the 2000 National Election Study.

CONTEXTS, NETWORKS, AND AUTOREGRESSIVE INFLUENCE

Our conception of autoregressive influence is located within a larger literature on context and network effects on individual behavior (Huckfeldt
and Sprague 1987). The development of contextual and network explanations has occurred around a central theme – that individuals formulate
their opinions, attitudes, and predispositions within particular settings.
These settings are, in turn, consequential for a wide range of political
behaviors, including not only attitudes and opinions, but also levels and
forms of political engagement and participation, as well as vote choice.
Hence, explanations for individual-level politics must take account of
both micro- as well as macro-circumstances connected to the individual (Huckfeldt 1986; Knoke 1990; Books and Prysby 1991; Achen and
Shively 1995; Huckfeldt and Sprague 1995).

At the same time, explanations for politics in the aggregate – for public
opinion, engagement, and electoral behavior in group settings – must similarly take into account these micro-macro relationships to make sense of
variations in the behavior of political groups (Eulau 1986). Durkheim's
lesson (1897: 321) for modern social science is that the groups formed
by interdependent individuals produce an empirical reality that is far
different from each individual considered independently. For purposes
of clarity and completeness, we simply add the corollary and derivative
implication – that individuals located in networks of interdependence also
produce an empirical reality that is far different from individuals understood as autonomous actors.

Hence, contextual and network theories of individual behavior are motivated by a common theoretical imperative – the importance of incorporating specifications of individual interdependence within explanations
for *both* group *and* individual behavior. The manner in which individual

interdependence is understood, either in terms of networks or in terms of contexts, has important implications for an understanding of agreement and disagreement within political communication networks. Hence, our discussion turns to alternative representations of contextual effects in politics.

REPRESENTATIONS OF CONTEXTUAL EFFECTS
ON COMMUNICATION

This discussion becomes more helpful if we translate the underlying ideas into several simply defined mathematical formulations that occur in the literatures on contextual and network effects on individual behavior. We begin with a contextual representation that is explicated most fully in the work of Boyd and Iversen (1979). Their development of the argument is particularly compelling because it is constructed on the basis of the seemingly simple relationship between an individual behavior and an individual characteristic. In their basic model,

$$Y_{ij} = a_j + b_j X_{ij}$$

where Y_{ij} is a particular political behavior, say support for the Democratic candidate by the ith individual in the jth context. And where X_{ij} is a relevant characteristic, say the income of the ith individual in the jth context.

Boyd and Iversen define the coefficients in the basic model as being functionally specific to the jth context:

$$a_j = a' + a'' X_{.j}$$
$$b_j = b' + b'' X_{.j}$$

where $X_{.j}$ is the mean of the relevant social characteristic summed over all individuals in the jth context.

Their model describes individual level support for the Democratic candidate as dependent on the presence or absence of an individual characteristic (X_{ij}) as well as the incidence of that characteristic in the surrounding population ($X_{.j}$). It is important to stress this point: Individuals are motivated not only by their own characteristics, but also by the characteristics of others in the surrounding context.

Additionally, the translation of the individual characteristic into a factor influencing individual behavior depends on the incidence of this characteristic in the surrounding population. Similarly, the translation of the population characteristic into a factor influencing individual behavior depends on the presence or absence of the individual characteristic. These contingent effects are perhaps seen more directly if the model is translated, by the appropriate substitutions, into a single equation form:

$$Y_{ij} = a' + b'X_{ij} + a''X_{\cdot j} + b''X_{ij}X_{\cdot j}.$$

Either by taking partial derivatives, or by simple algebraic arrangement, one can see that the effect of the individual characteristic is $(b' + b''X_{\cdot j})$, and the effect of the population characteristic is $(a'' + b''X_{ij})$.

This representation portrays individual behavior as dependent on the presence of an individual trait, as well as the incidence of that trait in the surrounding population. Moreover, the individual level behavioral effects of both the individual trait and the distribution of the individual trait in the larger population are conditioned on one another. When treated as a statistical model for data analysis, this formulation produces some complex formulations of multi-level, hierarchical effects (Huckfeldt 1986; Huckfeldt and Sprague 1995), as well as insight into the nature of communication effects and individual interdependence.[1]

REPRESENTATIONS OF NETWORK EFFECTS
ON COMMUNICATION

Regardless of these advantages and insights, contextual models are of limited utility in pursuing some of the issues that we have introduced above. In particular, by conceiving political communication in terms of the central tendency for the distribution of a trait within a population, our ability to explain political communication in terms of complex social interaction patterns is compromised. Moreover, we are unable to consider individual exchanges of information within the larger context of other, cumulative information exchanges. Hence, we proceed to consider a parallel but separate literature regarding network effects on individual behavior.

This alternative network effects formulation is summarized in matrix form by Marsden and Friedkin (1994) as:[2]

$$y = \alpha Wy + X\beta + e.$$

Absent the term which includes the W matrix, this equation looks much like a standard least-squares regression model. X is a $(N \times K)$ matrix of individually based explanatory variables, y is a $(N \times 1)$ vector of

---

[1] Employing the model for purposes of data analysis produces complex implications for the structure of the error term (Boyd and Iversen 1979; Bryk and Raudenbush 1992). Important insights on these inherently hierarchical problems can be obtained from a Bayesian standpoint in Gelman, Carlin, Stern, and Rubin (1995); Congdon (2001, 2003); and Gill (2002).

[2] For closely related discussions see Anselin (1988), Besag (1974), Besag and Kooperberg (1995), Mollié (1996), and Wakefield, Best, and Waller (2000).

individually based response variables, and e is a $(N \times 1)$ vector of errors, where the $(K \times 1)\beta$ vector is the vector of coefficients that measures the effect of the exogenous explanatory variables included in the X matrix.

The innovation of this model lies in the formulation of the endogenous network effects on individual behavior, αWy. The W matrix is a $(N \times N)$ matrix of influence coefficients, such that each of the elements is greater than or equal to zero, and the sum of the coefficients for any individual is unity ($\Sigma w_{ij} = 1$, summed across j for any i). Finally, α is a weight operating on endogenous influence within the model. If α is zero, individual behavior is wholly a function of the exogenous factors and errors.

Assuming this is an appropriate characterization of influence for the population in question, omitting the term with the W matrix produces a model with autocorrelated error terms (Marsden and Friedkin 1994; Anselin 1988).

$$y = X\beta + \varepsilon,$$

where $\varepsilon = \rho W \varepsilon + \nu$.

These network formulations produce a number of advantages in the present context. First, rather than conceiving a contextual effect in which the central tendency of a population produces a direct effect, these models explicitly recognize that social influence comes in bits and pieces, in fits and starts, in a process where individuals typically encounter the other individuals within their network in serial fashion.

Second, this network formulation creates a social space that is not *necessarily* defined in terms of physical or geographic location.[3] A variety of populations might be analyzed in the context of these models. One might employ the models to consider network effects among colleagues in an academic department, policy makers in a set of governmental institutions, members of a religious congregation, residents of a neighborhood, and more. In short, although the population might be defined in terms of physical location and geography might play an important role in the definition of the network, this need not be the case.

A final advantage is that the model is formulated to consider network effects that arise through behavioral interdependence. The modern tradition of contextual effects was originally articulated by Blau (1960) and Davis, Spaeth, and Huson (1961) to consider more general milieu effects. One might therefore ask, how do the political consequences of being a member

---

[3] Contextual explanations need not be based on physical or geographic location either, but as a practical matter, most contextual analyses rely on data that are available based on physical boundaries (see Huckfeldt, Plutzer, and Sprague 1993).

of the Chilean working class compare to the political consequences of being located *among* the other members of the Chilean working class?[4]

As originally conceived, these contextual effects might be seen in terms of social interaction effects (or network effects) within the surrounding population, but they might also be seen more diffusely in terms of effects on social identities. This latter literature on diffuse contextual effects is vulnerable to the criticism offered by Erbring and Young (1979) in which a contextual effect becomes a matter of "social telepathy" – an instance in which some general population characteristic mysteriously becomes a factor affecting individual behavior. The Marsden and Friedkin formulation is less vulnerable because it explicitly makes individual behavior contingent on the behavior of others. At the same time, making individual behavior dependent on behavioral distributions within the network creates some challenging endogeneity problems, particularly if one's goal is to isolate asymmetric individual-level causal effects.

DYADS, NETWORKS, AND SOCIAL COMMUNICATION

The network effects model demonstrates some important advantages, but it also demonstrates limitations. First, and most important for present purposes, we are not studying political influence within a self-contained population. Rather, we are examining patterns of influence in the entire United States population during a presidential election campaign. In this setting, and in most other settings that are of interest to students of voting, elections, and public opinion, the populations are not usefully seen as being self-contained. In particular, the W matrix becomes enormous for anything other than small self-contained populations, and nearly all the entries are zero. What do we need instead?

Rather than mapping the network of relationships for an entire self-contained population, we are interested in the networks that are defined with respect to particular individuals within a larger and more extensive population. (Within the specialized study of social networks, these are known as egocentric networks.) Hence, we might define the network as: $N_i = \Sigma w_k d_k$, where N_i is the ith individual's communication network. Each network includes the k discussants with whom the particular individual regularly communicates, and the w_k are the complex undefined weights operating on communication patterns within the network.

Although it is possible that one discussant (one d_k) might serve as a discussant for more than one individual, the probability is extremely low for any random sample taken from a large population. And in addressing

---

[4] For a classic analysis of this problem, see Langton and Rapoport (1975).

a random sample of American citizens, we might judge this probability to be near zero.

Where does this formulation lead us with respect to our theoretical and substantive goals? First, rather than focusing on the individual's preference, we shift the focus to consider whether an individual's candidate preference corresponds to the candidate preferences of particular discussants within the network – to consider the probability that an individual agrees with any particular discussant in the network. Second, we address the flow of information and influence among and between the members of the network, and consider the flow of information within dyads as being contingent on the flow of information and influence within the larger network. In particular, we begin with the ith individual and her kth discussant. The probability of agreement depends on two general factors: (1) the distance between the discussant's candidate preference and the underlying partisan orientation of the respondent and (2) the candidate preference of the *particular* discussant with respect to the distribution of preferences in the remainder of the individual's network. Beginning with the first factor, the probability of agreement between the ith individual and her kth discussant may be written as:

$$P(A_{ik}) = f(\beta_o + \beta_1 P_k + \beta_2 O_i + \beta_3 P_k O_i)$$

where $P(A_{ik})$ is the probability of agreement regarding preferred candidates within a dyad formed by the ith individual and her kth discussant, O_i is the ith individual's underlying partisan orientation, and P_k is the candidate preference of the kth discussant in the dyad, measured in terms of the individual's perception. This formulation describes the probability of agreement in candidate preferences between an individual and any one of her discussants as a consequence of the discussant's preference, her own underlying partisan orientation, and the interaction between the two.

The autoregressive influence argument is that an individual will consider the information obtained from any particular discussant within the context of the information taken from all other discussants. In order to incorporate this argument, the model for the probability of agreement between the ith individual and the kth discussant is expanded to become:

$$P(A_{ik}) = f(\beta_o + \beta_1 P_k + \beta_2 O_i + \beta_3 P_k O_i + \beta_4 P_{.-k} + \beta_5 P_k P_{.-k})$$

where $P_{.-k}$ is the distribution of discussant preferences in the residual network – the remaining discussants, absent the kth discussant included in the dyad. Hence, this formulation expands the model to incorporate not only the idea that agreement depends on the political distance between discussion partners within a dyad, but also the idea that agreement depends on the political distance between the particular discussant and the remainder of the individual's communication network.

Dyads, Networks, and Social Communication

The same logic applies to each of the dyadic relationships within the network. Hence the same individual would also consider information taken from the second discussant within the context of information provided by the first and third discussants, as well as information taken from the third discussant within the context of information taken from the first and second discussants.

If this argument is correct, what would be the consequence of ignoring the fact that the impact of information taken from a single source is contingent on information taken from other sources? In the contingent view, the slope of the argument operating on P_k becomes $\beta_1 + \beta_3 O_i + \beta_5 P_{.-k}$, and hence the discussant's preference is contingent on the distribution of preferences in the residual network. A model that ignores this contingency produces autocorrelated errors within the social space where individuals reside. In particular, we are likely to overestimate the effects of discussants who hold minority preferences within networks, and underestimate the influence of discussants who hold majority preferences within networks (Huckfeldt and Sprague 1987).

In short, each individual's response to the information provided by any particular discussant depends on the opinions of a select group of other discussants, and it is unlikely that the informational effects that we seek to understand will be well represented by a simple summation (or any other index) that applies equally to all the discussants within the network. Hence, it is important to specify the nature of the informational linkages between the individual and the particular discussants within the communication network. In this way, each communication link in an individual's communication network is considered within the context of all the individual's remaining communication links.

Rather than characterizing the individual's correspondence with the central tendency of the network, we consider the level of correspondence within each dyad. Each observation within the resulting data matrix represents a dyad, and each individual's appearance in the matrix is multiplied by the size of her network. This means that, if the individual has four discussants, she would be represented within four different dyads within the matrix. Hence we are clustering within networks, and separate agreement measures for the same individual with different discussion partners appear as the regressands within multiple rows of the matrix. Clustering produces a situation in which the size of the matrix overstates the amount of information that is carried by the matrix, and thus in the statistical analysis below we employ a procedure that takes account of the clustering and produces robust estimates for the standard errors (Rogers 1993).

In summary, our argument is not simply that predicting individual behavior on the basis of individual characteristics produces individual errors that are correlated among associated individuals. Rather, we are arguing that *the consequences of dyadic information flows are conditioned on the remainder of the individual's network*. Hence, we imbed dyadic communication within the context of the larger network in order to avoid autocorrelation among the dyads within the same network. More important, by locating dyads within their larger networks, we provide a more compelling specification of political interdependence among citizens in democratic politics.

DYADS, NETWORKS, AND THE 2000 ELECTION

How do individuals respond to political heterogeneity within their communication networks? Our argument is that the views of individuals are discounted if they run counter to the dominant view within the network. In this way, the message conveyed by any particular discussant is weighted by the distribution of preferences in the remainder of the network (Huckfeldt et al. 1998a). Hence, we would expect agreement within dyads to depend not only on the political distance between the discussant's candidate preference and the respondent's political orientation, but also on the distance between the discussant's preference and the distribution of preferences in the remainder of the network.

We employ this model in analyzing the consequence of dyadic information flows within the networks of the respondents to the 2000 National Election Study. Recall that, in the post-election survey, interviewers asked each individual respondent to identify people with whom they discussed government, elections, and politics. As many as four discussants were identified for each respondent, and interviewers asked the respondents to provide information about each of the discussants, including their perceptions regarding the discussants' votes in the 2000 presidential election.

Each individual respondent provided self-report information regarding his or her own attitudes, opinions, voting behavior, and partisan identification. The respondents also provided their perceptions regarding each discussion partner's vote choice in the 2000 presidential election. Our goal is to ascertain the effect of the perceived candidate preference of the discussant on the respondent's own candidate preference. We hypothesize that the discussant effect is conditioned both on the individual respondent's own partisan orientation, as well as on the perceived preference distribution in the remainder of the communication network. This measure for the residual network is the number of remaining discussants perceived by the respondent to hold the same preference as the discussant being considered within the particular dyad.

Dyads, Networks, and the 2000 Election

Table 3.1. *Respondent agreement with discussants who support Bush,
Gore, and neither candidate by partisanship of the respondent and
distribution of preferences in the residual network. (Logit models;
t-values are in parentheses.)*

	Respondent Agreement with a Discussant Who Supports:		
	Bush	Gore	Neither
Constant	−.49	−.27	1.65
	(1.82)	(.98)	(4.45)
Party identification	.81	−.77	
	(10.03)	(8.14)	
Partisan strength			−.71
			(4.64)
Residual network support for:			
Bush	.65	−.18	−.65
	(3.21)	(1.32)	(3.63)
Gore	−.35	.64	−.93
	(2.15)	(2.81)	(4.50)
Neither	−.18	−.30	.04
	(.98)	(1.64)	(.20)
N (clusters)	1183(665)	1071(649)	545(395)
Chi-square/df/p	125/4/.00	86/4/.00	43/4/.00

Respondent agreement within dyad: 1 = if respondent perceives that the discussant
supports his or her own candidate choice, 0 = other. Party identification: seven point
scale = −3 (strong Democrat) to 3 (strong Republican). Partisan strength: four point
scale = 0 (independent) to 3 (strong partisan). Residual network support for Bush:
number of discussants in remainder of network that are perceived to support Bush.
Residual network support for Gore: number of discussants in remainder of network
that are perceived to support Gore. Residual network support for neither: number of
discussants in remainder of network that are perceived to support neither candidate.
Source: 2000 National Election Study; unit of analysis is dyad; data are weighted;
standard errors are corrected for clustering.

The presence or absence of agreement within each of the identified
dyads is considered in terms of our argument in Table 3.1, where the
functional form is defined in terms of the logistic distribution. In each
of the dyads analyzed in the first model, the respondent perceives that
the discussant voted for Bush, and hence agreement is defined as an instance in which the respondent also reported voting for Bush. Similarly
in the second model, the respondent perceives that each of the discussants supported Gore, and agreement exists if the respondent also reports
voting for Gore. Finally, in the third model, respondents perceive that
these discussants voted for neither Bush nor Gore, and agreement exists
if the respondent reports voting for neither candidate. (Based on these

measurement procedures, the participants in 60 percent of all dyads in the sample hold the same political preferences.)

Several explanatory variables are included in the models: the respondent's partisanship, as well as the numbers of discussants in the remaining network whom the respondent perceived as voting for Bush, Gore, or neither. In the models for discussants who are perceived to support Gore and Bush, respondent partisanship is measured on the traditional 7-point scale, where 0 represents independence or neutrality, -3 is strong Democrat, and 3 is strong Republican. In the model for discussants who support neither candidate, respondent partisanship is measured as strength absent direction — as the absolute value of the party identification measure. Recall that a maximum of four discussants is recorded for each respondent, and hence the maximum number of discussants in the residual network is three.

These models allow us to address the conditions that enhance and diminish the probability of agreement within particular dyads. The models consistently produce statistically discernible coefficients for respondent partisanship. Strong Democrats are more likely to agree with Gore voters and less likely to agree with Bush voters. Correspondingly, strong Republicans are more likely to agree with Bush voters and less likely to agree with Gore voters. Strong partisans of either variety are less likely to agree with discussants who support neither of the major party candidates.

The preference distributions within the residual networks produce results that are more complex (and perhaps more interesting). Support for Bush in the residual network enhances the probability of agreeing with a discussant who supports Bush and attenuates the probability of agreeing with a discussant who supports neither of the major party candidates. Similarly, residual support for Gore enhances the probability of agreement with a discussant who supports Gore and diminishes the probability of agreement with a discussant who supports neither candidate. In addition, increased Gore support attenuates the probability of agreeing with a discussant who voted for Bush. Finally, the number of discussants who support neither candidate fails to produce a discernible coefficient in any of the three models.

The magnitudes and implications of these patterns of relationships are seen most readily in Figure 3.1, which displays the estimated probabilities of agreement within dyads for respondents who identify as political independents. The independent respondents are more likely to agree with discussants who voted for Bush to the extent that support for Bush occurs in the remainder of their networks. Similarly, they are more likely to agree with Gore-voting discussants to the extent that Gore voting is more common in the remainder of their networks. In both instances, the agreement probability is only modestly attenuated by the distribution of

A. Discussant is Bush supporter   B. Discussant is Gore supporter

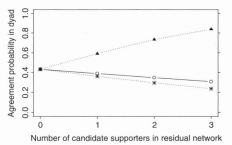

C. Discussant supports neither candidate

○   Bush support
▲   Gore support
✳   Support for neither

Figure 3.1. Contingent probability of agreement within network dyads, by the candidate preference of the discussant in the dyad and the levels of candidate support in the remainder of the network. All respondents are independents. *Note:* When the level of support for a particular candidate preference in the residual network is held constant at 0, 1, 2, or 3 discussants, support for the other preferences is held constant at 0. *Source:* Table 3.1 estimates.

other preferences or non-preferences. Finally, and in contrast, the probability of agreement with a discussant who supports neither candidate is not enhanced by the presence of other non-supporters in the remainder of the network, but is diminished by the presence of either Bush or Gore voters.

Figures 3.2 and 3.3 replicate Figure 3.1, but for respondents who identify as strong Republicans and strong Democrats respectively. These figures demonstrate the strong bias toward (1) agreement with discussants whose vote preferences correspond with the respondents' partisan loyalties and (2) disagreement with discussants whose vote preferences run counter to the respondents' partisan loyalties. The pattern of agreement and disagreement that depends on preference distributions in the residual network is also present in these figures, but its magnitude is greatly reduced.

A. Discussant is Bush supporter

B. Discussant is Gore supporter

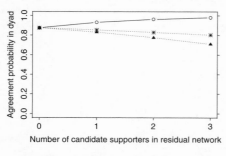

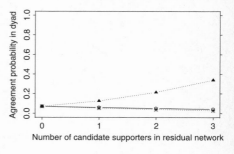

C. Discussant supports neither candidate

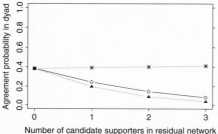

○ Bush support
▲ Gore support
✳ Support for neither

Figure 3.2. Contingent probability of agreement within network dyads, by the candidate preference of the discussant in the dyad and the levels of candidate support in the remainder of the network. All respondents are strong Republicans. *Note:* When the level of support for a particular candidate preference in the residual network is held constant at 0, 1, 2, or 3 discussants, support for the other preferences is held constant at 0. *Source:* Table 3.1 estimates.

In summary, this analysis shows that:

1. A strong partisan is highly likely to *agree* with a discussant who supports her own party's candidate – and to *disagree* with a discussant who supports the opposite party's candidate – *regardless* of the partisan division in the remainder of the network.
2. As the strength of partisanship decreases, the probability that individuals will agree or disagree with a discussant who supports either candidate increasingly becomes contingent on the distribution of candidate preferences in the remainder of the communication network. In particular, the probability of agreement is enhanced by the presence of other discussants who hold the same political preference.

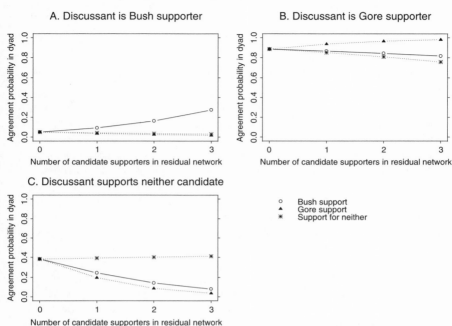

Figure 3.3. Contingent probability of agreement within network dyads, by the candidate preference of the discussant in the dyad and the levels of candidate support in the remainder of the network. All respondents are strong Democrats. *Note:* When the level of support for a particular candidate preference in the residual network is held constant at 0, 1, 2, or 3 discussants, support for the other preferences is held constant at 0. *Source:* Table 3.1 estimates.

3. The probability of agreeing or disagreeing with a discussant who supports *neither* of the major party candidates is also contingent on preference distributions in the remainder of the network. Although the probability is not enhanced by the presence of other discussants who support neither candidate, it is dramatically diminished by the presence of discussants who support either of the candidates.

What do these results suggest? Agreement within dyads is typically sustained by larger networks of communication that simultaneously support the preferences of *both* individuals within the dyad. Hence, disagreement is also socially sustained, but – as we argue in Chapter 5 – by politically *divergent* networks that serve to pull the two members of the dyad in politically *opposite* directions. In summary, the survival of disagreement within dyads is profitably seen within larger patterns of association and communication that occur at the intersection between the networks that surround individual citizens.

Thus far we have seen that the correspondence in vote choice between a respondent and a particular discussant is often contingent on the distribution of candidate support in the remainder of the network. At the same time, these patterns of relationships depend on the individual respondent's partisanship in some interesting and important ways. In particular, strong partisans appear to be less influenced by the flow of information in their networks – they are unlikely to agree with a discussant who supports the opposite party's candidate, regardless of the distribution of candidate preferences in the remainder of the network.

Do these same patterns persist for opinions regarding the candidates? That is, do we see the same patterns of effects for respondents' candidate evaluations as we do for their ultimate vote choices? This is an important issue that is directly related to the nature of the informational effects that we are observing. One interpretation, based on the results in Table 3.1, is that strong partisans are much less likely to be affected by socially communicated information. In particular, Figures 3.2 and 3.3 suggest that it is very difficult to convince a strong partisan to vote for the other party's candidate.

An alternative interpretation suggests that, in such instances, the effects of socially communicated information are still present. The fact that strong partisans do not cross over to vote for the opposite party's candidate is not evidence that social communication is lacking in influence, but rather that the information effect is overwhelmed by partisan loyalty. If the strong Democrat of 2000 approximates the yellow dog Democrat of an earlier era, she might indeed vote for a yellow dog rather than for a Republican. But if her Republican associates convince her that the Democrat is indeed a yellow dog, it seems a mistake to suggest that partisans are insulated from socially communicated information. In other words, strong partisans may be *loyal* to their party's candidates, but that is not the same thing as saying that they are *enthusiastic* supporters of their party's candidates.

Hence, we give attention to the dynamics of candidate evaluation during the campaign. In particular, what are the consequences of network preference distributions for changes in the respondents' evaluations regarding George Bush and Al Gore during the course of the campaign? One of the most compelling results from the early Columbia studies was the manner in which volatility was produced in situations where individual preferences ran contrary to the dominant opinions within networks

(Lazarsfeld et al. 1948; Berelson et al. 1954; McPhee et al. 1963; Huckfeldt and Sprague 1995). We explore that issue here, by comparing respondents' pre- and post-election feeling thermometer scores for the candidates.

The dependent variable in Part A of Table 3.2 is the individual change in the feeling thermometer over the course of the campaign – the post-election thermometer measure minus the pre-election thermometer measure. Using an ordinary least-squares model, the resulting difference measure is regressed on two sets of variables: (1) the respondent's party identification, the discussant's vote, and their interaction, as well as (2) the percent of the residual network that agrees with the discussant and its interaction with the discussant's vote. (The pre-election thermometer score is also included as a control variable.) As the results show, three explanatory variables produce consistently discernible coefficients – the pre-election thermometer score, individual partisanship, and the interaction between the discussant's vote and the remainder of the network that shares the discussant's vote.

How are these effects interpreted? First, partisans are likely to become more favorable toward the candidate of their own party and less favorable toward the candidate of the opposite party. For example, the thermometer score for Gore is likely to increase by more than 10 points across the general election campaign among strong Democrats ($-3X-3.86$), and it is likely to decrease by more than 10 points among strong Republicans ($3X-3.86$). These effects are wholly in keeping with the insights of the Columbia studies – election campaigns have the effect of increasing the differences in preference distributions among politically relevant groups (Berelson et al. 1954).

Second, respondents are likely to become more favorably disposed toward the candidate supported by any one of their discussants, but only when that candidate preference is reflected among the other discussants within the remainder of the network. If the discussant is the sole supporter of a candidate within a network, the results for both feeling thermometers suggest that respondent's preference demonstrates *no* discernible correspondence with the discussant's preference. In contrast, if the discussant's preference is shared throughout the network, the Gore discussant's preference produces a 4.95 point increase in the main respondent's feeling thermometer score toward Gore, and the Bush discussant's preference produces a 6.75 point increase in the feeling thermometer score toward Bush. In summary, these results suggest that the events of the campaign are not only filtered through the prism of individual partisanship, but also through the partisan networks within which individuals are located. Moreover, the information coming from any single discussant would appear to be filtered through information coming from the remainder of the network.

Table 3.2. *Change in feeling thermometers toward candidates by respondent party identification, discussant vote, the percent of the residual network that agrees with the discussant, and initial feeling thermometer score.*

A. Difference in thermometers: post-election minus pre-election. Least squares

	Bush Feeling Thermometer		Gore Feeling Thermometer	
	Coefficient	t-value	Coefficient	t-value
Constant	25.00	9.08	24.34	7.74
Party identification	3.51	7.44	−3.86	7.45
Discussant vote	−.78	1.48	−.52	.96
Party id. X disc. vote	.79	2.60	−.31	1.17
Percent in residual net agreeing with discussant	−1.03	.63	−.09	.06
Residual net agreement X discussant vote	6.75	3.99	−4.95	2.90
Pre-election feeling thermometer	−.44	9.74	−.48	10.04
N (number of clusters) =	2493 (831)		2484 (828)	
R^2 =	.23		.24	
Standard error of estimate =	16.81		17.39	

B. Direction of change: increase, stay the same, decrease? Ordered logit

	Bush Feeling Thermometer		Gore Feeling Thermometer	
	Coefficient	t-value	Coefficient	t-value
Party identification	.38	7.68	−.31	5.74
Discussant vote	−.032	.53	−.057	1.02
Party id. X disc. Vote	.062	2.04	−.061	1.93
Percent in residual net agreeing with discussant	−.12	.71	.10	.57
Residual net agreement X discussant vote	.50	2.75	−.31	1.77
Pre-election feeling thermometer	−.040	9.71	−.038	9.25
First threshold	−3.26	s = .29	−2.82	s = .28
Second threshold	−1.49	s = .27	−1.00	s = .26
N (number of clusters) =	2493 (831)		2484 (828)	
χ^2/df/p =	123/6/.00		94/6/.00	

Direction of change: 1 = thermometer increased more than 5 points, 0 = change in thermometer is 5 points or less, −1 = thermometer decreased more than 5 points.
Source: 2000 National Election Study; unit of analysis is dyad; data are weighted; standard errors are corrected for clustering.

Conclusion

In order to assess the mediating impact of partisanship on these information flows, we employ an ordered logit model to consider the probability that the individual's level of support for Gore and Bush either increased, decreased, or stayed the same. Increases and decreases in support constitute individual level differences in the pre-election and post-election feeling thermometers of more than 5 points in the appropriate direction, and a lack of change is an instance in which the two feeling thermometer ratings are within 5 points of each other. Based on these definitions, 40 percent of the respondents did not change their Bush evaluations and 39 percent did not change their Gore evaluations; 30 percent report decreased levels of support for Bush and 36 percent reported decreased levels of support for Gore; 30 percent report increased levels of support for Bush whereas 25 percent reported increased levels of support for Gore.

The ordered logit model is nonlinear, with the effect of each explanatory variable depending on the effect of every other explanatory variable. Hence the model incorporates contingent effects among the explanatory variables by virtue of its construction, allowing us to see whether network effects persist across partisan categories.

In Part B of Table 3.2, the resulting measures of individual change in Bush and Gore support are regressed on the same explanatory variables as in Part A, and the pattern of t-values for the coefficients is very similar to the earlier results. In order to assess the magnitude of network effects across individual partisan categories, we vary the respondent's partisanship across its range while varying network and discussant variables across their ranges. This strategy allows a comparison of discussant and network effects across partisan categories, as well as a comparison of partisan effects across discussant and network categories.

Figures 3.4 and 3.5 show comparable patterns of discussant and network effects across partisan categories. In general, the presence of a Bush (or Gore) discussant enhances the probability of increased favorability toward Bush (or Gore), but only in situations where the remainder of the network supports the discussant's candidate preference. Although the effects are somewhat larger among independents, the differences in the magnitudes of these effects between partisans and independents are not dramatic. Hence, it would appear that strong partisans are not immune to the political messages that are filtered through networks of political communication.

CONCLUSION

The results of the analyses show that disagreement was a common event among citizens during the 2000 presidential election campaign, even within closely held networks of political communication. At the end of

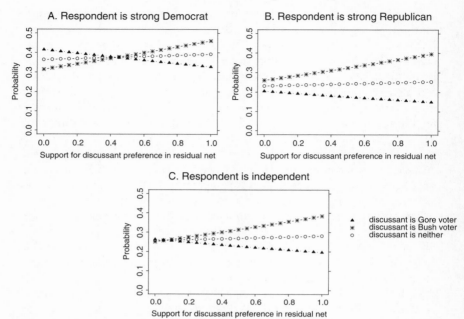

Figure 3.4. Predicted probability of increased favorability toward Bush from pre-election to post-election. *Note:* The pre-election Bush feeling thermometer is held constant at the pre-election mean for the partisan category: 80 for strong Republicans, 55 for independents, and 39 for strong Democrats. *Source:* Table 3.2b estimates.

the campaign, after people have been bombarded by the events of the campaign for many months, heterogeneous preferences continue to survive among people who interact on a regular basis. On this basis, it would seem to be clear that political homogeneity within communication networks does not constitute an equilibrium condition in democratic politics. Hence the question naturally arises, if socially communicated political information is influential, how is it that disagreement is able to persist?

A central part of the answer to this question relates to the low density characteristics of political communication networks. In networks characterized by weak ties (Granovetter 1973) and structural holes (Burt 1992), associated individuals are frequently located in networks that intersect but do not correspond. Regardless of the fact that two individuals communicate with each other on a regular basis, their remaining lists of contacts may be non-overlapping. That is, Tom and Dick may regularly eat lunch together at work, but neither of them may associate with the other's non-workplace associates (see Fuchs 1955).

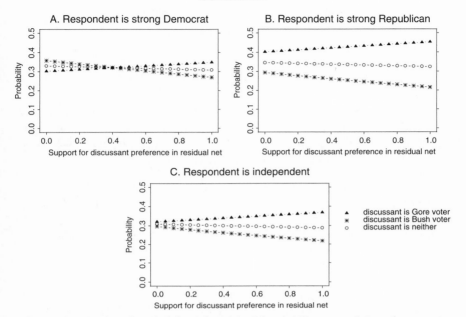

Figure 3.5. Predicted probability of increased favorability toward Gore from pre-election to post-election. *Note:* The pre-election Gore feeling thermometer is held constant at the pre-election mean for the partisan category: 33 for strong Republicans, 53 for independents, and 80 for strong Democrats. *Source:* Table 3.2b estimates.

These sorts of low density networks create a high potential for accommodating and even sustaining disagreement. Suppose that Tom is a strong Democrat and Dick is a strong Republican. They regularly disagree about politics, but when Tom goes home at night and undertakes his other activities, he is regularly surrounded by other strong Democrats. Correspondingly, when Dick leaves work he is regularly located among other strong Republicans. Neither of them is persuaded by their lunchtime discussions because they discount the information communicated within the dyad based on information communicated through the remainder of the network.

In short, the political dynamic within dyads is contingent on the political dynamic within the remainder of each individual's network. This means, in turn, that the influence of particular discussants is autocorrelated within networks. Not only do individually based models of political preference generate autocorrelated errors by failing to take account of interdependence among individuals within the same network, but dyadic models of communication also produce autocorrelated error by failing to locate dyads within the larger preference distributions that are present within networks. Correspondingly, models of communication and influence that rely on the central tendencies within networks and contexts do not capture the non-linear systems of weights that operate on patterns of communication within those settings.

How do Tom and Dick manage to maintain their relationship in the face of disagreement? The answer depends on the particulars of the individuals and the relationship. For some individuals, politics is simply not at the center of the relationship. Tom and Dick may spend most of their time talking about baseball or fly fishing.

Other individuals may not be particularly troubled by the disagreement because they have perfectly suitable idiosyncratic explanations to account for their lunch partner's wrong-headed views. As Ross and his colleagues suggest (1976), the powers of social conformity pressures are inversely proportional to the availability of explanations to account for disagreement. Hence, Tom may think that Dick is a Republican because he is unduly influenced by his rich uncle, and hence it becomes much easier to dismiss his views.

In summary, the management of political disagreement within the dyad depends on the circumstances of the individuals within the relationship. The important point for our analysis is that the structure of a given network may actually sustain disagreement. Hence we might say that both agreement and disagreement are capable of being socially sustained by the structural details of particular settings. And the persistence of political heterogeneity within networks of political communication is not, by itself, evidence of either a social influence failure or a lack of interdependence among citizens.

The analytic results of this chapter are primarily descriptive, but they provide a compelling case for an account of citizens in democratic politics that is thoroughly rooted in interdependence. At one level, a long tradition of political analysis points out that individuals should be understood within a context that arises due to the composition of the particular groups within which individuals are located (Eulau 1963). At a more immediate level, another body of work shows that these contexts should be understood in terms of the specific networks of relationships that connect individuals within and between these group contexts (Laumann and Pappi 1976). Finally, this chapter underscores that the influence of each relationship within an individual's network of relationships should be understood relative to the remaining relationships.

In Chapters 4 and 5 we employ the Indianapolis–St. Louis Study to provide a more thorough examination of the specific network effects that arise on communication and influence. The analysis of Chapter 4

Conclusion

focuses on the clarity, accuracy, and effectiveness of communication between and among citizens during the course of the 1996 election campaign. Chapter 5 focuses on the persuasiveness of communication. In both
chapters, we pursue a similar set of themes – autoregressive patterns of
influence within networks and the consequences of disagreement within
networks.

4

Disagreement, Heterogeneity, and the Effectiveness of Political Communication

The Columbia studies revolutionized the study of democratic politics, inspiring a view of the electorate based on interdependent citizens who reach decisions through a shared process of collective deliberation. This perspective led many to expect that citizens would be imbedded within homogeneous micro-environments of politically like-minded associates, but as we have seen, citizen communication networks demonstrate remarkably high levels of political heterogeneity. Within this context, we examine the implications of disagreement and political heterogeneity for the effectiveness of political communication and deliberation among citizens during a presidential election campaign. In order for communication to be effective, messages conveyed through social interaction must be unambiguous, and the person receiving the communication must readily, confidently, and accurately perceive the intent of the sender. Hence, we address a number of factors that might influence communication effectiveness among individual citizens: the dynamic of the election campaign, the accessibility and extremity of the political preferences held by individual citizens, the distribution of preferences within political communication networks, and the presence of disagreement between the senders and receivers of political messages. The analysis is based on the 1996 Indianapolis–St. Louis election study, based on interviews with citizens and their discussants conducted during the campaign.

Presidential election campaigns are among the most widely recognized events in American politics, inevitably capturing the attention of anyone who watches the evening news, reads the newspaper, or listens to news reports on the car radio. But these election campaigns are not simply or even primarily significant as media spectacles based on primary election horse races, televised debates, campaign scandals, or public opinion polls. Rather, presidential election campaigns are more fundamentally important as they relate to the process of democratic politics – a process characterized by *interdependent* individuals who *collectively* reach a summary political judgment on the first Tuesday past the first Monday of every leap

This chapter is coauthored with Jeffrey Levine, based on an earlier effort in Huckfeldt, Sprague, and Levine (2000).

year. In this chapter we are primarily concerned with the consequence of presidential election campaigns for the collective deliberations of democratic politics. In particular, how do these election campaigns alter the effectiveness of political communication among citizens?

A number of important and influential efforts have questioned the capacity of democratic institutions to sustain a deliberative politics in which citizens are more than passive and isolated individuals who are pushed and pulled and manipulated by symbolic appeals and limited alternatives. Various reform efforts point to the relationships between and among citizens as central to the creation of a more vibrant democratic politics. Barber (1984: 155) argues for the creation of a "strong democracy" in which "to be a citizen is to participate in a certain conscious fashion that presumes awareness of and engagement in activity with others." Fishkin (1991: 2) proposes a reformed presidential nominating process in which a "deliberative opinion poll" brings together a national sample of citizens to debate the issues "with the candidates and with each other." These are politically and intellectually worthy arguments and proposals, and they raise a number of important issues with respect to the effectiveness of democratic deliberation among and between citizens in American politics. The problem is that most research on campaigns, voters, and electorates conceives the citizen as an independently self-contained decision-maker. Hence we know very little about patterns of shared deliberation among citizens, or about the effectiveness of political communication within the electorate, or about the consequences of political campaigns for the effectiveness of political communication and deliberation.

How should we conceive the effectiveness of communication and collective deliberation among citizens? At a minimum, political messages that are conveyed effectively through social interaction must be unambiguous, and the person receiving the communication must *readily, confidently,* and *accurately* perceive the intent of the sender. Even effectively communicated messages may be received unsympathetically: effective communication provides no guarantee of agreement or influence, and neither disagreement nor rejection constitutes communication failures among citizens. It might well be argued that effective communication in the context of disagreement lies at the heart of a healthy democratic discourse (McPhee et al. 1963). Thus, effective political communication is usefully conceived as the absence of distortion in one person's judgment regarding the politics of another, wholly apart from influence or agreement. The hallmark of effectiveness is the extent to which the receivers of political messages are readily able to make accurate, unambiguous, and confident judgments regarding the politics of the senders.

A variety of factors might give rise to systematic patterns of distortion in the political communication that occurs among citizens, and thus the natural dynamics of social interaction may not be wholly coincidental with the requirements of effective political communication. This chapter examines the factors that give rise to effective and unambiguous political communication among citizens. How is the effectiveness of political communication dependent on the changing political–temporal context of a presidential election campaign? To what extent does the effectiveness of political communication depend on the strength and extremity of political preferences held by the senders and receivers of political messages? Does effectiveness depend on the distribution of preferences in the receiver's surrounding environment? Is the effectiveness of political communication compromised by disagreement between the senders and receivers of political messages?

Thus we are particularly concerned to understand the political campaign as an institution that stimulates effective communication among citizens. Similarly, we are interested in the characteristics of individuals that lead to the effective transmission and receipt of political messages. In other words, who are the good listeners, and who are the good talkers, in the collective deliberations of democratic politics? We address these issues based on a study conducted during the course of the 1996 campaign. Nearly 2,200 respondents and almost 1,500 of their associates were interviewed during the ten-month period beginning in March of 1996 and ending in early January of 1997. On the basis of the resulting data set, we are able to study the flow of information between citizens as it occurred within their larger networks of association at particular temporal points during the campaign.

SYSTEMATIC SOURCES OF DISTORTION IN COMMUNICATION

What are the factors that systematically give rise to clarity and ambiguity within the context of socially communicated political information? A variety of factors might render political communication ineffective by distorting the political messages being sent from one person to another.

Preferences of the Sender. First, we might expect preferences of the *sender* to be important in determining the effectiveness of communication. In particular, strong attitudes should communicate more clearly than weak ones (Latané 1981; also see Fazio 1990). People who have developed firmly grounded opinions and commitments are more likely to communicate in a direct and unambiguous manner, and their opinions are more likely to be interpreted accurately and unambiguously. In this particular context, however, the defining ingredient of a strong opinion is less than obvious: Do opinions communicate more effectively when the sender of a political message holds political preferences that are more intense or extreme

(Abelson 1995)? Or do opinions communicate more effectively when they are readily accessible within the cognitive structure of the sender (Fazio 1995)?

Frequency of Exposure. Second, the accuracy and effectiveness of communication should depend on exposure frequency. The more frequently one citizen is exposed to the preferences of another, the more likely it is that distortion will be reduced and clarity enhanced (Latané 1981: 334). What are the factors that affect the number of opportunities for receiving a political message from a particular discussant? Some individuals are constant companions – spouses and members of the immediate family, co-workers on the assembly line, and so on. Other individuals are frequent sources of political information – the friend with whom you enjoy talking politics (Finifter 1974). Opportunities for political discussion and exchange are not wholly defined by the idiosyncratic characteristics of the individuals involved in a relationship, however. The political–temporal setting of social interaction defines the potential for effective political communication within these relationships. At the end of a year-long election campaign, the stage has been set for effective communication through the accumulation of frequent opportunities for political exchange.

False Consensus Effects. Third, characteristics of the receiver and the receiver's preference are also important in affecting the clarity of political communication. In particular, a great deal of evidence accumulated in a broad range of settings points to the existence of a "false consensus effect" in which people perceive the opinions of others in terms of their own beliefs, wrongly assuming that their beliefs are shared (Granberg and Brent 1983; Granberg 1987; Krueger and Ziegler 1993; Krueger and Clement 1994; Fabrigar and Krosnick 1995). Hence, perceptions are biased in the direction of inferring consensus, and political messages are more likely to be interpreted accurately when there is objectively defined agreement in political preferences between the sender and the receiver of communication.

The larger question for this analysis is related to the various ways in which the presence of agreement or disagreement might be related to accuracy. One interpretation focuses on dissonance reduction and the tendency of citizens to avoid the psychic discomfort of political disagreement through selective perception (Festinger 1957). We might expect this discomfort to be especially pronounced when the receiver holds more extreme, less ambivalent opinions that are difficult to reconcile with the perception that someone else holds a different opinion. A second interpretation of false consensus suggests that disagreement might give rise to ineffective communication because the sender communicates an ambiguous political message in order to sidestep potential conflict. Once again, this particular problem should become more pronounced when the receiver of communication is committed to more extreme partisan viewpoints that inhibit the flow of communication by increasing the potential for conflict.

A third explanation for the false consensus effect is that citizens perceive the preferences of others in the context of *their own* preferences and, lacking strong evidence to the contrary, infer agreement. Faced with the task of making a judgment under uncertain circumstances, individuals resort to the use of a personal experience heuristic (Kahneman and Tversky 1973): my co-worker Joe is a lot like me; I am voting for Clinton; Joe is probably voting for Clinton as well. In short, the false consensus effect may be a residue of the fact that people generalize on the basis of their own very personal experience – the experience of their own preferences (Fiske and Taylor 1991: 75–8).

Network Effects. Finally, to the extent that citizens form political expectations based on their own personally realized patterns of social interaction, distortion is more likely to arise when a sender's preference is less common within the remainder of the receiver's social network. How might such a mechanism work? The argument is that individuals generalize on the basis of the environment they know best – the environment they experience through their own patterns of social interaction (Huckfeldt and Sprague 1995). If Joe perceives that the vast majority of the people he knows are Clinton supporters, he is more likely to miss the fact that one of them actually supports Bob Dole.

Thus, the logic of the social network explanation runs parallel to the personal experience explanation for the false consensus effect. People understand ambiguous political messages in a social context created by their own preferences as well as by the preferences of others. In this way, an individual's own preference is simply one more piece of information to use in forming a generalization based on personal experience. Not all political messages are ambiguous, but to the extent that a message *is* ambiguous, individuals may very well resort to their own personal sample of observations in forming a judgment regarding its political content (Huckfeldt et al. 1998a).

ELECTION CAMPAIGNS AND SOCIAL COMMUNICATION

What are the consequences of election campaigns for the effectiveness of political communication among citizens? The answer to this question is problematic, and it depends on the underlying theory of social communication regarding politics. At the same time that elections stimulate political discussion and communication, they also encourage individuals to develop stronger preferences regarding the candidates. Thus, depending on the relative effects of strong attitudes for the receivers and senders of political messages, the campaign might either enhance or inhibit the effectiveness of communication.

On the one hand, election campaigns stimulate effective political communication among citizens both by (1) clarifying political choices and (2) focusing patterns of collective deliberation. At the beginning of the campaign, before the agenda of candidate choices had crystallized fully, we would expect many individuals to be uncertain, not only regarding the voting intentions of others, but also regarding their *own* preferences. Early in March of 1996, when we began our interviewing, the incumbent President Bill Clinton was in control of the Democratic nomination, but the Republican nomination was still up for grabs. Moreover, no one was certain whether Ross Perot would be a factor in the 1996 campaign. As the campaign progressed, however, the agenda of choices became increasingly clear. By early in the summer of 1996, it was obvious both that the Republicans would nominate Bob Dole and that the Perot campaign was experiencing difficulty in regenerating the enthusiasm of 1992. As a consequence, the campaign quickly evolved into a choice between a moderate Democrat with emerging legal problems and a moderately conservative Republican with age and personality problems.

The progress and visibility of the campaign also meant that individual and collective attention inescapably turned to the unfolding competition among the candidates. It invaded the newspaper articles citizens read, the television programs they watched, and, inevitably, the discussions they had with friends and associates. Thus, as the campaign developed and choices became clear, individuals were forming judgments regarding the political preferences of their associates as they were formulating their own opinions regarding the candidates. *To the extent that these strongly held individual opinions encourage the more effective communication of preferences, the campaign should serve to stimulate effective communication.*

On the other hand, people with strongly held opinions might be less likely to recognize the opinions expressed by others, either because they selectively perceive the message being communicated, or because their strong opinion discourages the expression of disagreement by others. Thus, *to the extent that strongly held opinions serve to obscure or inhibit free and effective communication, election campaigns would actually serve to diminish the effectiveness of communication by encouraging individuals to develop the strong opinions which limit the free flow of political discussion and discourse.*

How should we assess the effect of the campaign on political communication among citizens? If election campaigns stimulate effective communication, citizens should increasingly become aware of their associates' preferences over the course of the campaign, and on this basis we generate several expectations. As a consequence of the campaign, (1) individuals should more readily make judgments regarding the preferences of others, (2) they should become more confident in their own ability to make these judgments, and (3) the accuracy of their judgments should increase.

THE CENTRALITY OF POLITICAL DISAGREEMENT

Hence, the theoretical centrality of disagreement and conflict is variable and problematic within alternative interpretations regarding the effectiveness of political communication. One interpretation stresses conflict avoidance as a central motivating factor in patterns of communication. In an effort to avoid conflict, people talk about politics less frequently, and they send obscure messages that are likely to be misinterpreted. Patterns of selective perception add to the problem by creating situations in which the receivers of messages rewrite the scripts of their own conversations, further attenuating the likelihood that disagreeable political communication will be correctly understood.

These problems are further exacerbated in the context of strongly held opinions. Those people who are most committed and engaged by partisan viewpoints are the same people who would be most disturbed by disagreement, and hence they are the least likely to recognize disagreement when they encounter it. To the extent that election campaigns encourage the strengthening of opinion and the formation of strongly held preferences, they might actually inhibit communication by creating politically polarized populations that are unable to transmit messages to one another.

The inhibiting effects of disagreement are less central to an alternative view of political communication, with less severe biases in communication arising due to the psychic and social discomfort of political disagreement. This alternative view does not deny the importance of systematic biases in patterns of communication, but it locates these biases within the context of mechanisms that are used to perceive and communicate political information. These mechanisms have less to do with psychic discomfort regarding political disagreement, and more to do with the ways that people interpret political information. In particular, political communication may be *inherently autoregressive* – people may understand political messages within a context created by their own preferences as well as by the preferences of others. As a consequence, the effectiveness of communication may be attenuated, not because citizens are incapable of confronting political disagreement, but rather because they lack an interpretive frame of reference for understanding communicated messages – particularly the messages that are less common within this socially defined frame of reference.

74

Data and Research Design

DATA AND RESEARCH DESIGN

We evaluate these issues and expectations on the basis of the 1996 Indianapolis–St. Louis Study, conducted by the Center for Survey Research at Indiana University. We are primarily concerned with political communication over the course of the campaign, and thus we employ interviews that began early in March of 1996 and ended in early January of 1997. The study includes two samples: a sample of main respondents (N = 2,174) drawn from the lists of registered voters, combined with a one-stage snowball sample of these main respondents' discussants (N = 1,475). Main respondent samples are drawn from the voter registration lists of two study sites: (1) the Indianapolis metropolitan area defined as Marion County, Indiana; and (2) the St. Louis metropolitan area defined as the independent city of St. Louis combined with the surrounding (and mostly suburban) St. Louis County, Missouri. The pre-election main respondent sampling plan was to complete interviews with approximately 40 main respondents each week before the election, equally divided between the two study sites. After the election, an additional 830 respondents were interviewed, once again divided between the St. Louis and Indianapolis metropolitan areas. Discussant interviews were completed at a rate of approximately 30 interviews each week during the pre-election period, with an additional 639 interviews conducted after the election. In the pre-election period, the discussant interviews for a particular main respondent were completed within two subsequent interview weeks of the main respondent interview.[1]

Every respondent to the survey was asked to provide the first names of not more than five discussion partners. A random half of the sample was asked to name people with whom they discuss "important matters"; the other half was asked to name people with whom they discuss "government, elections, and politics" (Burt 1986; Huckfeldt and Sprague 1995; Huckfeldt, Levine, Morgan, and Sprague 1998b). The experimental condition that is imbedded within the design of this name generator allows us to examine the extent to which political information networks are separate from social communication networks more broadly considered. That is, are political discussants different from important matters discussants, and what are the consequences for the effectiveness of political communication?

After compiling a list of first names for not more than five discussants, the interviewers asked a battery of questions about each discussant in the sequential order in which the discussant was named. After asking the battery of questions for the last-named discussant, the interviewer asked

---

[1] Additional details regarding the study are available in Appendix A.

the respondent to identify the presidential candidate supported by each of the discussants, but the order in which respondents were asked this final question about particular discussants was varied across main respondents. Immediately after asking the question about each particular discussant, the interviewer used a key stroke to start a computer clock. As soon as the respondent answered the question, the interviewer used a second key stroke to stop the clock before recording the respondent's answer. The CATI system then asked the *interviewer* whether the timing was successful, and the interviewer asked the respondent a follow-up question: "How difficult or easy was it to say how [discussant first name] voted?"[2] At the end of the interview, the interviewer asked the main respondents for identifying information to use in contacting and interviewing their discussants. Based on their responses we interviewed 1,475 discussants, employing a survey instrument that was very similar to the instrument used in the main respondent interview. The analyses of this chapter draw on information taken from both the main respondents and their discussants, where each observation in the resulting data set is a dyadic relationship between a main respondent and a discussant.[3]

ACCESSIBILITY AND THE EASE OF JUDGMENT

When a survey interviewer asks a respondent how she expects one of her discussants to vote in November, the respondent is being asked to connect that discussant with a particular political preference. In many instances this is likely to be an easy task. Many individuals are quite vocal regarding their strongly held preferences, and their politically attentive associates are thus able to predict their behavior quite readily. In other instances, however, the task may be more difficult for a variety of reasons: the discussant is less forceful and decisive in political discussion, the discussant has no preference, and so on.

In the first instance we might say that the respondent possesses a strong association in memory between the discussant and a particular voting behavior, and this strong association yields a highly accessible perception

---

[2] The median response times for the five discussants were, for the first discussant: 1.73 seconds (n = 462); for the second: 1.27 seconds (n = 325); for the third: 1.18 seconds (n = 250); for the fourth: 1.04 seconds (n = 104); for the fifth: 1.43 seconds (n = 83).

[3] Each discussant (n = 1,475) only appears once in this data set, but main respondents (872) appear multiple times: 469 appear in one dyad, 250 in two, 112 in three, 35 in four, and 6 in five. Hence we employ a standard error correction for clustering that takes account of this fact. This correction produces only minor changes (see Rogers 1993) – an unsurprising result given the very modest degree of clustering. All results are obtained with Stata, Release 7 (Stata Corp. 2001).

regarding the discussant. In the latter case, we might say that the association in memory is weak, yielding a perception that is much less accessible. In this way, accessibility is defined as the strength of association between two objects in memory. To the extent that political communication between two citizens is more effective, the cognitive association between a particular individual and a particular political preference should become stronger in the memory of the person who communicates with that individual. And hence the cognitive accessibility of a judgment regarding a discussant should thereby be enhanced (Fazio 1995).

In this section of the analysis, we are concerned with the factors that give rise to more or less accessible judgments regarding the political preferences of discussants, but how do we know whether such judgments are accessible within the memory of the person making the judgment? Pioneering work on the measurement of attitude accessibility has shown that accessibility reveals itself in terms of response latencies, defined in the metric of response time – the time required for an individual to provide a response to a question or stimulus (Fazio 1990; Fazio, Chen, McDonel, and Sherman 1982). Whereas the earliest work on attitude accessibility took place in a laboratory setting, more recent efforts employ the computer-assisted telephone interview and the computer clock to record response times in the context of an otherwise conventional telephone interview (Bassili 1993; 1995; also see Fazio and Williams 1986). By recording the time that is required for a respondent to provide judgments regarding each of their discussants, we obtain a measure for the accessibility in memory of respondent judgments regarding their discussants.

Before proceeding with the analysis, we must address two issues related to the use of latency (response time) measures: the baseline speed of response and the problem of learning curves (Fazio 1990). First, some people answer questions more rapidly than others, and thus it becomes important to take account of this fact by establishing an individually idiosyncratic baseline speed of response when analyzing particular response latencies. As an analytic strategy, we employ this baseline measure as a statistical control when assessing various effects on the speed with which respondents offer judgments regarding their discussants' political preferences. In the present context, this baseline measure is based on the mean time that is required for a respondent to report their judgments regarding the political preferences of the discussants in their residual network – all the discussants other than the one currently being considered.[4] This

---

[4] Latency data are typically skewed with an extended tail of slow response times. Thus, in constructing a measure for the baseline speed of response, we first take the log of the times and then compute the mean of these logs. Respondents who identify fewer

means, in turn, that main respondents who name less than two discussants are eliminated from the analysis.

Second, as people progress through a battery of questions, their speed of response accelerates as they become familiar with the question format. Thus, all else being equal, it takes longer to make the first judgment regarding a discussant than it does to make the fifth judgment regarding a discussant. The effect of such a learning curve is a potentially severe problem in the present analysis due to the fact that the sociometric order in which discussants are named may carry substantive meaning (Burt 1986; Huckfeldt et al. 1998b). We anticipated this problem by altering the order in which we asked the questions across respondents. The battery always begins with a question about the first discussant's voting preference. If the respondent named two discussants, this meant that we asked about the first and then the second. If the respondent named three discussants, we asked about the first, the third, and the second. For respondents who named four, we asked about the first, the fourth, the third, and the second. Finally, respondents with five discussants were asked about the first, the fifth, the second, the fourth, and the third. This means that there is a perfect correlation between being the first discussant named and the first discussant about whose preference the respondent is asked, but the correlation between discussant order and question order drops to –.14 for the remaining discussants.

EXPLAINING ACCESSIBILITY

Baseline Speed of Response. A range of factors that might affect accessibility is considered in Column A of Table 4.1. The first set of factors includes the baseline speed of response and the order in which respondents are asked to provide judgments regarding the various discussants, as well as a dummy variable control for the first named discussant. A faster baseline speed of response is associated with a more rapid response time for each of the individual judgments regarding discussant preferences. Moreover, the measure for question order produces a substantial effect in which response time shortens with respect to judgments regarding discussant preferences asked later in the sequence. Finally, the additional dummy variable for the first discussant in the sequence fails to produce a statistically discernible effect, and thus it would not appear that the first named discussant has an independent effect on response time over and above that captured in the variables measuring the sequence in which the questions are asked and the mean network response time.

than two discussants are excluded from the analysis, and for those with only two discussants, the baseline speed is based on a single response time.

Explaining Accessibility

Nature of Relationships. The second set of factors incorporates several variables which measure the nature of the relationship between the main respondent and the discussant. Three dummy variables summarize the closeness of the relationship between the main respondent and the discussant: whether the discussant is a spouse, some other relative, or a close friend. (The excluded baseline category is a nonrelative who is less than a close friend.) As the results show, these variables produce effects which lie in the expected direction, but the t-values for the coefficients are small, suggesting statistically indiscernible effects.

Agreement Effects. The third set of factors is related to the presence of agreement or disagreement between the discussant, the main respondent, and the remainder of the main respondent's communication network. A dummy variable is included for whether or not the respondent and the discussant hold the same candidate preference, based on their own self-reports. As the table shows, agreement has no effect on the accessibility of the judgment. That is, the ease (or speed) with which respondents are able to render a judgment regarding the preference of the discussant is unaffected by whether or not the discussant and the respondent agree.

These results provide some insight regarding the nature of the false consensus effect. If false consensus is the consequence of dissonance reduction, we would expect individuals to experience personal difficulty in forming a judgment regarding the political preference of someone with whom they disagree. Indeed, the concept of dissonance reduction points toward an individual effort to reduce such difficulty! But at least when we conceive increased difficulty in terms of decreased accessibility, these results indicate that disagreement has no effect on the ease or difficulty of judgment.

Similarly, these results show no discernible effect on the accessibility of the judgment when the remainder of the social network is perceived to hold the preference reported by the discussant.[5] As we will see, these results do not mean that people are unaffected by their own personal experience in forming judgments of other discussants (Kahneman and Tversky 1973; Tversky and Kahneman 1974). The results do show that network disagreement has no demonstrable effect on the accessibility of particular judgments regarding discussants.

---

[5] For respondents with only one additional discussant, the measure is 0 if the respondent perceives that the additional discussant holds a preference that is different from the one reported by the discussant in the dyad and 1 if the respondent perceives that the additional discussant holds the same preference. For respondents with more than one additional discussant, the measure provides the proportion that is perceived to hold the preference reported by the discussant in the dyad.

Table 4.1. *Accessibility, confidence, and accuracy of main respondent judgments regarding the vote preferences of their discussants.*

	A. Accessibility (OLS)		B. Confidence (OLS)		C. Accuracy (logit)	
	Coeff.	(t)	Coeff.	(t)	Coeff.	(t)
Constant	343.177	(3.27)	.166	(.48)	−4.214	(5.32)
1. Baseline Response Controls						
Mean network response time	53.666	(4.37)				
Question order for perceptions	−21.774	(2.81)				
First named discussant (dummy)	28.897	(1.11)				
2. Nature of Relationship						
Spouse (dummy)	−50.185	(1.81)	.366	(2.98)	.559	(1.62)
Other relative (dummy)	−42.862	(1.85)	.279	(2.80)	.186	(.79)
Close friend (dummy)	−17.467	(.75)	.110	(1.07)	−.006	(.02)
3. Agreement Measures						
Agreement in dyad (dummy)	−13.050	(.65)	.059	(.54)	.995	(5.14)
Network agreement proportion	−33.309	(1.35)	.260	(1.96)	1.912	(6.60)
4. Main Respondent Preferences						
Partisan extremity	−16.511	(1.51)	.097	(1.76)	.119	(1.09)
Candidate evaluation extremity	.266	(.04)	.086	(2.43)	−.002	(.03)
Partisan accessibility (party ident. response time)	.126	(2.85)	−.011	(.69)	−.074	(1.87)
5. Discussant Preferences						
Partisan extremity	−36.699	(3.04)	.115	(2.72)	.317	(3.42)
Candidate evaluation extremity	−11.065	(1.46)	.107	(3.50)	.288	(3.74)
Partisan accessibility (party ident. response time)	.030	(.97)	−.010	(.59)	−.030	(.76)

6. Other Characteristics

Imputed discussant knowledge	6.517	(.38)	.103	(1.58)	.130	(.82)
Reported discussion frequency	−26.735	(2.32)	.314	(5.80)	.229	(1.90)
Political discussant network (dummy)	−15.996	(1.01)	.164	(2.14)	.357	(2.02)
7. Campaign Dynamic						
Campaign week	−3.437	(2.27)	.022	(3.19)	.043	(2.76)
Primary season (dummy)	−76.972	(2.09)	.361	(1.99)	.662	(1.61)
N (number of dyads) =	902		994		996	
R^2 =	.15		.18			
s =	242		1.08			
chi²/df/p-value =					227/16/.00	

Note: Response times are in hundredths of seconds, except the dependent variable in column A, which is measured in whole seconds. Estimates are corrected for clustering (Rogers 1993). *Accessibility of main respondent judgment* regarding discussant candidate support measured as response time (dependent variable for Table 4.1A). *Accuracy of judgment:* 1 if there is agreement between self-reported candidate choices of main respondent and discussant; 0 otherwise (dependent variable for Table 4.1C and Table 4.2B). *Agreement in dyad:* 1 if there is agreement in the self-reported candidate preferences of main respondent and the dyad; 0 otherwise. *Campaign week:* Week of interview, where 1 is first week in March and 36 is the week of the election or later. *Candidate evaluation extremity:* Absolute value of difference between evaluations of the two major party candidates; range is 0 (indifferent) to 4 (most opinionated). *Close friend:* 1 if discussant is close friend; 0 otherwise. *Confidence in judgment:* Main respondent self-report regarding how difficult or easy it was to make a judgment regarding discussant's candidate preference (dependent variable for Table 4.1B and Table 4.2A). *First named discussant:* 1 for the discussant who is named first by the respondent – always the first discussant in question order sequence; 0 otherwise. *Imputed discussant knowledge:* Main respondent evaluation of discussant's political knowledge on a scale of 1 (least knowledgable) to 3 (most knowledgable). *Mean network response time:* Mean of logged response times for candidate preference questions regarding the remaining discussants. *Network agreement proportion:* Proportion of the remaining network perceived by the main respondent to hold a candidate preference that agrees with the discussant's self-reported preference. *Other relative:* 1 if discussant is some other relative; 0 otherwise. *Partisan accessibility:* Response time for party identification question. *Partisan extremity:* 0 = Independent or nonidentifier; 1 = leans toward Democrats or Republicans; 2 = not strong identifier; 3 = strong identifier. *Political discussant network:* 1 if discussant is named in response to political discussion probe; 0 if important matters probe. *Primary season:* 1 if week of interview is earlier than first week of July; 0 otherwise. *Question order:* Sequence in which the respondent is asked about each discussant. *Reported discussion frequency:* Main respondent report regarding frequency of discussion with the main respondent on a scale of 1 (least frequent) to 4 (most frequent). *Spouse:* 1 if discussant is spouse; 0 otherwise.
Source: Indianapolis–St. Louis Study.

Preference Effects. The fourth and fifth sets of variables include factors related to the strength and extremity of political preferences held by the main respondent and the discussant. The challenge of this undertaking is to assess the particular dimensions of partisan preference that relate to political communication (Converse 1995; Abelson 1995). Is communication regarding candidates affected by the extremity of generalized partisan orientations, or by the extremity of opinions regarding the candidates, or by the accessibility in memory (the strength) of partisan orientations? By posing these questions, we are self-consciously separating the extremity and strength of partisanship (Weisberg 1980). For these purposes, extremity refers to the distance from their own partisan orientation to the midpoint of indifference with respect to partisan alternatives. In contrast, strength is defined in terms of accessibility: individuals demonstrate stronger partisan orientations if they can more readily define themselves with respect to the two major parties. In this way it is analytically possible to define a strong independent or a strong non-identifier – someone who readily identifies himself apart from the major parties.[6]

Moreover, it is just as important to consider how these factors differentially affect the sender and the receiver of political messages. The effective communication and receipt of political messages may require very different characteristics on the part of senders and receivers. Thus, for both sides of the dyads, we include the extremity of partisanship, the extremity of candidate preference, and the accessibility of partisanship. The extremity of partisanship is measured as a 4 point transformation of the traditional party identification scale, where 0 is independent or non-identifier and 3 is strong Republican or Democrat. The extremity of candidate preference is measured as the absolute difference between the individual's evaluation of the two major party candidates, each of which is measured on a 5-point (1–5) scale. Finally, the accessibility of partisanship is measured in terms of the response latency for the question stem of party identification – the time in hundredths of a second required for the respondent to answer.

Thus we are able to ask, how do the strength and extremity of partisan preferences, both on the part of the senders and the receivers of political messages, affect the ease with which inferences are made regarding the preferences of the senders? The results suggest that the pattern of effects is different for the sender and the receiver. The only statistically

---

[6] Krosnick and Petty (1995) argue that attitude strength can be measured and conceived in a number of different ways – as accessibility, extremity, certainty, and so forth – even though each of these measures a different aspect of attitude strength. In contrast, Fazio (1995) defines attitude strength in terms of the associational strength in memory, and thus attitude strength reveals itself in terms of accessibility, measured in terms of response latencies.

discernible effect of the respondent's (receiver's) partisan preference is the accessibility of party identification. Respondents with accessible partisan orientations also have more accessible perceptions of their discussants' preferences, even after we control for the baseline speed of response. In contrast, the only discernible effect of the discussant's (sender's) preference is the *extremity* of partisanship – discussants who hold more extreme partisan orientations are more easily perceived by the main respondents.

This pattern of effects, suggesting that extreme partisans make the best talkers whereas accessible partisans make the best listeners, is quite interesting and entirely reasonable. It is not the strength of partisanship measured as accessibility but rather the extremity of partisanship which communicates well. Thus, even strong (accessible) independents are less likely to send clear political signals regarding their own preferences. Extreme partisans, even if their own partisan orientations are not readily accessible, are more likely to send unambiguous political messages. In contrast, the individuals who are best able to decode political messages may very well be those individuals who hold highly accessible conceptions of their own partisan loyalties. In short, both extremity and accessibility are separable aspects of partisanship that merit close analytic attention. Most important, *there is no evidence here to support an argument that strong attitudes inhibit political communication,* regardless of whether such attitudes are held by the sender or the receiver, and regardless of whether attitude strength is measured in terms of extremity or accessibility.

These are important results along two different dimensions. First, they call into question the extent to which strong attitudes lead individuals to disguise, misinterpret, or misperceive political disagreement. Second, the results support a general view which argues that the strength of attitudes can be conceived apart from attitude extremity (Krosnick and Petty 1995). More specifically, the analysis supports the importance of accessibility as a measure of attitude strength, and it shows that alternative conceptions of attitude strength perform in ways that are theoretically meaningful and distinguishable.

Other Political Characteristics. Several other political characteristics of the discussant are introduced into the analysis as the sixth set of explanatory factors. Two variables are based on the perceptions of the main respondent: the relative frequency with which the respondent reports discussing politics with the discussant and how much the respondent thinks the discussant knows about politics. Although there is no effect for the imputed knowledge of the discussant,[7] the statistically discernible

---

[7] Other analyses of these data (Huckfeldt 2001) suggest that the actual (as opposed to perceived) expertise of the discussant – measured in terms of the discussant's score

effect for the reported frequency of political discussion lies in the expected direction – more frequent discussion reduces the response time. A dummy variable is introduced to measure which of the network name generators was used to ask for names of discussants, but it fails to produce a statistically discernible effect. These results do not necessarily imply an absence of differentiation between political networks and more generalized social networks. Rather, we are already taking into account the differentiating characteristics of a political network, and other analyses show that the politics name generator is more likely to produce people who are casual acquaintances and more frequent political discussants – factors we are already considering.

Campaign Dynamics. Finally, two different variables are used in Table 4.1(A) to index campaign time: the week of the interview and a dummy variable that measures the primary season. The primary season is defined to continue through the end of June, and thus the primary season dummy variable indexes all respondents who are interviewed during this period. The week of the interview begins (at 1) with the first week of interviewing early in March and reaches its maximum (at 36) during the week of the election. (Respondents interviewed after the election are also given the maximum value.) Thus, the week of the interview (campaign week) indexes the temporal accumulation of opportunities for respondents to communicate politically within their networks of association

During the primary season we asked respondents whether they thought their discussant would vote for the Democratic candidate, the Republican candidate, or an independent candidate. After the primary season, we asked whether their discussant would support Bill Clinton, Bob Dole, or some other candidate. (See Appendix A.) The coefficient for the primary season dummy variable (-76.972) suggests that asking about *specific* candidates rather than simply asking about support for the party candidates *increased* the time required to answer by approximately three-fourths of a second. The increased specificity of choices offered by the campaign may have made it more difficult for some respondents to form judgments regarding the behavior of their discussants. In other words, it may be easier to say that Joe will vote for the Republican than it is to say that Joe will vote for Bob Dole!

Regardless of any effect that arises due to the specification of candidates at the end of the primary season, the model suggests a fairly strong, clarifying effect due to campaign time – measured as the week of

on a political knowledge battery – does predict the effectiveness with which the discussant communicates.

84

interview – even after all the other factors have been taken into account. If we ignore the effect of the primary season, response time decreases by 1.2 seconds across the 36 weeks (-3.437×35) – the accessibility of the judgment increases. Alternatively, if we only consider the period after the end of primary season – the first week of July and beyond – response time decreases by approximately two-thirds of a second (-3.437×19).[8]

In summary, the overall consequence of the election campaign is to make these judgments more accessible in memory. A number of other factors also produce more accessible judgments on the part of the respondents, and none is more important than the extremity of the discussant's partisan identification and the accessibility (or strength) of the respondent's party identification. The model predicts that response time decreases by more than a full second if the discussant is a strong Republican or Democrat rather than an independent (-36.699×3). Moreover, the accessibility of the main respondent's judgment is directly related to the accessibility of the main respondent's partisanship: Response time for the judgment increases by approximately three-fourths of a second across the lower 95 percent of the range of the main respondent's response time on the party identification measure ($.126 \times 615$),[9] even after we take account of the baseline speed of response. In short, strong attitudes – measured either in terms of accessibility or extremity – serve only *to enhance rather than impede* the effectiveness of communication.

REFLECTIVE CONFIDENCE IN POLITICAL JUDGMENTS

Accessibility is one important aspect of the judgments that citizens render regarding the preferences of other citizens, but it is certainly not the only aspect of such judgments. In particular, it is entirely possible that an individual will hold a highly accessible opinion regarding the likely vote of a discussant that is not sustained on further reflection. For example, a respondent may have a strong association in memory between "Joe"

[8] If we include the primary season coefficient in the calculation, predicted response time still decreases across the campaign, from week 1 to week 36 or higher, by approximately .4 seconds. The combined effect in week 1 is: $-76.972 - (3.437 \times 1)$; and in week 36 it is: $-(3.437 \times 36)$.

[9] The median time of response for the party identification question is 1.2 seconds, but the response times are characteristically skewed with an extended tail of higher values. In a conservative effort to avoid overstating the effect that arises due to partisan accessibility, the range of the response time measure is truncated for these purposes by eliminating the top 5 percent of the response times. The resulting response time distribution has a range that extends from 17 (or .17 seconds) to 632 (or 6.32 seconds) for a difference of 615 (or 6.15 seconds).

and "support for Republican candidates," but on further reflection the respondent may recall that Joe holds an antipathy toward politicians from Kansas, and hence the respondent may have a low level of confidence in her judgment about Joe's support for Dole. Alternatively, the respondent may have a highly inaccessible opinion regarding Joe's voting behavior, but further reflection based on a variety of factors – a dimly recalled conversation, a generalization based on other people the respondent knows – may lead the respondent to express a great deal of confidence in her judgment regarding Joe's political preference.

In short, accessibility is the product of associative strength, cognitive structure, and the ease with which judgments are reached. In contrast, judgmental confidence is based on individuals' reflective evaluations of their own judgments. Bassili (1996) refers to these sorts of evaluations as meta-attitudes – attitudes regarding attitudes. We anticipate that people will, in general, have more confidence in judgments that are more accessible, but confidence and accessibility might also be subject to very different sets of effects that arise due to other exogenous factors.[10] To the extent that accessibility and judgmental confidence are subject to the *same* explanatory variables, it is helpful to think in terms of direct and total effects. For example, the campaign may have a direct effect on judgmental confidence that is independent of its effect on judgmental accessibility, but we anticipate that such a direct effect would be less than the total effect of the campaign – the direct effect combined with the indirect effect on confidence that is mediated through judgmental accessibility. In Column B of Table 4.1, we estimate the total effects on confidence, but later in the analysis we consider direct effects by introducing a control for accessibility.

EXPLAINING JUDGMENTAL CONFIDENCE

After the main respondent provided a judgment regarding the discussant's voting preference, the interviewer asked the respondent "how difficult or easy it was to say" which candidate the discussant supports. We treat this question as a measure of the respondent's reflective confidence in the judgment. A scale is constructed where "very easy" is 4; somewhat easy is 3; somewhat difficult is 2; and very difficult is 1. Respondents who were unable to offer a judgment – and hence were not asked the confidence question – are assigned the value of 0.

---

[10] The correlation between accessibility and confidence is .48, the correlation between accessibility and accuracy is .28, and the correlation between confidence and accuracy is .43.

Explaining Judgmental Confidence

Nature of Relationships. Unlike the results in Column A of Table 4.1, the model in Column B shows statistically discernible effects due to the nature of the relationship between the discussant and the main respondent. In particular, the main respondents are more confident in their judgments regarding the political preferences of spouses and other relatives. Thus, although people may not have more accessible judgments regarding a spouse or relative, they *are* more confident in the judgments they render. It remains unclear, however, whether such confidence is justified.

Agreement Effects. Table 4.1(B) also shows no effect on judgmental confidence due to the presence of agreement or disagreement with the discussant. Thus, neither accessibility nor judgmental confidence is affected by disagreement within the dyad. Confidence *is* enhanced by a higher level of correspondence between the self-reported preference of the discussant and the perceived preference of *other* discussants, but the effect is relatively modest. None of this suggests that the false consensus effect is absent or lacking in importance, but the presence of political disagreement has no inhibiting effect on the ease with which people make inferences regarding the political preferences of others, and it has little effect on the confidence they place in these judgments.

Preference Effects. In terms of partisan preferences among discussants and main respondents, Table 4.1(B) results show that the extremity of candidate preferences, for *both* discussants *and* main respondents, appears to enhance judgmental confidence. People are more likely to be confident in their judgments if they hold an extreme position regarding the candidates, or if their discussant holds an extreme position. Moreover, confidence is also enhanced by higher levels of partisan extremity on the part of the discussants.

Other Political Characteristics. Column B of the table also shows that the confidence of respondents' judgments is unaffected by whether the discussant is named in response to the political discussion name generator or the important matters name generator. In contrast, effects are produced for the imputed knowledge of the discussant and for the reported frequency of political discussion, and this latter effect is quite pronounced.

Campaign Dynamics. Finally, the effect of campaign time is sustained for the respondent's judgmental confidence. Across the campaign, respondents become three-quarters of a point more confident in their judgments (.022 X 35), but this effect is partially offset by the effect of the primary

87

season, when respondents are only asked whether their discussants will support the Democratic candidate, the Republican candidate, or some other candidate.

THE ACCURACY OF POLITICAL JUDGMENTS

Finally and fundamentally, the effectiveness of political communication among citizens depends on the accuracy of one citizen's judgment regarding the preferences of another citizen (Huckfeldt and Sprague 1995; Huckfeldt et al. 1998a). If Joe thinks that Sam supports Dole when Sam is actually a Clinton voter, the collective deliberations of democracy have malfunctioned. Accurately perceived communication becomes a defining ingredient of effective communication, and hence a defining ingredient of collective deliberation in democratic politics.

What is the relationship between the accessibility of a political judgment on the one hand, and the accuracy of that judgment on the other hand? To the extent that strong associations in memory between the discussant and a particular political preference are the residue of past communication with the discussant, one might expect accessibility to enhance accuracy. In contrast, we have no expectation regarding an effect on accuracy due to confidence. Hence, we begin by considering total effects on accuracy, but in a later analysis we control for accessibility to consider the direct effects alone.

EXPLAINING ACCURACY

Accuracy is conceived in terms of the correspondence between the main respondent's judgment and the discussant's reported preference, thereby producing a binary response – accurate or inaccurate. Thus, in the analysis that follows, a nonlinear logit model replaces the linear least-squares model. Because the logit model is nonlinear in parameters, the effect of any single variable is best evaluated with respect to a particular point on the probability distribution for accuracy. The procedure that we generally employ, therefore, is to examine the magnitude of change in the probability across the range of one variable while all other variables are held constant at typical values.

Nature of Relationships. The first issue that arises is how the effects on accuracy in Table 4.1(C) compare with the earlier results. For example, is the pattern of effects for accuracy the same as the pattern of effects for confidence? Is accuracy simply a surrogate for confidence? We immediately see that this is not the case with reference to the nature of the relationship between the main respondent and the discussant. People have more confidence in their assessments of spouses' and relatives' political preferences, but there is no comparable effect with respect to accuracy. Thus, the lack of effect on accuracy parallels the lack of effect on accessibility. People are more likely to *believe* that they do a better job making judgments with respect to spouses, relatives, and close friends, but their confidence is misplaced!

Agreement Effects. The consequences of agreement show an even more pronounced divergence from earlier patterns of effects. *The accuracy of the main respondent's judgment is dramatically enhanced by the presence of agreement between the main respondent and the discussant, as well as by agreement between the discussant and the remainder of the respondent's network.* The magnitudes of these effects are shown in Part A of Figure 4.1, where we see particularly strong effects that arise due to agreement within the residual network. Thus, although there was little evidence of an agreement effect on accessibility or judgmental confidence, we see strong evidence for such an effect on accuracy.

Preference Effects. The pattern of effects arising due to discussant and main respondent partisan orientations parallels many of the earlier results. In particular, accuracy is enhanced to the extent that the discussants' partisan preferences are extreme – both with respect to partisanship and with respect to candidate evaluations. As Part B of Figure 4.1 shows, discussants are much more likely to be perceived accurately if they send clear and unambiguous messages. Strong partisans with extreme views regarding the candidates are more than 40 points more likely to be perceived accurately than independents who are neutral regarding the candidates. Finally, there is no evidence here to suggest that main respondents with strong or extreme preferences are unable to perceive their discussants' preferences accurately.

Other Political Characteristics. Neither the imputed political knowledge of the discussant, nor the reported frequency of political discussion, nor membership in explicitly political networks displays statistically discernible effects on accuracy. This is the first instance in which reported frequency of political discussion fails to produce a discernible effect, but for both latent indicators – accessibility and accuracy – the effect lies at the borderline of null hypothesis rejection criteria. It is only in the case of perceived judgmental confidence that perceived frequency produces a substantial and crisp effect.

Campaign Dynamics. Column C of Table 4.1 shows that the election campaign has a substantial effect on the accuracy of main respondent

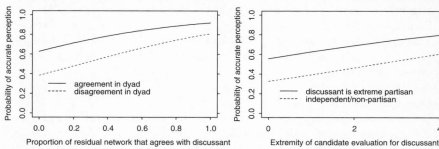

A. Agreement in dyad and residual network.

B. Extremity of discussant preferences.

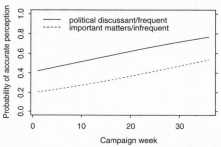

C. Campaign week and discussant type/discussion frequency.

Figure 4.1. The effect of various factors on the predicted probability that the main respondent accurately perceives the discussant's vote intention. In each part of the figure: The discussant is held constant as a non-relative who is not a close friend. Partisan accessibility for the main respondent and the discussant is held constant at the 1.2 seconds. Main respondent partisan extremity is held constant at 2 and candidate evaluation extremity is held constant at 2.1. Imputed discussant knowledge is held constant at 2.3. And the primary season dummy variable is held constant at 0. In Part A of the figure: Dyadic agreement and residual network agreement are varied across their ranges. The campaign week is held constant at 25. Frequency of discussion is held constant at 3. The discussant is held constant as a political discussant. Partisan extremity of the discussant is held constant at 2. And candidate evaluation extremity of the discussant is held constant at 2.1. In Part B of the figure: The partisan extremity and candidate evaluation extremity of the discussant are varied across their observed ranges. The dyad is held constant at disagreement. And the residual network is held constant at a disagreement level of .5. Other variables are held constant as in Part A. In Part C of the figure: The campaign week is varied across its range for political discussants with whom the respondents often discuss politics and for important matters discussants with whom they never discuss politics. Discussant partisan extremity is held constant at 2 and candidate evaluation extremity is held constant at 2.1. Other variables are held constant as in Part B. *Source:* Table 4.1(C) logit estimates.

judgments regarding the preferences of the discussants. The magnitude of the effect due to the campaign week during which the respondent was interviewed is shown in Part C of Figure 4.1, both for non-political network discussants with whom the main respondent reports infrequent political discussion and for political network discussants with whom the main respondent reports frequent political discussion. Discussants are nearly 40 points more likely to be perceived accurately at the end of the campaign than at the beginning.[11]

As the campaign progresses, people develop more readily accessible perceptions regarding their associates' preferences, and these campaign effects are directly reflected in the accuracy of their judgments. Thus the campaign stimulates political communication not only by making respondents more confident in more highly accessible judgments, but also by improving the quality of people's judgments, where quality is measured in terms of accuracy.[12]

In contrast, there are some effects that are *only* reflected in accuracy, most notably the false consensus effects that arise due to the distribution of preferences both within the dyad and within the remainder of the network. Disagreement does not seriously compromise the confidence or accessibility of judgments, but it *does* compromise the *accuracy* of these judgments.

[11] If we were tracking the consequences of the campaign for public opinion regarding the candidates, we would certainly want to take account of idiosyncratic campaign events – debates, scandals, and so forth. This is not our goal, however. Our focus is on the campaign as an institution which stimulates public communication and deliberation quite apart from the particular events and dramas that characterize particular moments along the way. Thus, we conceive of the campaign's temporal metric in terms of the accumulated opportunities for political communication among citizens. Within this context, it is appropriate to consider various periods during the campaign. We therefore include a control for the primary season. Other analyses, not shown here, fail to demonstrate an effect due to the interaction between the campaign week and the primary season. The campaign week has no differential impact before or after the primary season. Another analysis shows that the effects of the campaign week are substantially sustained even when the post-election interviews are eliminated.

[12] These analyses have shown that respondent judgments regarding the political preferences of their associates are systematically affected by the election campaign. What of their own preferences? As part of the study we asked the respondents for whom they intended to vote, and, after the election, for whom they voted. When we control for their evaluations of the candidates, the strength of their partisan identification, and the baseline speed of response, the campaign produces a pronounced effect on the accessibility of their intended or reported vote. Indeed, the speed of response increases by a full half second from the period before the election to the period after the election.

TAKING ACCOUNT OF ACCESSIBILITY

In Table 4.1 we ignored the possibility that confidence and accuracy depend on accessibility. In the analyses of Table 4.2 we include controls for accessibility, thereby considering only the direct effects on judgmental confidence and accuracy that operate separately from accessibility.

Table 4.2. *Confidence and accuracy of main respondent judgments regarding the vote preferences of their discussants, with accessibility control.*

	A. Confidence (OLS)		B. Accuracy (logit)	
	Coeff.	(t)	Coeff.	(t)
Constant	1.100	(3.12)	3.701	(3.97)
1. Response Time and Controls				
Accessibility of judgment	−.183	(9.96)	−.191	(4.06)
Question order	.025	(.72)	.310	(3.06)
First named discussant	.174	(1.74)	.808	(2.77)
2. Nature of Relationship				
Spouse (dummy)	.391	(3.55)	.477	(1.24)
Another relative (dummy)	.225	(2.37)	.021	(.08)
Close friend (dummy)	.104	(1.06)	−.123	(.45)
3. Agreement Measures				
Agreement in dyad (dummy)	−.046	(.47)	1.021	(4.66)
Network agreement proportion	.172	(1.52)	1.841	(5.92)
4. Main Respondent Preferences				
Partisan extremity	.062	(1.36)	.065	(.56)
Candidate evaluation extremity	.075	(2.41)	−.017	(.20)
Partisan accessibility (party ident. response time)	.015	(.92)	−.074	(1.88)
5. Discussant Preferences				
Partisan extremity	.047	(1.26)	.271	(2.57)
Candidate evaluation extremity	.086	(3.24)	.273	(3.22)
Partisan accessibility (party ident. response time)	−.012	(.82)	−.025	(.60)
6. Other Characteristics				
Imputed discussant knowledge	.134	(2.28)	.039	(.22)
Reported discussion frequency	.282	(5.77)	.176	(1.35)
Political discussant network (dummy)	.094	(1.45)	.348	(1.85)
7. Campaign Dynamic				
Campaign week	.016	(2.62)	.035	(2.11)
Primary season (dummy)	.274	(1.63)	.516	(1.20)
N =	913		915	
R^2 =	.35			
s =	.94			
chi^2/df/p =			215/19/.00	

Note: Response times are in hundredths of seconds. Estimates are corrected for clustering (Rogers 1993).
Source: Indianapolis–St. Louis Study.

Taking Account of Accessibility

Effects of Accessibility on Confidence. The first set of factors in Column A of Table 4.2 makes it possible to consider the effect of accessibility on confidence, controlling for question order and whether the discussant is named first by the respondent. Quite clearly, there is a very strong relationship – the strength of the association in memory between a discussant and a political preference gives rise to higher levels of confidence in judgment.

A number of factors have effects on judgmental confidence that are decreased by approximately 50 percent due to the control for accessibility: correspondence between the discussant and the remainder of the network; the partisan extremity of the respondent and the discussant; whether the discussant is named as a member of the political discussion network; and the temporal effects of the campaign. What does it mean that some variables' effects are diminished by the introduction of the accessibility control? These factors affect *both* accessibility *and* judgmental confidence, and their direct effects on confidence are reduced by taking into account the indirect effect on confidence that operates by way of accessibility.

Such reasoning encourages an analytic separation between the factors that primarily affect accessibility and the factors that primarily affect judgmental confidence. Some factors primarily affect judgmental confidence via accessibility. The best example of this is perhaps the partisan extremity of the discussant. Other variables primarily affect judgmental confidence without any effect on accessibility. The best example of this is perhaps the extremity of the discussant's evaluation of the two candidates. These effects are eminently reasonable. Over the long haul, we develop strong preconceptions regarding the political preferences of our extremely partisan associates. Perhaps ironically, their preferences of the moment – their actual evaluations of candidates – may have less consequence for the accessibility of our judgments. In contrast, when the main respondents are asked to stop and think (Zaller 1992), the discussants' current opinions may have a better chance of surfacing, perhaps due to the recollection of particular conversations and expressions of sentiment.

Another example of an asymmetrical effect operating only on judgmental confidence is the higher level of confidence regarding the preferences of spouses and relatives. To the extent that spouses and relatives are more frequent sources of political communication, we might expect their opinions to be more accessible, but the effects on accessibility are at most marginal. To the extent that respondents *are* more confident regarding their judgments of spouses and relatives, the confidence may be generated by the respondents' own expectations that they *should* have more complete knowledge about these associates' political preferences.

Finally, some factors have direct effects on *both* accessibility *and* judgmental confidence, and thus the total effect on the judgment is cumulative across direct and indirect effects. The best example of this is the effect of

93

the campaign. As the campaign progresses, respondents develop more accessible judgments regarding the preferences of their discussants, and this heightened accessibility leads to a heightened level of judgmental confidence as well. At the same time, the campaign also has a direct and independent effect on judgmental confidence. When we ask people to consider their opinion and to tell us how hard it was to make the judgment, we are asking them to reflect on the evidence. As the campaign progresses, they have more evidence to consider, and hence they become more confident in their judgments.

Effects of Accessibility on Accuracy. Column B of Table 4.2 shows that higher levels of accessibility also translate into higher levels of accuracy – people who hold more accessible judgments regarding their discussants' political preferences tend to be more accurate in their perceptions. When other factors are held constant at typical values, the model estimates are capable of producing a more than 30 point increase in the probability of accurate judgment across the lower 95 percent of the range in accessibility.[13]

This is an important relationship: To the extent that accuracy is enhanced by accessibility, it would appear that judgmental accessibility is anchored primarily in an evidentiary base, and hence is not the residue of selective perception. In short, the level of accessibility which lies behind these judgments provides a good index to the accuracy of the judgments, and thus accessibility is unlikely to be a simple product of an effort to reconstruct reality so as to minimize cognitive dissonance.

By including the control for accessibility, we eliminate effects on accuracy that operate indirectly through the accessibility of judgment. The general pattern of effects is quite similar, but several effects are reduced in comparison to Table 4.1(C), including the effect of the campaign.

CONCLUSION

Two very different models of political judgment are imbedded within most analyses of political communication and cognition among citizens. One model assumes that people see what they want to see and hear what they want to hear. Taking inspiration from the early work on cognitive dissonance and selective perception by Festinger (1957), it is assumed that

---

[13] In order to avoid overstating the effect that arises due to partisan accessibility, the range of the response time measure is truncated by eliminating the top 5 percent of the response times. See the note to Figure 4.1 for the control values of the other explanatory variables.

individuals are capable of rewriting reality in order to avoid the unpleasant and unsettling experience of political disagreement.

A second model emphasizes the cues and strategies that individuals employ in reaching political judgments. According to this model, individuals are able to employ inferential devices in order to reach political judgments in ambiguous and uncertain circumstances (Sniderman, Brody, and Tetlock 1991; Kahneman and Tversky 1973; Tversky and Kahneman 1974). Of course, not all decision-making situations involve ambiguity or uncertainty, and reaching a judgment is a fairly straightforward matter in many circumstances.

Our own analysis conforms with this latter interpretation. First, we see no effect of main respondent partisan extremity on either strategic avoidance or selective perception. If extreme partisans were less likely to make accurate judgments regarding their discussants' preferences, we might conclude either (1) the discussant was sending an ambiguous political signal in order to avoid disagreement and conflict with a highly opinionated associate, or (2) the highly opinionated main respondent was selectively perceiving the discussant's preference in order to avoid the distress of cognitive dissonance. But we see no effect of main respondent extremity on either the accuracy or the accessibility of judgment. The extremity of main respondent candidate preference *does* enhance judgmental confidence, but in the absence of any distorting effect on accuracy, such an effect offers little support for a cognitive dissonance interpretation regarding the distortion of political communication.

Second, although there is no evidence to suggest that extreme partisans are bad listeners, it is quite clear that the extreme partisans *are* more effective communicators. Main respondents are more likely to offer accessible, confident, and accurate judgments regarding the political preferences of discussants who hold more extreme views. But this is just another way of saying that people's political perceptions of one another are subject to the *actual flow of information* that occurs through social communication, and people with extreme preferences are more likely to communicate unambiguous information. Once again, political judgment depends on the quality of political information – it is not an artifact of selective perception.

Third, this analysis encourages us to rethink the nature of false consensus as it applies to political communication among citizens. If political disagreement is dissonance producing, it might be expected to produce political judgments that are hesitant, inaccessible, and lacking in certainty. Instead, we see no effects on accessibility and confidence that arise due to perceived agreement or disagreement between the respondent and the discussant. Moreover, we see relatively weak and inconsistent effects on accessibility and confidence that arise due to agreement or disagreement between the discussant and the remainder of the respondent's social frame of reference – the remaining members of her communication network. In short, political disagreement does not appear to unsettle our respondents, and they are not seriously hindered in the ease or confidence with which they offer political judgments regarding discussants who hold politically disagreeable views.

In contrast, the distribution of preferences within the dyad and the residual network registers a profound effect on the accuracy of judgment: *People are much less likely to make an accurate judgment regarding a rare preference.* If they do not hold the preference, and if they do not believe that others hold the preference, their own personal experiences are telling them that the discussant in question probably does not hold the preference either.

Moreover, the effect of personal disagreement within the dyad is not so pronounced as the effect of perceived agreement in the residual network. But if disagreement is so personally unsettling, its effects should be more dramatic within the dyad. Thus it would appear that an individual's own political preference is as primarily important as another piece of information that the individual uses to make an informed judgment regarding the likely preference of some other person. In this context, we might very well see false consensus effects as the consequence of judgmental errors that occur when people use a reasonable decision-making device that happens to fail in a particular circumstance.

None of this is meant to take issue with theories of cognitive dissonance as they relate to the perceptual biases that arise due to personal distress or discomfort over *inexplicable* differences of opinion (see Ross et al. 1976). Rather, these results regarding communication among citizens in an election campaign lead one to question the extent to which political disagreements are actually troubling sources of dissonance in the lives of most citizens. Indeed, for several reasons, political disagreement may produce *very little* of the personal distress that is associated with cognitive dissonance and selective perception. Many people do not care enough to be alarmed. Others see political opinions as idiosyncratic expressions of personal preference that do not require explanation, similar to the ways in which consumer choices between Chevrolets and Fords do not require explanation. Moreover, differences in preference and opinion often *are* readily explained: Tom votes for Democrats because he is a liberal; Jane voted for Dole because she is rich; Sally voted for Clinton because she comes from a family of Democrats; and so on. In short, political differences and disagreements are easily reconciled, readily accommodated, and simply explained by many citizens, and hence they are unlikely to be dissonance producing.

Conclusion

Finally, the political judgments of citizens are susceptible to the temporal context of information created by the unfolding of a presidential election campaign. The outcomes of many elections may be highly predictable even before the campaign takes place (Gelman and King 1993), but this does not erase the role of campaigns as important deliberative devices in democratic politics. At any given moment during the campaign, any given citizen may be more than willing to offer her own opinion regarding the candidates, and even to provide her own expected vote. Moreover, these expected votes may be highly predictive of ultimate voting behavior, but this does not eliminate the deliberative role of even the most predictable presidential election. Citizens talk to one another; they express their preferences; and over the course of the campaign they develop judgments regarding the preferences of others. The successful candidate must survive this collective process of public scrutiny, and stimulating such a process is arguably the most important function of democratic elections.

5

Disagreement, Heterogeneity, and Persuasion: How Does Disagreement Survive?

The previous chapter demonstrates that people are less likely to recognize a preference accurately if they do not hold the preference, or if they perceive the preference to be less common within their communication networks. At the same time, the presence of this autoregressive bias in patterns of communication does not protect citizens from the experience of political disagreement, and a number of questions thus arises. If campaign stimulated processes of political communication and influence do not eliminate disagreement, what are the factors that sustain political heterogeneity and disagreement? What are the consequences of political heterogeneity within these communication networks for patterns of political influence between and among citizens? Finally, in what manner is the influence of one citizen on another conditioned by the structure of communication networks and the distribution of preferences in the remainder of the these networks? We address these questions based on the study of electoral dynamics in the 1996 presidential campaign as it took place in the Indianapolis and St. Louis metropolitan areas.

Citizens are typically aware of the political disagreements that exist within their personal networks of communication, even though results in the previous chapter indicate the existence of autoregressive biases that sometimes attenuate communication effectiveness. Disagreements over politics and policy arise even in the smallest and most closely held social groups. Although the political preferences of citizens tend to reflect the partisan composition of their micro-environmental surroundings, few citizens are completely insulated from interaction with others who will disagree with them. The simple fact is that disagreements occur on a regular basis, and that simple fact forces a reassessment of (1) the common wisdom suggesting that political homogeneity is the inevitable outcome of self-selection and conformity pressures within small groups, and (2) the models and mechanisms of political communication and influence among citizens.

Students of public opinion and political participation adopt very different models to explain the dynamic consequences of political communication among and between citizens. According to one model, social communication and social influence provide the underlying fabric of a resilient political order. Individual preferences are imbedded within politically homogeneous networks of social relations, and hence they are anchored in a stable collective sentiment. An alternative model suggests that individual choices and preferences are subject to the diverse and fluctuating sentiments of a heterogeneous mix of public opinion. Whereas individuals are imbedded within networks of social relations, the preference distributions within these networks are politically heterogeneous and dynamic, and hence the socially contingent preferences of particular individuals are highly dynamic as well.

The divergence between these models is especially relevant to processes of democratic deliberation as they unfold in the context of an election campaign (Barber 1984; Fishkin 1991). In particular, the models predict dramatically different consequences for the dynamics of individual preference formation and for the convergence of aggregate opinion in the campaign. The central issues revolve around the survival of political disagreement and the extent to which higher levels of interdependence among citizens serve to shield individuals from, or expose them to, the events of the campaign. Several questions become crucial.

Do campaign stimulated processes of collective deliberation result in the elimination of disagreement within networks of social communication? If not, what are the factors that sustain political heterogeneity and disagreement within these networks? And what are the consequences of political heterogeneity within communication networks for patterns of political influence between and among citizens? Is the influence of one citizen on another conditioned by the distribution of preferences in the remainder of the micro-environment? Finally, what are the implications of the analysis for the penetration of individual patterns of communication and deliberation by the larger dynamics of the campaign? How does this penetration affect the dynamic consequences of communication among and between citizens?

We address these questions based on a study of electoral dynamics in the 1996 presidential campaign as it took place in the Indianapolis and St. Louis metropolitan areas. Attention focuses primarily on citizens and their networks of political communication. Network data were gathered throughout much of the campaign and beyond, from early March of 1996 through early January of 1997, and again in the fall of 1997. Hence we are able to address the dynamic political relationships among citizens within their networks of political communication.

POLITICS, INTERDEPENDENCE, AND THE SURVIVAL OF DISAGREEMENT

As we have seen, the classic statement of the socially and politically conservative consequences that arise due to social communication in politics is contained in the work of Lazarsfeld and his colleagues, based on their field work in Elmira and Erie County during the 1940s (Lazarsfeld et al. 1948; Berelson et al. 1954). According to their argument, political preferences become individually idiosyncratic as political communication among citizens becomes less frequent during the period of time between election campaigns. In response to the stimulus of the election, the frequency of political communication increases, idiosyncratic preferences become socially visible, and hence these individuals are brought into conformity with micro-environmental surroundings. In this way, social communication creates political stability as it provides a buffer against the political volatility of the external political environment (Huckfeldt and Sprague 1995).

Pressures toward conformity should drive out disagreement in several ways (Festinger 1957; Huckfeldt and Sprague 1995): The discomfort of disagreement should encourage people to modify their patterns of social relations so as to exclude people with whom they disagree; people should avoid political discussion with those associates who hold politically divergent preferences; partially as a consequence of discussion avoidance, people should incorrectly perceive agreement among those with whom they actually disagree; perhaps most important, individuals should bring their own preferences into correspondence with the preferences that they encounter within their networks of social relations.

These theoretical expectations confront an awkward empirical problem. Campaigns do *not* extinguish disagreement within networks of social relations. Perhaps citizens should avoid the experience of disagreement, but they do not. The persistence of disagreement has been documented by studies of respondents and their discussants in multiple locales and at various times: South Bend in 1984 (Huckfeldt and Sprague 1995), a national American sample in 1992 (Huckfeldt et al. 1998a), Indianapolis and St. Louis in 1996 (Huckfeldt, Johnson, and Sprague 2000), and in the 2000 National Election Study (see Chapter 2). Main respondents who supported a major party candidate perceived agreement in about two-thirds of the dyads identified by these studies.

Recall that such a measure understates the overall levels of disagreement that exist in the networks in which citizens are situated. If the probability of dyadic disagreement is .7, and if the likelihood of disagreement is independent across the dyads within a network, then the probability of agreement across all the relationships within a two-discussant network drops to $.7^2$ or .49. Hence, even when an individual only has two discussants, the odds of heterogeneity are as high as the odds of homogeneity.

The pervasiveness of disagreement within networks of social relations forces a reassessment of social conformity as a mechanism of social influence, as well as a reconsideration of the aggregate implications of political interdependence among citizens. The theory of the consequences of social communication for the dynamics of an election campaign might be transformed fundamentally. Rather than serving as a source of insulation from the external political environment, social communication might even serve to magnify the consequences of the external environment by exposing individuals to nonredundant, politically disparate information.

DATA AND RESEARCH DESIGN

We address these issues on the basis of the Indianapolis–St. Louis Study, conducted by the Center for Survey Research at Indiana University during and after the 1996 presidential election campaign. The study was expressly designed to examine the dynamic consequences of the campaign. The primary focus of the study is on political communication and preference formation over the course of the campaign, and thus campaign interviews began in early March of 1996 and ended in early January of 1997. The campaign study includes a sample of 2,174 main respondents drawn from the lists of registered voters, combined with a one-stage snowball sample which produced interviews with 1,475 of these main respondents' discussion partners.[1]

In an effort to establish a *post hoc* baseline for campaign effects on political activation, we returned to the field in October and November of 1997 using the same questionnaire and sampling design. During this period we completed 438 interviews with main respondents and 265 interviews with their discussants. For purposes of our discussion, main respondent interviews conducted before the end of primary season (prior to July 1, 1996) are referred to as first wave cases. Subsequent main respondent interviews taken *before* the end of the campaign are referred to as second wave cases. Main respondent interviews conducted immediately after the election are third wave cases. The *post hoc* baseline interviews, conducted in the fall of 1997, are fourth wave cases.

In order to collect social network information, every main respondent to the survey was asked to provide the first names of his or her discussion partners.[2] A random half of the sample was asked to name people with whom they discuss "important matters"; the other half was asked

---

[1] Main respondent samples are drawn from the voter registration lists of two study sites: (1) the Indianapolis metropolitan area defined as Marion County, Indiana; and (2) the St. Louis metropolitan area defined as the independent city of St. Louis combined with the surrounding (and mostly suburban) St. Louis County, Missouri. Details of the study design can be found in Appendix A.

[2] The discussants were also asked to provide social network information, but no effort was made to interview the discussants of the discussants.

to name people with whom they discuss "government, elections, and politics" (Burt 1986; Huckfeldt et al. 1998b).[3] After compiling a list of first names of not more than five discussion partners, the interviewers asked a battery of questions about each discussion partner. At the end of the interview, main respondents were asked for identifying information that might be used to contact and interview these discussants.

POLITICAL ACTIVATION EFFECTS IN THE CAMPAIGN

Presidential election campaigns are the marathon events of the American electoral Olympics, not only for direct participants but even for passive observers (Witcover 1977). News media attention to the campaign is both intense and long running. No one escapes media coverage via newspapers, news shows, talk shows, and comic monologues. Moreover, it is very difficult to get in front of the campaign, or even to say when the campaign begins, with candidates lining up support and planning strategy long before the preceding midterm congressional elections.

In such a setting it is less than clear when the public becomes attentive, or more important for our purposes, when communication processes among citizens are activated. Are channels of political communication and deliberation activated at the first primary election, or at the politicians' announcements of their candidacies, or at the beginning of the general election campaign? Alternatively, does political attentiveness and deliberation ever stop, or is it an ongoing state of affairs for many citizens?

We examine these questions from two different vantage points, by considering both the level of political discussion within communication networks as well as the size of the communication networks. After identifying the respondent's network of social contacts, we asked a battery of questions regarding each discussant, and one of the questions was: "When you talk with (discussant's first name), do you discuss political matters: often, sometimes, rarely, or never?" Values of 1 through 4 are assigned to the responses in ascending order of discussion frequency, and a mean level of political discussion is computed for each respondent based on their responses for all discussants. A second criterion of deliberation is based on the number of discussants named by each main respondent, scaled from 0 to 5.

Campaign effects on both these deliberative criteria are considered in the two models included in Part A of Table 5.1. Several individual level predictors of political involvement are incorporated in each

[3] The experimental condition imbedded within the design of this name generator allows us to examine the extent to which political information networks are separate from social communication networks more broadly considered.

Political Activation Effects in the Campaign

Table 5.1. *Campaign activation effects on political communication.*

A. Simple effects of campaign

	Mean Political Discussion		Number of Discussants	
	Coefficient	t-value	Coefficient	t-value
Constant	2.04	22.88	−.03	.16
Partisan extremity	.05	3.50	.07	1.87
Education	.03	5.79	.14	10.29
Org. memberships	.04	5.19	.16	7.94
Political discussion name generator	.20	7.48	−.10	.53
Wave 1	−.04	1.02	.02	.17
Wave 3	−.06	1.78	−.02	.18
Wave 4	−.11	2.74	−.24	2.22
N =	2006		2490	
R^2 =	.08		.10	
S.E.	.59		1.72	

B. Campaign effects contingent on type of discussant

	Mean Political Discussion		Number of Discussants	
	Coefficient	t-value	Coefficient	t-value
Constant	2.01	23.09	−.04	.20
Partisan extremity	.05	3.51	.07	1.86
Education	.03	5.83	.14	10.26
Org. memberships	.04	5.15	.16	7.95
Political discussion name generator	.18	6.37	−.08	1.12
Wave 4 X important matters discussion	−.11	2.31	−.17	1.36
Wave 4 X political discussion	−.04	.75	−.30	2.26
N =	2006		2490	
R^2 =	.08		.10	
S.E. =	.59		1.72	
t-value for difference in wave 4 effects	1.01		.70	

Partisan extremity: 0 = independent; 1 = independent leaning toward party; 2 = not strong partisan; 3 = strong partisan. Education: years of school. Org. memberships: number of organizations to which the main respondent reports being a member. Political discussion name generator: 1 = respondent is asked with whom she discusses government, elections, and politics; 0 = respondent is asked with whom she discusses important matters. Wave 1, wave 3, wave 4: 1 = respondent was interviewed at the particular wave; 0 otherwise. Wave 4 X important matters discussion: 1 = respondent was interviewed at wave 4 and asked the important matters name generator; 0 otherwise. Wave 4 X political discussion: 1 = respondent was interviewed at wave 4 and asked the political discussion name generator; 0 otherwise.

Source: Indianapolis–St. Louis Study.

model: partisan extremity, education, and organizational involvement. Partisan extremity is based on the standard party identification measure, with strong partisans coded as 3, weak partisans as 2, independents who lean toward a party as 1, and independents who do not lean as 0. Education is coded as years of formal education, and organizational involvement is coded as the number of organizations in which the respondent reports being a member. A dummy variable control is also included for the form of the network name generator: "political discussion" is set to 1 if the respondent is asked to supply the first names of political discussants and 0 if the respondent is asked to supply "important matters" discussants. Finally, the campaign is coded as a series of three dummy variables, with the second wave cases treated as the (excluded) baseline condition. The second wave constitutes the heart of the campaign, after the end of the primary season and before the election, and hence it would appear *a priori* to be the period of highest activation.

The first model in Table 5.1A shows positive effects on discussion frequency arising due to partisan extremity, education, and organizational involvement. Moreover, the reported level of discussion is higher for those discussants provided in response to the political discussion name generator. The only statistically discernible *campaign* effect comes in the form of the *post hoc* baseline. That is, the mean level of political discussion is lower in the fall of 1997 than it is in the fall of 1996. None of the other campaign dummies produces statistically discernible effects, although the signs for the coefficients all lie in the expected direction, suggesting depressed levels of discussion in comparison to the heart of the campaign.

The second model in Table 5.1 shows similar effects on network size due to individual involvement variables, although the t-value for partisan extremity is of marginal size. In contrast, no effect arises due to the network name generator. Main respondents do not name more or less discussants in response to the politics or important matters name generators. Once again, the only statistically discernible effect of the campaign occurs with respect to the *post hoc* baseline. In the fall of 1997, main respondents provide fewer discussant names, thereby indicating smaller communication networks.

What do these results suggest? First, it would appear that our sampling strategy failed to get in front of the campaign. That is, channels of public deliberation had already been activated early in 1996. Second, we *do* establish the campaign's activation effect on public deliberation by establishing a *post hoc* baseline that produces smaller networks and lower levels of political discussion. Thus, while we cannot demonstrate the precise period during which the activation occurred, this analysis does document heightened levels of attentiveness and social communication during the campaign. In short, the campaign serves to activate channels of social communication among citizens, the activation effect occurs early, and it is long in duration.

CONTINGENT EFFECTS OF CAMPAIGN ACTIVATION

The campaign might produce differential effects on patterns of social communication depending on the particular focus and construction of communication networks. To the extent that networks of political communication are specialized and hence separate from networks of communication more generally defined, the stimulus of the campaign might either be irrelevant or redundant to one or the other. Thus, for example, people are more likely to talk about politics with others whom they have defined as political discussants, and the campaign may thus be irrelevant to the further stimulation of political discussion within these relationships. Alternatively, to the extent that discussions of the campaign invade every relationship, we might expect to see effects on more generalized patterns of communication. Hence, the campaign effect on political discussion might be especially pronounced within communication networks that are normally consumed by topics other than politics.

We evaluate these expectations regarding the frequency of political discussion in the first model of Table 5.1B. This model is parallel in construction to the model considered in Table 5.1A, but the *post hoc* baseline is the only campaign dummy variable that is included, and its construction is contingent on whether the main respondent named political discussants or important matters discussants. The model shows a discernible effect among important matters discussants but no discernible effect among political discussants. In other words, the frequency of political discussion is reduced among important matters discussants, but it is not reduced among political discussants.[4] Thus, the directions and magnitudes of effects support an argument which suggests that the stimulus of the campaign is especially influential in increasing levels of political deliberation within discussion networks that are not politically defined.

The second model of Table 5.1B provides a comparison of the contingent effects due to the campaign on the size of political networks. The stimulus of the campaign does not serve to increase the frequency of political discussion within political communication networks, but it might serve to increase the *size* of political communication networks. Once again, the Table 5.1B model parallels the corresponding model in Table 5.1A, but the only included campaign variable is the *post hoc* baseline. As before,

---

[4] Although the effect is discernible among important matters discussants and not discernible among political discussants, the difference between effects is not statistically discernible (t = 1.01).

the construction of the *post hoc* baseline is contingent on whether the respondent named political discussants or important matters discussants. In this instance, the model shows a discernible effect on the number of political discussants, but no discernible effect on the number of important matters discussants. Hence the directions and magnitudes of effects support an argument suggesting that the campaign serves to increase the size of political discussion networks.[5]

In summary, these results suggest that the campaign clearly increases the size of discussion networks and the frequency of political discussion. There is some evidence to suggest that the campaign effect on political discussion frequency is primarily important within networks that are not defined with respect to political communication. Evidence is also present to suggest that the campaign effect on network size is primarily important in increasing the size of political discussion networks.

CAMPAIGN EFFECTS ON HOMOGENEITY WITHIN NETWORKS

We have seen evidence to suggest that the election campaign stimulates political deliberation and communication among citizens. In comparison to the *post hoc* baseline, communication networks increase in size during the campaign, and the frequency of political discussion increases as well. A separate but related question addresses the consequence of political communication for the creation of political homogeneity within discussion networks. That is, does the campaign serve to eliminate political disagreement among individuals who are connected within networks of social communication?

We are particularly interested in the survival or elimination of disagreement among citizens *during the course of the campaign*, and the *post hoc* baseline correspondingly becomes less relevant to our task. Hence we limit the analysis to an examination of the campaign sample taken in waves 1 through 3, and we focus on the respondents' perceptions of their discussants' partisan preferences. Our analytic strategy is to examine variation in the strength of the relationship between (1) the main respondent's perceptions regarding the partisan composition of her networks and (2) the main respondent's partisan orientation. We are making no argument regarding the direction of causation, which undoubtedly runs both ways. People select associates on the basis of partisan orientations, and these orientations are simultaneously affected by associates (Huckfeldt and Sprague 1995). Our only purpose is to see whether the campaign increases political

---

[5] The effect on size is discernible for political discussion networks and not discernible for important matters networks, but the difference between effects is not statistically discernible ($t = .71$).

Campaign Effects on Homogeneity within Networks

Table 5.2. *Campaign effects on political homogeneity within networks.*

A. Partisan composition of network by respondent's party identification

	Network Clinton Proportion		Network Dole Proportion	
	Coefficient	t-value	Coefficient	t-value
Constant	.63	27.72	.09	4.05
Wave 1	.01	.38	−.01	.28
Wave 3	−.03	1.13	.02	.77
Party identification	−.09	14.81	.09	16.09
Party id. X wave 1	−.01	1.02	.004	.48
Party id. X wave 3	.01	.95	−.01	1.14
N =	1692		1692	
R^2 =	.28		.30	
S.E.	.32		.33	

B. Partisan composition of network by respondent candidate evaluation

	Network Clinton Proportion		Network Dole Proportion	
	Coefficient	t-value	Coefficient	t-value
Constant	−.07	2.24	−.07	2.10
Wave 1	−.01	.29	.02	.42
Wave 3	.06	1.50	.08	1.71
Candidate evaluation	.15	15.94	.16	14.24
Cand. eval. X wave 1	−.003	.23	−.001	.08
Cand. eval. X wave 3	−.03	2.06	−.03	2.20
N =	1731		1724	
R^2 =	.27		.22	
S.E.	.32		.34	

Network Clinton proportion: The proportion of all discussion partners perceived by the main respondent to support Clinton (mean is .35). Network Dole proportion: The proportion of all discussion partners perceived by the main respondent to support Dole (mean is .38). Party identification: Measured on a 7 point scale, where 0 is strong Democrat and 6 is strong Republican (mean is 3.03). Wave 1, wave 3: 1= respondent was interviewed at the particular wave; 0 otherwise. The distribution across the three waves was 28%, 34%, and 38%, respectively. Candidate evaluations: Measured on a 5-point scale, where 1 is most unfavorable and 5 is most favorable. Clinton is evaluated in the left-side model, and Dole is evaluated in the right-side model. The mean for Clinton is 2.9, and the mean for Dole is 2.8.
Source: Indianapolis–St. Louis Study.

homogeneity within networks of communication. If the campaign has the effect of eliminating disagreement, then the level of correspondence between individual preferences and surrounding preferences should be enhanced over the course of the campaign.

In Part A of Table 5.2, the partisan composition of the network is regressed on the respondent's party identification. The first model uses the perceived network proportion supporting Clinton as a criterion variable, and the second model uses the perceived network proportion supporting Dole. In both instances, strong relationships appear between the political composition of the network and the respondent's party identification. The change in the homogeneity of the networks across the campaign is measured by the coefficient estimates for the time of interview (or wave) variables in interaction with the main respondent's party identification. For purposes of this analysis, main respondent interviews conducted before the end of primary season (prior to July 1, 1996) are first wave cases. Subsequent main respondent interviews taken before the election are second wave cases. And main respondent interviews conducted after the election are third wave cases. Statistically discernible coefficients fail to appear, thereby indicating that levels of homogeneity within the networks do not depend on the dynamics of the campaign.

A parallel analysis is conducted in Part B of Table 5.2, but the respondent's party identification is replaced by the respondent's evaluation of the major party candidates – Clinton in the first model and Dole in the second. In both instances, the candidate evaluations are based on a five-point scale, where a score of 5 is most favorable and a score of 1 is most unfavorable. The relationships between the respondent's political preference and the partisan composition of the network are once again pronounced, but in this instance we see a slight campaign effect for the post-election period. The relationship between the respondent's candidate evaluation and network partisanship is *reduced* by about 20 percent in the post-election wave. At the end of the marathon campaign, respondents are actually *less* likely to report a candidate preference that is in correspondence with their own perception regarding the partisan composition of the network. Hence, there is little evidence here to suggest that a process of motivated conformity enhances political homogeneity within networks over the course of the campaign.[6]

An alternative interpretation of these data is that pressures toward conformity reach their peak during the election campaign (waves 1 and 2) and relax thereafter (during wave 3). The problem with this interpretation is that it is not supported by an alternative analysis that focuses on objectively defined agreement based on self-reported opinions within discussion dyads. For the 1,475 dyads in which discussion partners were interviewed, we are able to determine whether main respondents and discussants report

---

[6] A post-election consensus effect is well documented, where those who supported the loser become more favorable to the victorious candidate. This would have the net effect of reducing the relationship between an individual's own evaluation of the candidate and the perceived distribution of preferences in the surrounding network (Joslyn 1998).

the same vote preference, and the levels of agreement across the three waves are: 63 percent, 52 percent, and 60 percent. Hence, agreement *increases* between the general election and the postelection waves, the highest level of agreement occurs during the primary wave, and the lowest level occurs during the general election campaign. Hence, we see no compelling evidence to suggest that political disagreement is substantially reduced within communication networks as a consequence of the campaign.

What *does* happen during the course of an election campaign? People generally talk with more people, and they talk about politics more frequently. In contrast, disagreement does not disappear or even diminish. Does this mean that communication is ineffective?

The analyses of Chapter 4 demonstrate substantial campaign effects on the *effectiveness* of political communication, where effectiveness is defined in terms of the clarity and accuracy with which political messages are conveyed among citizens. At the end of the campaign, citizens are more likely to perceive their associates' preferences accurately. They are more confident in their own assessments of associates' preferences. And their judgments regarding the preferences of others are more accessible – they come to mind more readily.

In summary, the survival of disagreement is not the result of a communication failure. The campaign not only encourages people to engage in more *extensive* communication, but it also results in more *effective* communication. The questions thus remain, how does disagreement survive, and what are the circumstances under which communication is *influential* as well as effective? At the same time, the simplest, most direct tests for the homogenizing impact of political interaction do not bear fruit. A more subtle, contingent model of communication and persuasion must be pursued in order to understand the impact of individual level communication processes on patterns of opinion formation (Axelrod 1997a). In the next section, we investigate the possibility that disagreement survives as a systematic consequence of the particular network configurations within which citizens are located.

COMMUNICATION AND THE SURVIVAL OF DISAGREEMENT

The fact that election campaigns serve to increase the frequency and enhance the effectiveness of political communication among citizens is wholly in keeping with the spirit of the analyses carried out by Lazarsfeld and colleagues (1949) and Berelson and colleagues (1954). In contrast, these citizens are *not* more likely to be imbedded within homogeneous networks of politically like-minded citizens – we see no evidence that disagreement and politically diverse views are being squeezed out of citizens' networks of political communication. How should we understand the persistence of political diversity within the context of these campaign-induced increases in the frequency and effectiveness of political communication?

Our argument is that the *influence* of political communication depends in very important ways on the *effectiveness* of the communication, as well as on the configuration of the larger networks within which the communication occurs. Hence, we are deliberately separating the effectiveness of communication from the influence of communication. Unless people communicate effectively, they cannot hope to exercise influence within their networks of communication (Latané 1981; Huckfeldt and Sprague 1995). Election campaigns activate networks of political communication, thereby enhancing the effectiveness of communication among citizens. The potential is thus created for influential communication, but the realization of this potential is problematic due to contingencies operating on political influence within communication networks.

In order to evaluate our argument, we introduce a series of models that investigate whether a person's evaluation of a presidential candidate is influenced by the political outlook of an associate. In each model of Table 5.3, the main respondent's evaluation of Bill Clinton is regressed on a range of individually based factors related to the main respondent – partisanship, ideology, income, education, race and ethnicity, religion, and church attendance. In addition, the self-reported partisanship of the discussion partner is also included as a regressor, along with various contingencies.

In the first model, we consider the simple, nonconditional effect of discussant partisanship. The partisanship variable is coded on the familiar seven-point scale, where 0 signifies a strong Democrat and 6 signifies a strong Republican. As one would expect, the coefficient for the main respondent's partisanship is negative and statistically discernible (-.34). In comparison, the coefficient for the discussant's partisanship is also negative and discernible (-.03), but it is quite small in magnitude. Although we would certainly expect the effect of the respondent's own partisan identification to be more influential than the discussant's partisanship in affecting the evaluation, the more important issue revolves around the factors that inhibit or enhance the influence of the discussion partner.[7]

---

[7] This model only considers the direct effects of discussant partisanship on the main respondent's evaluation of Bill Clinton, without taking account of any indirect effects due to discussant partisanship that might be operating through main respondent partisanship. Such a modeling strategy is appropriate because we are only concerned with the short-term campaign effects that arise due to the discussion partners' political preferences, and we are treating the partisanship of both the main respondent and the discussion partner as exogenous.

Table 5.3. *Discussant effects on Clinton evaluation, contingent on the accuracy and ease of judgments regarding discussants, as well as the correspondence between discussant and the remainder of network. (Least squares; coefficient t-values are in parentheses.)*

	Discussant Effects Contingent on				
	1. Baseline Model	2. Judgment Accuracy	3. Judgment Ease	4. Network Corresp.	5. Ease & Corresp.
Constant	4.89	4.74	4.64	4.57	4.39
	(23.38)	(21.23)	(21.37)	(20.38)	(19.08)
Partisanship	−0.34	−.33	−.33	−.33	−.33
	(21.01)	(20.24)	(20.54)	(19.05)	(18.81)
Ideology	−0.14	−.15	−.14	−.14	−.14
	(7.56)	(7.74)	(7.47)	(7.00)	(6.93)
Income	0.01	.01	.01	.02	.02
	(.45)	(.67)	(.43)	(1.00)	(.98)
Education	−0.02	−.02	−.01	−.02	−.02
	(1.21)	(1.09)	(1.05)	(1.32)	(1.16)
African-American	.32	.43	.31	.40	.39
	(3.04)	(3.87)	(2.93)	(3.65)	(3.59)
Other ethnic minority	1.00	.98	.99	1.02	1.02
	(6.19)	(6.16)	(6.25)	(6.26)	(6.28)
Church attendance	−.06	−.06	−.06	−.05	−.05
	(3.14)	(2.95)	(2.98)	(2.62)	(2.47)
Protestant	−.13	−.12	−.13	−.12	−.12
	(1.70)	(1.54)	(1.71)	(1.50)	(1.51)
Catholic	.002	−.002	.001	.004	.002
	(.02)	(.03)	(.02)	(.04)	(.02)
Jewish	.32	.34	.30	.38	.37
	(1.86)	(1.96)	(1.78)	(2.17)	(2.12)
Discussant partisanship	−0.03	.005	.02	.03	.07
	(2.42)	(.19)	(.99)	(1.66)	(3.05)
Judgmental accuracy		.11			
		(.98)			
Accuracy X disc. part.		−.04			
		(1.31)			
Judgmental ease			.28		.26
			(2.93)		(2.60)
Judg. ease X disc. part.			−.08		−.08
			(3.41)		(3.06)
Network correspondence				.38	.31
				(2.93)	(2.33)
Network corr. X disc. part.				−.12	−.10
				(3.70)	(3.16)

(*continued*)

Table 5.3 (*continued*)

	Discussant Effects Contingent on				
	1. Baseline Model	2. Judgment Accuracy	3. Judgment Ease	4. Network Corresp.	5. Ease & Corresp.
N =	1,131	1,084	1,129	1,042	1,040
R^2 =	.62	.63	.63	.64	.65
S.E. =	.88	.88	.88	.87	.87

Partisanship: Seven-point party identification scale, where 0 is strong Democrat and 6 is strong Republican (The mean is 3.15). Ideology: Seven-point ideological self-placement, where 0 is strongly liberal and 6 is strongly conservative (The mean is 3.49). Education: Years of school. (The range is 7–19, and the mean is 15.1). Income: Family income on a 6-point scale (The range is 1–6, and the mean is 4.2). African-American: 1 = African-American; 0 = other. (African-Americans constitute 8 percent of the sample. The baseline category is non-Hispanic white.). Other ethnic minority: 1 = any ethnic minority other than African-American; 0 = other. (Other ethnic minorities constitute 3 percent of the sample. The baseline category is non-Hispanic white.). Protestant: 1 = respondent identifies as a Protestant; 0 otherwise. (Protestants constitute 51% of the sample, and the baseline category is nonreligious or other religious – not Catholic, Protestant, or Jewish.). Catholic: 1 = respondent identifies as a Catholic; 0 otherwise. (Catholics constitute 27% of the sample, and the baseline category is nonreligious or other religious – not Catholic, Protestant, or Jewish.). Jewish: 1 = respondent identifies as Jewish; 0 otherwise. (Jews constitute 3% of the sample, and the baseline category is nonreligious or other religious – not Catholic, Protestant, or Jewish.). Church attendance: Frequency of attendance, where 5 = every week, 4 = almost every week, 3 = once or twice a month, 2 = a few times a year, 1 = never. (The mean is 3.4). Judgmental accuracy: 1 = main respondent accurately judges the discussant's self-reported vote preference; 0 = not accurate. (65% are accurate.). Judgmental ease: 1 = very easy to judge discussant vote; 0 = somewhat easy, somewhat difficult, or very difficult. (56% report very easy.). Network correspondence: proportion of other discussant partners perceived by the main respondent to hold the vote preference that is reported by the discussant in the dyad. (The range is 0–1, and the mean is .47.).
Source: Indianapolis–St. Louis Study.

In the second and third models of Table 5.3, the effect of the discussion partner is contingent on two different indicators of effective communication, each of which is related to the nature of the main respondent's judgment regarding the discussion partner's presidential vote. In the second model, the effect of the discussant's partisanship is contingent on the accuracy of the main respondent's judgment regarding the discussant's voting behavior. As the model shows, the effect of discussant partisanship is only modestly enhanced by accuracy, and the enhancement effect produces a relatively small t-value.

In the third model, the effect of discussant partisanship is contingent on the ease with which the main respondent is able to judge the discussion partner's vote preference. This ease of judgment measure is based on the respondent's response to a question regarding "how difficult or easy it was" to make a judgment regarding the particular discussion partner's vote choice. Once again, this measure provides an indicator of effective communication, where communication that is more effective makes it easier for the respondent to render a judgment regarding the discussion partner's preference. As the third model estimates indicate, the effect of discussant partisanship is substantially enhanced (−.08) in circumstances where the main respondent is able to render a judgment easily. And the main effect, which measures the discussant effect in circumstances where it was difficult to render the judgment, is statistically indiscernible. In short, the discussant effect is conditional on the ease with which the main respondent is able to render a judgment regarding the politics of the discussion partner.

Thus, taken together, the second and third models suggest that influence is enhanced to the extent that communication occurs effectively. Why does judgmental ease serve to produce a larger enhancement effect? Recall that our criterion variable is the main respondent Clinton evaluation, the explanatory variable is discussant partisanship, and the contingency is the effectiveness of communication regarding *vote choice*. It is entirely possible that a main respondent might correctly recognize that a normally Democratic discussion partner plans to vote for Bob Dole, but we would not necessarily expect the effect of discussant partisanship to be enhanced in such a situation. The main respondent has been able to make an accurate judgment regarding the discussion partner's vote regardless of the disagreement between partisanship and vote choice. In contrast, it is generally easier for respondents to make judgments regarding the voting preferences of strong partisans who vote in line with their partisan loyalties, and these are also the circumstances that enhance influence.

POLITICAL INFLUENCE AND HETEROGENEITY WITHIN NETWORKS

As we have seen, the impact of dyadic communication depends on factors that exist beyond the narrow confines of the dyad. For example, respondents are much more likely to recognize the preference of a particular discussion partner accurately when they perceive the preference to be more widespread among other discussion partners. In this way the majority within a particular network realizes an advantage in effectively communicating its preference, and the obvious question becomes whether the majority *also* realizes an advantage in terms of influence. Are discussion partners more influential if their political preferences enjoy higher levels of support within respondents' networks of communication?

The fourth model of Table 5.3 addresses this question by making the effect of discussant partisanship contingent on the perceived distribution of preferences among the main respondent's other discussion partners. In particular, we are concerned with the proportion of the remaining network discussion partners who hold preferences that, according to the respondent's judgment, correspond with the self-reported preference of the discussion partner being considered within the dyad.[8] This measure of network correspondence produces a substantial enhancement in the effect of discussant partisanship. The effect of a politically isolated discussant is reversed in sign (.03), thus suggesting that a socially unsupported preference actually encourages a reactive response on the part of main respondents. In other words, the presence of a lone Democratic discussion partner within a network otherwise composed of Republicans may actually discourage Clinton support. At the same time, this effect is more than nullified by the negative enhancement effect (−.12) for discussion partners whose preference is perceived to be held by all the other discussants – the Clinton discussion partner in the context of other discussants who are also perceived to support Clinton. The important point is that discussion partners who hold minority preferences have, at best, no influence on main respondents, whereas the expected effect of discussion partners who hold the majority preference is substantially enhanced.

The final model of Table 5.3 gives joint attention to *both* judgmental ease *and* the configuration of preferences in the remaining network as factors conditioning discussant effects, and the results parallel those found earlier. Substantial enhancement effects on discussion partner influence are produced by both factors. Discussion partners are more likely to be influential if they hold preferences that are perceived to be dominant within the network *and* if it is easier for the respondents to render judgments regarding their political preferences, and the cumulative enhancement effect is particularly substantial. The net effect for easily perceived discussants holding a preference that reflects a network consensus is −.11 (.07 − .08 − .10 = −.11), a nearly fourfold increase in the discussant effect of the baseline model (−.03).[9]

---

[8] Network correspondence is a proportional measure defined in terms of vote preference. If the discussion partner in the dyad reports a vote preference that the respondent believes is shared by all the other discussants, network correspondence is set to 1. At the other extreme, if the discussion partner reports a vote preference that the respondent believes is shared by none of the other discussants, network correspondence is set to 0.

[9] The alternative models in Table 5.3 do not produce enormous differences with respect to the explained variation and standard errors of estimate. Rather, the added value lies in a better specification of the conditions that give rise to political influence.

MAJORITARIAN BIASES AND THE SURVIVAL OF DISAGREEMENT

These results add to a significant body of evidence suggesting that political minorities operate under pronounced disadvantages in democratic politics (Miller 1956). Several efforts show that minority preferences are less likely to be communicated effectively, and hence they are less likely to be recognized, even by fellow members of the minority (Huckfeldt and Sprague 1995; Huckfeldt et al. 1998a; Huckfeldt, Sprague, and Levine 2000). This chapter adds to these efforts, showing that the individuals who hold minority preferences are less likely to be politically influential within networks of social communication. In other words, the influence of the discussion partner's preference is weighted by majority–minority standing within networks of social communication. Hence, the preferences of those in the political majority count more heavily in the deliberative process than the preferences of those in the minority.

Regardless of this cumulatively bleak picture for the communication and influence of minority preferences, there is no evidence here to suggest that minorities tend to be eliminated as part of the deliberative process (see Moscovici, Mucchi-Faina, and Maass 1994). This is especially striking because we are defining minority and majority preferences relative to closely held social environments created through the communication networks of individual citizens. Within this context, only 36 percent of the main respondents who supported Dole or Clinton perceived that all their discussion partners held the same candidate preference. In other words, a lack of political agreement is the modal condition among our respondents, even within enduring networks of communication and association.

This raises an important question – how is the minority opinion able to survive? Like the gene pool, the opinion pool is subject to a number of different forces which act both to eradicate and sustain diversity. At an aggregate level, perhaps the minority is sustained by something as simple as the Markov principle. A small defection rate operating on a large (majority) population will at some point be at equilibrium with a large defection rate operating on a small (minority) population.

We suspect other processes are at work, however, which serve to both maintain individual-level disagreement and sustain minority opinion in the aggregate. A discussion partner who holds a minority opinion in one of our main respondent's networks may be part of a majority in her *own* network and thus sustained in her opinion. Although such a person encounters disagreement, she receives sufficient support for her opinion to withstand the drift toward conformity. Correspondingly, although people who hold opinions that receive minority support in the aggregate are more likely to experience disagreement within networks of political communication (Huckfeldt et al. 1998a; Huckfeldt and Sprague 1995), they are often located within political micro-environments that tend to support their views.

Hence, in order for disagreement to survive within political communication networks, it is vital that the micro-environments created through networks of communication are not closed systems that are identically experienced by all participants. In particular, even if two discussion partners, say Joe and Bill, are reciprocally related to one another as regular discussants and close friends, their micro-environments may be almost completely independent. Hence, Joe and Bill may hold different political preferences, and yet both may be part of a political majority within their own respectively defined networks.

Several simple network structures, as well as their implications for the survival of disagreement, are considered in Figure 5.1. Individuals are represented as ovals, discussant relationships as connecting lines, and the presence of a particular political preference as the presence or absence of shading in the oval. In Part A of the figure, each individual is connected

A. Conformity and the socially heroic holdout.

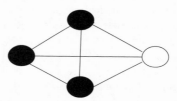

B. Socially sustained disagreement.

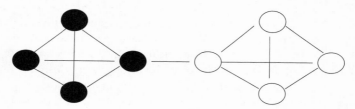

C. Social connections giving rise to political change.

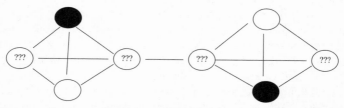

Figure 5.1. Patterns of social connection and implications for electoral change.

to each of three other individuals in a self-contained network of relations. In such a situation, the logic of Table 5.3 suggests that disagreement is quite likely to disappear, and only the heroic individual is likely to sustain an unpopular belief. In contrast, Part B of Figure 5.1 shows two subnetworks of four individuals each, where every individual is connected to every other individual within the subnetwork. In addition, one individual within each subnetwork is connected to one individual in the other subnetwork, thereby providing a bridge that spans a structural hole between subnetworks (Burt 1992). In this setting, the logic of Table 5.3 suggests that agreement will be socially sustained *within* each of the subnetworks, but *dis*agreement will be socially sustained *between* the individuals who bridge this particular type of structural hole.

SOCIALLY SUSTAINED DISAGREEMENT

How important are such networks to the survival of disagreement? One way to address this question is by examining the networks of *both* main respondents *and* their discussion partners. The interview with the discussion partners included the same network name generator that was employed in the interview with the main respondents. Thus we are able to compare (1) the main respondent's perception regarding the political composition of the main respondent's network with (2) the discussion partner's perception regarding the political composition of the discussion partner's network. Guided by Part B of Figure 5.1, we are particularly interested in the composition of the residual networks – the networks that remain when the two members of the dyad are removed.

Two questions arise. First, how closely related is the political composition of the discussion partner's residual network to the political composition of the main respondent's residual network? Second, does this relationship depend on the existence of political agreement or disagreement between the main respondent and the interviewed discussion partner?

In Part A of Table 5.4, the percentage of the discussion partner's residual network supporting Clinton is regressed on the percentage of the main respondent's residual network supporting Clinton. The regression is estimated twice – once for all dyads in which interviewed discussion partners and main respondents each name at least two discussants, and a second time for all dyads in which the main respondent and the discussion partner each identify more than two discussion partners. In both instances we see a positive slope with a large t-value and a small R^2. In short, the political composition of the main respondent's residual network generally resembles the political composition of the discussion partner's residual network.

Table 5.4. *The proportion of the respondent's network perceived (by the respondent) to support Clinton regressed on the proportion of the discussant's network perceived (by the discussant) to support Clinton, conditional on whether the main respondent perceives agreement within the respondent-discussant dyad.*

	Number of Discussants Named by Both the Respondent and the Discussant	
	2 or More	More Than 2
A. All Dyads		
Constant	.32	.30
	(20.15)	(15.75)
Slope	.16	.22
	(5.28)	(5.53)
R^2	.03	.04
S.E.	.38	.36
N	1006	640
B. Agreeing Dyads		
Constant	.26	.22
	(13.46)	(9.61)
Slope	.36	.47
	(9.23)	(9.78)
R^2	.12	.19
S.E.	.37	.34
N	605	401
C. Disagreeing Dyads		
Constant	.39	.42
	(16.03)	(14.24)
Slope	−.08	−.15
	(1.73)	(2.34)
R^2	.01	.02
S.E.	.36	.34
N	378	223

Note: In constructing perceived network support for Clinton, the main respondent in the dyad is extracted from the discussant's network, and the discussant in the dyad is extracted from the main respondent's network. Hence, we index the political composition of the remaining networks absent the preferences of the particular dyad. The measure is based on perceptions regarding whether each remaining member of the networks voted for Clinton in the 1996 presidential election. The mean level of network Clinton support is .37 for main respondents and .33 for discussants.

Source: Indianapolis–St. Louis Study.

These simple regressions are repeated in Parts B and C of Table 5.4, first for main respondents and interviewed discussion partners reporting the same candidate preferences, and then for main respondents and interviewed discussion partners reporting different candidate preferences. For the agreeing dyads, we see an enhanced relationship in the form of a larger regression slope, as well as a larger t-value and an enhanced R^2. In contrast, for the disagreeing dyads, we see a reversed slope of smaller absolute value with a nearly non-existent R^2, but with a coefficient t-value that supports the presence of a discernible negative relationship.

What do these results suggest? Agreement within dyads is typically sustained by larger networks of communication that simultaneously support the preferences of *both* individuals within the dyad. In contrast, we see at least some evidence to suggest that disagreement is also socially sustained, but by politically *divergent* networks that serve to pull the two members of the dyad in politically *opposite* directions. At the very least, disagreement within dyads is characterized by political independence between the two participants' larger networks of association and communication.

As a practical matter, removing the interviewed discussion partner from the main respondent's network is a straightforward task. Removing the main respondent from the interviewed discussion partner's network is not straightforward because we do not have a direct measure of reciprocity – we do not know with certainty whether the main respondent serves as an information source for her discussion partner. In the present analysis we adopt the procedure of assuming that the main respondent is included in the discussion partner's network if the main respondent reports a candidate preference that is perceived by the discussion partner to be present in the network. And then, in these situations, a residual network is constructed by removing a discussant with this preference.

In order to confirm these results, we pursued other analyses, not shown here, employing an estimate of reciprocity based on correspondence between the main respondent's first name and the first names provided by the interviewed discussant for *her* discussants.[10] In one analysis, we removed the main respondent from the discussant's residual network when the dyad was judged to be reciprocal – when the interviewed discussant named a discussant with the same first name as the main respondent. In another analysis, we omitted the reciprocal dyads entirely, carrying out

---

[10] Hence, reciprocity is defined as an instance in which the interviewed discussant provides a list of first names that includes the main respondent's first name. Defined in this way, the overall reciprocity level is 33 percent: 51 percent among spousal dyads, 29 percent among dyads that involve nonspousal relatives, and 31 percent among nonrelatives.

the analysis only for non-reciprocal dyads, thereby making it unnecessary to adjust the discussant's network.

These alternative analyses closely parallel the analysis shown in the text. The compositional correspondence between the residual networks is consistently strong and positive for dyads in which there is agreement, but weakly negative or independent for dyads in which there is disagreement. Hence, at a minimum these results show that agreement within the dyad is sustained by a strongly positive correspondence between the residual networks of the individuals in the dyad, whereas disagreement within the dyads is sustained by residual networks that are either independent or divergent.

In summary, the survival of disagreement within dyads is profitably seen within larger patterns of association and communication. The logic of social influence creates a bias in favor of majority sentiment, thereby making it difficult for disagreement to be sustained. To the extent that networks of communication and influence constitute closed social cells, characterized by high rates of interaction within these self-contained networks but very little interaction beyond, we would expect to see an absence of disagreement among and between associates. Hence, the survival of disagreement depends on the permeability of networks created by "weak" social ties (Granovetter 1973) and the bridging of structural holes (Burt 1992). As these ties lead to the dissemination of new information (Huckfeldt et al. 1995), they also bring together individuals who hold politically divergent preferences, thereby sustaining patterns of interaction that produce political disagreement.

IMPLICATIONS

What are the implications of this analysis for processes of social communication and democratic deliberation during election campaigns? Simply put, observed patterns in public opinion depend not only on individual predispositions and interpersonal communication, but also on the particular locations and configurations of individuals within networks of political communication. At one extreme, it is entirely possible to construct a hypothetical network in which majority opinion is, in the long run, held by all citizens. At the same time, it is also possible to construct a network in which minorities are not only able to survive, but are even able to overtake the majority.

The group conformity model, in which individuals are inevitably located within politically homogeneous networks, fails to accommodate *either* political disagreement *or* the ebb and flow of majorities and minorities that characterize the empirical reality of democratic politics. History shows that Democratic majorities replace Republican majorities, which in turn replace Democratic majorities. Does this happen outside the collective process of social communication and democratic deliberation? We think not, and our analysis points to the important dynamic implications of low density communication networks – networks characterized by individuals who serve as bridges of communication between and among otherwise independent networks (Granovetter 1973; Burt 1992). In networks such as these, individuals encounter disagreement at the same time that they find support for the opinions that they ultimately adopt, and therein lies the key to the survival of minority opinion.

Our analysis does not support or suggest a determinate outcome to the process of social communication and influence. Citizens not only respond to one another – they also respond to the real-life events in the external political environment. Individuals are continually being bombarded by the exogenous events of politics, and these events frequently lead to opinion changes that produce ripple effects within communication networks (McPhee et al. 1963). At the beginning of an election campaign, many individuals are uncertain regarding their preferred candidates. And as they formulate preferences in response to the campaign, their newly constructed opinions produce implications for other citizens. Part C of Figure 5.1 introduces this sort of individual uncertainty into the structural setting portrayed in Part B. And by introducing uncertainty, the outcome of the political dynamic within the network is rendered unpredictable and indeterminate.

Recall the traditional model of social influence in politics, whereby social communication and influence provide the underlying fabric of a durable political order, shielding individuals from the events and dramas in the external political environment. Consider such an explanation in the context of a political independent with three discussion partners – a strong Democrat, a strong Republican, and a fellow independent. Assume that the strong Democrat admires Bill Clinton, the strong Republican loathes Bill Clinton, and both independents are undecided at the beginning of the campaign. The role of the independent discussion partner is clearly crucial – she occupies a pivotal role in the formulation of the first independent's preference. If the independent discussion partner becomes a Clinton supporter, the persuasiveness of the strong Democrat is enhanced as the influence of the strong Republican is attenuated. Alternatively, if the independent discussion partner develops an animus toward Clinton, the entire pattern of influence is transformed.

Such an analysis suggests that the conversion of any single individual to a particular candidate's cause is not only important in terms of a single vote or a single unit of social influence. It is also important in terms of the enhancement and attenuation effects that it creates *throughout* the networks of relationships within which the individual is imbedded, quite literally transforming entire patterns of social influence. In this way, political interdependence among citizens might actually *magnify* the importance of events in the external political environment.

This alternative model of political influence is particularly important because many individuals do not reside in politically homogeneous microenvironments (Lipset 1981). Hence, for most citizens, the mix of political messages to which they are exposed – even at the most closely held levels of association – is heterogeneous, unstable, and subject to the impact of events in the external political environment. Rather than serving as a buffer between the individual and the external political environment, these networks of communication serve as transmitters and intermediaries that connect individuals to the events and circumstances of democratic politics.

None of this suggests that social communication and social influence are destabilizing forces in democratic politics. Rather, we are simply making two arguments. First, the collective processes of democratic communication and deliberation are not irrelevant to the outcome of the democratic process. Second, dyadic information flows must be seen in light of preference distributions within larger networks of communication, and thus individual preference arises in part as the complex and highly nonlinear product of larger patterns of association and communication (Huckfeldt and Sprague 1995). In summary and taken together, these results encourage a reconsideration of the role played in electoral politics by social communication and influence, as well as the manner in which events in the external political environment are socially as well as individually processed.

CONCLUSION

This chapter's analysis has addressed a number of specific questions regarding political communication and persuasion within election campaigns. Some of the results are important simply because they challenge long-standing common wisdom within public opinion research. In particular, we find that political communication occurs among people who disagree with each other, and contrary to expectations, disagreement is not inevitably diminished by interaction. We also find that political influence within discussion networks depends on two broad categories of factors. One category can be understood relative to the particular participants within an isolated dyad, but the other can be understood only with reference to the larger network within which the individuals and dyads are located. Perhaps most important, the political influence of *a particular discussion partner* depends in a very fundamental way on this second class of network-related factors.

Conclusion

These results provide grist for the debate regarding deliberative democracy and the importance of political communication among citizens during election campaigns (Barber 1984; Fishkin 1991). The empirical reality is that minority opinion and political disagreement are able to survive, and hence the group conformity model appears to be a bad fit with respect to the substance of political preferences and political communication. A central characteristic of political influence arises due to the subjectivity and hence comprehensibility of many political preferences, even when they are disagreeable. You may not like your best friend's politics, but the disagreement is frequently tolerable, in large part because you are able to understand the motivation behind her opinions (Downs 1957; Calvert 1985; Sniderman 1991).

A wide gulf separates most instances of *political* communication and persuasion from the communication and persuasion that are characteristic of the conformity studies conducted by Asch (1955) and others. As Ross and colleagues (1976) argue, it may be difficult to resist the majority when everyone is saying that the longer line is shorter than the shorter line due to the simple fact that no obvious explanation accounts for the divergence of their (incorrect) beliefs. In contrast, when an associate embraces the cause of Newt Gingrich or Bill Clinton, a variety of plausible justifications may arise for dismissing the associate's judgment. Thus, political disagreement is (perhaps ironically) much easier to tolerate and accommodate, pressures toward conformity are thereby reduced, and disagreement and minority preferences are better able to survive. Political disagreement is sustained not only by particular structures of social interaction, but also by the inherently subjective nature of democratic politics.

6

Agent-Based Explanations, Patterns of Communication, and the Inevitability of Homogeneity

Influential and long-standing theory predicts that political disagreement will be a rare event among people who communicate on a frequent basis, but accumulating evidence points to a different conclusion. We have seen that political disagreement is remarkably durable even within closely held networks of political communication. Although communication among interdependent citizens is politically influential, it does not eliminate diversity. This creates a puzzle that we pursue in this chapter and the next: How should we understand the dynamic mechanisms of communication and influence – mechanisms that guide individual decision even as they sustain diversity? Inspired by Axelrod's suggestion that an agent-based model can be a useful tool for "thought experiments" and the clarification of theory, we have used the Swarm simulation tool kit to investigate the formation of discussion networks and implications of theories about persuasion and information exchange. As in previous chapters, we treat communication and influence as interdependent yet separate mechanisms within the same process. Patterns of communication occupy center stage in the present chapter. We consider alternative devices through which political viewpoints and public opinion are communicated. The immediate question becomes, does the structure of communication among citizens account for the survival of diverse political preferences?

The mode of our analysis shifts quite dramatically in this chapter and the next. Prior to this point, our strategy of attack has been to dissect relationships and disassemble groups. Much like the child who takes apart the clock to see how it works, we have adopted an analytic approach that takes apart the larger aggregate reality of political groups and their underlying networks of communication and influence. The analysis has sought to identify the factors that sustain disagreement within processes of influence and communication among citizens – the characteristics of individuals, the properties of relationships, and the structures of networks that create durable patterns of agreement as well as disagreement in democratic politics.

We have defined the primary unit of analysis as the individual citizen before proceeding to consider the nature of the relationships that connect and combine these individuals into politically meaningful groups.

We have considered which individuals are best able to make their preferences known, which individuals are most likely to be influential, and which patterns of relationships are most likely to enhance and impede processes of communication and persuasion among and between multiple individuals. Based on these analyses, we have developed a series of strong expectations regarding factors that might be responsible both for creating influential patterns of communication among individual citizens, and sustaining disagreement within the larger community.

In this and the next chapter we pursue an analysis that permits an evaluation of these expectations. Rather than an observational analysis driven by data on individuals and their networks of communication, we employ simulations of interacting individuals – or, in the vocabulary of complexity theory – simulations built on agent-based models of dynamic interaction. These strategies make it possible to explore a range of questions regarding the factors that sustain disagreement among citizens. In the present chapter, our focus is on patterns of interaction and communication. Is the likelihood of sustained disagreement contingent on self-selected patterns of association? On the location of individuals in multiple overlapping environments? On levels of parochialism among individuals? In the next chapter our focus shifts to address several alternative mechanisms of persuasion. In particular, how is the likelihood of sustained disagreement affected by autoregressive patterns of political influence?

ANALYSIS VERSUS SYNTHESIS

James Coleman (1964) draws a distinction between analytic and synthetic research strategies. Analytic strategies are aimed at taking apart the clock and seeing how it works – at breaking down a larger reality into its component parts in order to understand it more completely. In contrast, synthetic strategies are aimed at understanding the macro-level consequences of micro-level constructions. In the context of this effort, we have two goals. First, we want to isolate the influential elements at the micro-level, in terms of both individual characteristics and the properties of the relationships that tie individuals together. Second, we want to recombine these micro-level elements in ways that make it possible to explain aggregate consequences (also see Boudon 1986).

Complex forms of interdependence among and between individuals produce an aggregate reality that is much more than a simple summation of its individual parts. Similarly, individual behavior cannot be inferred simply or directly on the basis of aggregate distributions. We believe that it is difficult to overstate the importance of complex interdependence for both fundamental political processes and compelling accounts of democratic politics. The implications of these complex micro–macro disjunctures lie at the heart of Durkheim's (1897, 1951) revolutionary contributions to social theory, as well as at the core of ongoing methodological literatures regarding individual-level inference based on aggregate data (Robinson 1950; Goodman 1953; Sprague 1976; Achen and Shively 1995; King 1997).

In short, we are neither inventing nor even rediscovering these distinctions, and one might argue that the social sciences were invented to address these very issues. The complexities of the "micro–macro manifold" within political science (Eulau 1986, 1963) are widely recognized in the larger field of contextual analysis (Boyd and Iversen 1979). McPhee and colleagues' vote simulator (1963) was an early and important effort at using a computer simulation to understand dyadic interactions among citizens within larger distributions of opinion, an effort that grew directly from the early efforts of the community-based election studies of the Columbia sociologists (Lazarsfeld et al. 1948; Berelson et al. 1954).

Later contributions by Abelson (1964, 1979), Przeworski (1974), Sprague (1976), Przeworski and Sprague (1986), Huckfeldt (1983), and Huckfeldt and Kohfeld (1989) were efforts at understanding the large scale aggregate consequences of interdependence among individuals. These latter efforts explored the dynamic and aggregate consequences of interdependence among citizens through the use of linear and non-linear difference and differential equation models. Much of this work was inspired by the contributions of mathematical ecologists such as May (1973) and Smith (1976, 1982) who were concerned with patterns of interaction among species and hence confronted their own version of the challenges presented by complex forms of interdependence. These models and their successors led to important progress in the areas of non-linear dynamics, stable limit cycles, and chaotic regimes. In the realm of politics, they produced a rich and variegated view regarding the political implications that arise due to individual interdependence (Boudon 1986; Huckfeldt 1990).

These models have also confronted two inherent limitations. First, the most interesting and relevant non-linear models are typically intractable, yielding no readily derived solutions, and hence their deductive implications must be pursued through simulation strategies. The use of simulation does not in itself constitute a liability, but it negates one advantage of the mathematical formalism – readily derived equilibria with attached stability conditions.

The second and more important liability of these models is that they are most readily understood on the basis of aggregate populations, and hence they do not allow a smooth and unifying transition between individuals and aggregates. This is the problem that has inspired much of the emphasis on individually based models in ecology (Parunak, Savit and

Riolo 1998; DeAngelis and Gross 1992). The macro–micro disconnect is a particularly telling liability with respect to network models that produce complex patterns of connections (and nonconnections) within aggregate populations of individuals. In such a context, the "group" becomes a complex representation of interconnected individuals, and each individual is potentially connected to a group that is idiosyncratically defined with respect to that particular individual. Agent-based simulation represents a workable alternative. In summary, synthetic models of networks must accommodate not only the inherently nonlinear basis of individual interdependence but also the highly complex and idiosyncratic relationships among and between groups and individuals.

Our approach is also differentiated from models based on cellular automata. In a cellular model (for example, Hegselmann, Flache, and Moller 1999; Hegselman and Krause 2002; Latané and Morio 2000; Nowak, Szamrej, and Latané 1990; Latané, Nowak, and Liv 1994; Latané and Nowak 1997), the numerical values of cells in a grid change in response to the condition of cells around them. Typically, updating is done by taking a snapshot of the grid and putting the values of the cells within a neighborhood of each cell through some sort of filter. The process through which the individual agents become aware of the conditions around them is not typically explained in these models. As such, they invoke a sort of "social telepathy" (Erbring and Young 1979) through which social conditions are brought to bear on individuals.

In contrast, we seek to develop an individually based theory in which the historical experience of an agent is brought to bear on the problem of attitude change and retention. Although the lessons of research on cellular automata are extremely useful and related in interesting ways (see Chapter 7), our own emphasis and approach are quite different.

AGENT-BASED MODELS

Recent developments in the use of agent-based models have created an opportunity to produce these seamless transitions between individuals and aggregates, at the same time avoiding the inherent problems of a theoretical specification relying on social telepathy. An agent-based model is a framework in which computer objects – objects that represent autonomous individuals – behave, interact, and adapt (Epstein and Axtell 1996; Johnson 1996, 2002). Agent-based models, sometimes referred to as individual-based models (IBM) or multi-agent systems (MAS), are perhaps ideally suited to the study of complex social and political organization (Johnson 1999). Many of the concepts of modern object-oriented programming naturally lend themselves to the study of large populations of interdependent, interacting individuals (see, for example, Eckel, 2000, or Apple Computer, Inc. 2002). The models define a collection of individual "agents" along with the setting (environment, or social milieu) in which the agents are embedded. The models explore the interaction among individual agents in order to uncover the complex combinatorial consequences.

In our agent-based models, individuals are self-contained agents that can move about, gather or offer information, learn from experience, and adapt in an individualistic way. It is implicit that we are referring to computer models, but these models are not necessarily confined to computers. It is conceptually possible to execute an agent-based model with pen and paper, since one could write down the position and data of each agent, pair them off for interactions and take note of any changes. Such an exercise might be informative, but it would also be impossibly tedious and time consuming. For all practical purposes, the complexity of calculations necessitates the use of a computer. And using a computer implies the choice of a computing language, software libraries, and modeling strategy.

Recent developments in computer programming, occurring within the past 15 years, have created a set of new concepts and tools that lend themselves quite naturally to models of multiple agent social systems. The agents themselves are represented, in the terminology of computer science, by *objects*. An object is a combination of data and method: variables representing the state of the individual agent, and methods (or commands) that the agent can execute. By repeatedly putting these artificial agents through their paces, we are able to ascertain the aggregate impact of various individual strategies, behavioral rules, and responses. This is the sense in which agent-based simulations are referred to as "bottom-up" modeling exercises (Epstein and Axtell 1996). The aggregate consequences are not imposed on the agents; rather the behavior of the agents produces the aggregate mosaic.

These large scale combinatorial consequences – the emergent properties of small scale organization – carry the potential to be quite surprising and highly counterintuitive. In the present analysis, we are concerned with one particular emergent property – the presence or absence of disagreement within the agents' networks of political communication. Based on the empirical record, we have seen that citizens typically do not escape the experience of disagreement. Multiple network studies at both national and local levels over the past 20 years document the existence of politically heterogeneous viewpoints within the networks that surround individual citizens. Our analyses here and elsewhere have produced a series of expectations regarding the factors that prove to be influential in enhancing and inhibiting political influence and agreement among and between citizens. In the analyses that follow, we construct a series of agent-based models to simulate the dynamic consequences of these political communication processes. Our goal is to identify the factors that give rise to the preservation of political diversity within networks.

Several disclaimers are in order, regarding both our research strategy and the lessons we intend to draw from the analysis. In the models and simulations that are produced here, we make no claims to achieve (and we have no intention of achieving) high levels of predictive accuracy. The simulations are inspired by empirical analyses, but they do not constitute direct translations of previously specified empirical models. Rather, in the spirit of McPhee and colleagues (1963) and Axelrod (1997a), our goal is to capture the insights of the empirical analyses in a way that will allow us to engage in a series of "thought experiments" (Axelrod 1997b: 4). For example, our empirical results repeatedly demonstrate a process of political introversion in which citizens would appear to seek out like-minded individuals as political informants (Huckfeldt and Sprague 1995: chapter 8). One of the questions we pursue is whether self-selection and introversion inhibit or enhance the survival of disagreement among citizens. The answers to questions such as these are neither intuitive nor obvious, and the simulations based on agent-based models provide us with extremely helpful analytic leverage.

A second disclaimer is related to the distinction between adaptive behaviors and rational behaviors. It is quite easy to make too much of this distinction. As Axelrod (1997b) suggests, the distinction is more directly related to analytic strategies and opportunities than it is to epistemological anchorings and substantive arguments. Along with Simon (1985) and Weber (1966), we assume that individual citizens are rational unless proven otherwise, and there is nothing *within* our analyses to *suggest* otherwise. Indeed, we assert that it is entirely reasonable and sensible for citizens to rely on information obtained by other citizens in formulating their political judgments and preferences. At the same time, none of our analyses depends on individual rationality, and the results do not rise or fall on that basis.

THE MODELING STRATEGY

The models presented here have been implemented in Objective-C with the Swarm Simulation Toolkit (Minar, Burkhart, Langton, and Askenazi 1996). The Swarm project was initiated at the Santa Fe Institute under the leadership of Christopher Langton, and is now under the auspices of a nonprofit corporation known as the Swarm Development Group (http://www.swarm.org). Like Swarm itself, the source code for our models is freely available. Our software is highly modular, allowing the exploration of many possible rules for the behavior of agents. We have distributed several "snapshots" of this code, some more easily customized than others, to other researchers over the years. The most recent set is described in greater depth in Appendix B and is also documented within the source code itself.

As described here, we have implemented a wide variety of alternative models in order to explore the aggregate consequences of different rules for the behavior of agents. The most important differences across these alternatives involve variations in two separate design components. First, there is a "selection process" that puts agents together for a one-on-one interaction. In some versions of the model, the agents move about and select each other using personalized rules; in others, the agents are fixed in place and are forced together by chance. Second, there is a "persuasion process," characterized by particular opinion adjustment rules, which determines the outcome when an interaction occurs between two agents. In the opinion adjustment phase, our main focus has been on changes in the kinds of information that the agents take into account when they are confronted with a divergent opinion.

In addition, a range of subsidiary issues arises, and they are implemented within the computer code, even though they have not been the primary focus of the analysis. For example, if one agent initiates an interaction with another, and they exchange views, might both agents change their opinions? Or should only one of them change? We have designed the model so that a seemingly endless array of such possibilities can be investigated. The remainder of the model's design falls within the boundaries of a standard Swarm model, with agents implemented as separately instantiated objects that are contained in a collection, and with agent behavior that can be monitored in a number of ways.

The opinions of the agents are treated as integers. If there are three possible opinions about some particular issue, they are represented by the numbers 0, 1, and 2. Agents might hold opinions on multiple issues. Hence, if there are five issues in the political sphere, we represent an individual's stances on that collection of issues as a vector, such as $(0,1,0,2,2)$, where each entry in the vector represents the agent's opinion on an issue.

As agents interact, opinion values can change, and we are interested in knowing if the opinion vectors of the various agents are homogenized. In order to do so, we have sought to develop measures of diversity that capture both the level of diversity that is experienced by the individual agents and the level of diversity that is observed at the aggregate level – at the level of the entire system. For example, it is entirely conceivable that individual citizens never encounter diverse opinions within their networks of interaction, even though diverse preferences continue to survive at the aggregate level. We strive for a set of general tools that can describe the differences found among agents in a variety of circumstances across a variety of models. Hence, we have created aggregate level measures for the existence of diversity, as well as individual level (agent level) measures for the experience of diversity.

At the aggregate level, it is possible to tally and summarize the features of agents. This allows the calculation of several summary measures, such as the average and variance of each opinion. We also calculate a system-wide diversity measure, *entropy*, which is sometimes known as Shannon's information index. This measure of entropy is normed to an interval where it equals 0 if all objects in a set are identical and 1 if every possible type is equally represented in the set (Shannon 1949; Balch, 2000). If there are F different issues and T different values (or opinions) on each issue, then the number of possible issue stances is T^F. If the proportion of agents holding a given set of positions is pj, then the normed total entropy is given by:

$$Total\ Entropy = \frac{\sum_{j=1}^{T^F} p_j * \log_2(p_j)}{\log_2(\frac{1}{T^F})}$$

Hence, the normed entropy measure depends on both the number of issues and the number of opinions per issue. If the normed entropy measure tends toward 0, it means that the level of diversity observed in the opinions of the agents is reduced, and two *randomly chosen* agents are likely to agree on all of the issues. As we illustrate in the succeeding sections, these aggregate measures of diversity lead to some fairly stark statements, and it is a relatively straightforward task to determine the level of diversity at the aggregate level.

In addition to tracking aggregate levels of diversity, we are also interested in whether individual agents encounter diversity both within random patterns of encounters and within patterns of acquaintance. The agents formulate and adapt their opinions based on acquaintanceships that are produced through a continuing series of dyadic encounters, and it is possible for a gap to develop between individual experience and aggregate circumstance. Hence, we collect individual-level (agent-level) measures that are built up from the experiences of the individual agents.

The agent's experience of social interaction comes in two forms – encounters and acquaintances (see Huckfeldt 1983). One agent encounters another agent as part of a stochastic process in which the probability of a dyadic encounter is dependent on availability, where availability depends on shared locations in space and time. In the simplest form of the model, two agents are more likely to encounter one another if they reside in the same "neighborhood." In a more complex version of the model, two agents are more likely to encounter one another – even if they do not share a neighborhood – if they share the same "workplace" at the same time. In contrast to encounters, where the probability of an encounter depends on proximity and availability, the probability of an acquaintance depends on the existence of a shared opinion between two agents. When one agent encounters another agent, a choice is made regarding whether to become acquainted. This "choice" depends on the existence of a shared opinion, and in this way the models directly incorporate a self-selection component.[1]

In the model, each agent keeps a running tally of its social interaction experiences – of its encounters and acquaintances. These can be collected and summarized to build indicators of the extent to which random encounters between strangers involve opinions held in common, as well as the extent to which agents agree with their acquaintances. For our models, we present three individual-level measures.

1. *Acquaintance.* For each of the other agents encountered through the process of random encounters, the agent checks to see if the two agree regarding a randomly chosen issue. Because such agreement is a precondition for acquaintance, the proportion of encounters on which there is a shared feature is kept as a moving average that we call "acquaintance." This can be treated as the individual agent's expectation, based on accumulated experience, that it will agree on a random issue with another randomly chosen agent. In other words, it provides a measure of the individual agent's expectation regarding the probability that a random encounter might become an acquaintance.

2. *Harmony.* When an interaction occurs between two agents, the agents "compare notes" and discover how much they have in common. Hence, the level of "harmony" is the proportion of opinions across all issues shared between two agents that are acquainted.

3. *Identicality.* Similar to "harmony," identicality is based on a comparison across all the opinions held by two agents that are acquainted with one another. For an individual agent, a moving average is retained for 20 interactions, and a 1 is added if another agent is identical, and 0 if it is not. A value of the moving average of, say, 0.70, indicates that seven-tenths of the others with which the agent has interacted are exactly the same as the agent itself.

---

[1] Hence, we conceive of an interaction sequence in which an encounter becomes a precondition for an acquaintance. Encounters are stochastic events within particular settings, and they may or may not lead to the formation of an acquaintance. In this way, encounters and acquaintances are specifically defined aspects of a more generally defined interaction process.

In summary, "harmony" and "identicality" indicators reflect information regarding only those other agents with which a particular agent is acquainted, and hence it provides a measure of the agents' networks of political communication. In contrast, the "acquaintance" measure is collected across all the other agents that are encountered by a particular agent, regardless of whether the encounter actually becomes an acquaintance. Please note that these measures do *not* necessarily provide accurate summaries for the simple aggregate states of the system. Rather, they are based on the experiences of individual agents. Generally, we calculate averages and standard deviations as summary measures of experience across all the agents in the system. Although agents cannot experience diversity when the aggregate is homogeneous – when entropy is complete – it is entirely possible for agents to experience homogeneity even when the aggregate is characterized by high levels of diversity. The measurement procedures thus described allow us to explore these possibilities.

THE AXELROD CULTURE MODEL

The starting point for our investigation is provided by Robert Axelrod in the formulation and analysis of his Culture Model (1997a, 1997b). The Axelrod Culture Model (ACM) is a computer simulation in which individual agents interact with their neighbors, and a culture of commonly shared features is spread through these individual interactions. In the ACM, there is a square grid on which agents are distributed, one per cell. (An illustration is presented in Figure 6.1.) Axelrod calls these cells "villages." Each village has a set of discrete-valued features, where these values are called traits. A feature might be thought of as an opinion, issue stance, political party allegiance, or any other similar construct. For concreteness, suppose there are five features with three possible traits for each feature. If the three possible traits are 0, 1, or 2, then the culture of a village might be represented as $(0,1,0,2,0)$ or $(1,2,1,0,1)$, and so forth. At the outset, each village has a vector of features in which each trait is assigned randomly from a uniform distribution. Our own efforts address Axelrod's formulation, but in order to avoid confusion, we address his contribution in the vocabulary of neighborhoods, issues, opinions, encounters, and acquaintance that is relevant to our own effort.

In the original Axelrod approach, an agent is randomly selected and a neighbor from the von Neumann neighborhood – consisting of cells on the east, west, north, and south borders – is randomly encountered. In the second step of this interaction sequence, the agents become acquainted with probability equal to their agreement on features. If two agents share the same value on two of five features, then they form an acquaintance

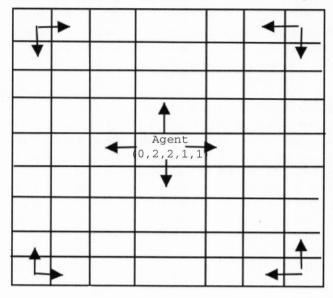

Basic Model:
- Grid of agents (villages)
- Feature (opinion) array of each agent, e.g., (0, 2, 2, 1, 1) for a five-feature model
- Interaction within truncated von Neumann neighborhoods

Figure 6.1. The design of the Axelrod Culture Model.

with probability 0.40. If they become acquainted, *influence is automatic.* The agent that initiated the encounter copies one feature on which the two agents differ. Cells that lie on the outside boundaries of the grid can only interact with cells that lie on within-the-grid boundaires, so they have fewer neighboring agents with which to interact.[2]

Since our own computer model explores some variations on the ordering of interactions among agents (a general topic known in Swarm as "scheduling"), we have designed the code with many features that can be changed when the program is created (compiled) and when it is run. Axelrod's original code repeatedly selects one agent at random and conducts the interaction. Because of anomalies observed in the follow-up study (see Axtel et. al. 1996), it is perhaps prudent to employ a Knight's tour approach, in which the agents are randomly sorted at the beginning of each cycle and each is given an opportunity to interact before

---

[2] We have implemented an option to have the grid "wrap around" to form a torus, and thus eliminate these edges, but have found nothing interesting to report on that variation.

starting through the list again. We have implemented a run-time feature to select either the one-at-a-time (Axelrod's original) scheduling or the tour through the list. In this report, we present models in which the tour approach is used.

The number of issues (Axelrod's "features") as well as the number of opinions on each issue (Axelrod's "traits") can be varied. Axelrod observed that, when the number of traits is small, the tendency toward system-wide homogeneity is greatest. In contrast, an increase in the number of traits may allow the formation of homogeneous subgroups. Diversity is preserved only when neighbors have nothing in common, so they do not become acquainted and hence cannot influence one another. When there are many possible traits, the chance that two randomly chosen agents will find something in common is lower, and thus diversity is preserved by preventing the formation of an acquaintance. Axelrod summarized the observed diversity by counting the number of homogeneous subgroups of cells within the model, but that approach does not generalize to the models we present here. Instead, we summarize diversity by employing the previously described measures.

After a series of experiments with our implementation of the Axelrod model, we find strong support for his conclusion that, over the long run, diversity tends to disappear. The tendency toward homogeneity is greater for some parameter settings than others, but it is powerful in all cases. As Axelrod observed, the number of traits is a vital element. If the number of possible traits on a feature is small, then the agents are likely to become acquainted, individual change is a certainty, and diversity disappears. On the other hand, if the number of traits is large, the chance that two agents will have nothing in common is increased, thereby attenuating the likelihood of acquaintance. Pockets of culture develop which are completely isolated from one another because, lacking any point of agreement, individual members of one culture cannot become acquainted with members of other cultures. Diversity is preserved in the aggregate sense, but *none of the individual agents is acquainted with other agents holding divergent opinions* – none of the agents experiences diversity within its networks of acquaintance.

The summary of 100 runs of a model in which there are five features and three traits per feature is presented in Table 6.1. The simulation continues until 10 passes are made through the list of agents without any changes of opinion. In every single run, the final level of entropy was 0, meaning all agents were identical in the end. The variance of opinion across the population is 0. The measures of agent experience necessarily indicate a complete lack of diversity. Every agent has something in common with every other agent, and every agent agrees with every other agent about just about everything.

Table 6.1. *Axelrod culture model. Five issues with three opinions per issue.*

	Summary Statistics for 100 Simulations	
	Mean	Standard Deviation
Iterations at end	441.89	146.49
Variance for each issue:		
Issue 0	0	0
Issue 1	0	0
Issue 2	0	0
Issue 3	0	0
Issue 4	0	0
Total entropy	0	0
Average for all agents across all runs		
Acquaintance	0.99	0
Harmony	0.99	0
Identical	0.97	0.01

A primary benefit of agent-based modeling is that the scientist can interact with the simulation, observing its development in a variety of ways. It is not easy to convey the richness of the experience in a printed format, but that does not stop us from trying! When run interactively, the model generates time-plots and color-coded "rasters" to display the state of the grid for each feature. A view of the distribution of opinion in the grid can be seen in the top part of Figure 6.2. The value of a feature at each spot in the grid is represented by a colored square. Values of the feature are color coded, with the dark representing the value of 0, and lighter shades used to indicate a progression of values. (In a model with more traits, we use all shades between the extremes.) As the model run is illustrated on the computer screen, it becomes readily apparent that the features are homogenized one at a time. As soon as a single feature is homogenized, we know for certain that all other features will be homogenized. If one feature is homogenized, it means that all agents have at least one feature in common, and so there is always a positive probability that encounters will produce acquaintance. The process of homogenization accelerates as each piece of the puzzle (each feature) falls into place. In Figure 6.2a, we show the starting conditions of each of the five features in its own grid. The typical outcome of the simulation is the second part of the figure, showing that each feature has been homogenized because the grid is filled with only one color.

In the bottom panel of Figure 6.2, we present the time plots of some of the diagnostic variables. Note that entropy begins at 0.8, near the maximum, and then falls to a value of 0. Individual experiences are roughly

The Axelrod Culture Model

a) Initial Conditions

Feature: 0   1   2   3   4

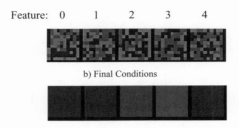

b) Final Conditions

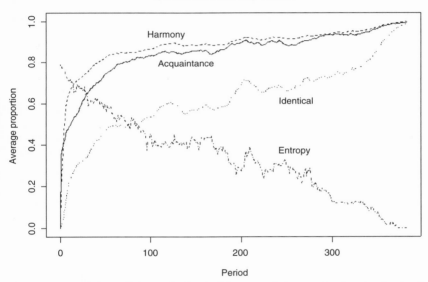

c) Time Paths of Summary Variables

Figure 6.2. Initial conditions, final conditions, and time paths for the Axelrod Culture Model.

in line with that aggregate indicator. The indicators of acquaintance, harmony, and identicality begin with values near zero and gradually climb to near 1.0. They do not quite reach 1.0 because the agents use a 20-period moving average to keep their records, and when the simulation stops after 10 periods without any culture changes, some agents can still remember past periods when disagreement was experienced. If we let the simulation continue 10 more time steps, then the individual experience indicators would converge to 1.0.

In his original presentation, Axelrod pointed out that it is possible to find parameter settings such that the grid is not homogenized, but rather subdivided into groups that do not become acquainted across group boundaries. This never happens in our batch of 100 runs when there are five features and three traits per feature, and hence this outcome appears to be theoretically possible but unlikely. Such an outcome becomes more likely if the number of traits is increased because it creates more separate cultures and reduces the chances of acquaintance across cultures. Outcomes of that sort are highly unstable, in the sense that any disturbance which allows acquaintance across the boundaries is likely to reduce diversity. Studies by Shibanai, Yasuno, and Ishiguro (2001) and Greig (2002) explore extensions of the ACM in which there are 10 possible values for each feature. We have chosen to focus most of our attention on the difficult case, one in which there are a small number of traits, and agents are less likely to be insulated from an acquaintance with diversity by the fact that they are *completely* different from other agents.

The problem we face, then, is exactly the same one discovered by Robert Abelson 35 years ago. His differential equations of social influence led to the prediction that "any compact group of individuals engaged in mutual dyadic interactions at constant rates will asymptotically tend toward complete homogeneity of attitude positions" (1964: 152). Later he observed that there is a "virtually inexorable consensus" (1979: 244), one that he seeks to avoid (with only a qualified amount of success) by exploring various changes in the design of the model. Like Abelson, we have explored a number of variants related to the contacts to which agents are exposed as well as the ways in which agents adjust to one another. We have one advantage in this pursuit, however: the recent development of agent-based modeling, which allows one to explore the implications of hypotheses about truly autonomous agents.

ALTERATIONS IN THE SELECTION PROCESS

The agent-based modeling approach allows experimentation with novel ideas about the way individuals might interact. We are able to investigate a number of "what if" questions by substituting in new assumptions about the agents and their environments. It has already been observed that in the context of the model, there are only two alternatives: We can change the process through which agents come together, or we can change the way they react to one another. Recall that, in the Axelrod model, agents randomly encounter a neighbor; they form an acquaintance with probability equal to their similarity; and if an aquaintance is formed, one opinion on which they disagree is copied from the second agent to the first. In this section we explore changes in the structures of interaction that affect the communication process among agents, and we consider the persuasion (or reaction) process in the next chapter.

Alterations in the Selection Process

Our objective is to discover whether it is possible to redesign the model so that communication among agents with diverse opinions can occur without the elimination of disagreement. In addition to the design features that maintain aggregate diversity, we also explore the features that might maintain the individual experience of diversity – the circumstances that might give rise to persistent heterogeneity within networks of acquaintances. As a practical matter, we are interested in the conditions under which agents with divergent opinions maintain patterns of acquaintance without eliminating disagreement – circumstances in which the indicators of harmony and identicality stay lower than 1.0. That is to say, we are interested in whether agreement must be the inevitable outcome of sustained patterns of acquaintance.

We have explored the interaction and communication process from a number of perspectives, which we now describe. Our conclusion will be that, short of erecting "fire walls" that completely block patterns of communication among agents that disagree, thereby eliminating the *individual* experience and communication of disagreement, little can be done to preserve diversity in the *aggregate* by altering the selection and interaction components of the model.

Multi-Agent Cells

In adopting the agent-based paradigm for extending this model, we begin by investigating a natural question: What if a single "village" (or cell) contains many individual agents? If the agents are most likely to become acquainted with others inside their cells, perhaps self-reinforcing "opinion clusters" will form.[3]

Hence, the model is redesigned to consider the possibility that reconceptualizing the cells as multi-agent groups will lead to diversity over the long term. As in so many programming problems, the devil is in the details, but at a conceptual level the approach is quite elegant. Think of a grid in which each cell contains a collection of agents. We assign features at random to each cell, but then create many identical agents within the cell. Our goal is to stay as close to the original logic of the ACM as possible, while adjusting in a way that allows agents to encounter and become acquainted with other agents *within their own cells*.

This new component of the model requires the introduction of a new concept, *parochialism*. Parochialism is the likelihood that an agent will look within its own neighborhood or cell when it seeks to form an

---

[3] In order to implement this version of the model, we have developed a general purpose multi-agent grid called MultiGrid2d, which allows us to create containers in the grid into which many agents can be inserted and removed.

acquaintance, and thus parochialism becomes a key parameter in the interaction–communication process. When an agent has the opportunity to initiate interaction, it does so in a two-step process. First, a random draw (probability equal to the parochialism parameter) dictates whether the agent seeks another agent within its own cell or from one of the adjoining cells. Agents seeking interaction within their own cells will randomly encounter others in their cell. The other, non-parochial agents will choose an adjoining cell at random and then randomly encounter an agent from that cell. Here we intend only to explore modifications in the interaction–communication component of the Axelrod model, not in the persuasion component. As in the original ACM, acquaintance occurs with probability equal to the similarity of the two agents. If the level of parochialism is sufficiently high, meaning agents interact with their "own kind" frequently enough, then perhaps the homogenizing impact of contact with outsiders can be ameliorated.

We have run batches of simulations with multi-agent cells, and while the homogenization of opinion takes longer, it still occurs. Contrary perhaps to some expectations, this model does not lead to the development of self-reinforcing clusters. Table 6.2 displays the summary statistics for an extreme case in which parochialism is equal to 0.95, meaning that agents encounter other agents from their own cells almost all the time. When the simulation stops because no agent has changed its culture features for 10 successive time steps, the agents are located in patterns of acquaintance that are highly harmonious.

Table 6.2. *Multi-agent grid. Five agents per cell (10 × 10 grid). Five issues with three opinions per issue; parochialism = 0.95.*

	Summary Statistics for 100 Simulations	
	Mean	Standard Deviation
Iterations at end	8220.61	2511.32
Variance for each issue:		
Issue 0	0.00168	0.0011
Issue 1	0.00038	0.0038
Issue 2	0	0
Issue 3	0.00008	0.0008
Issue 4	0	0
Total entropy	0.000408	0.002008
Average for all agents across all runs:		
Acquaintance	0.999	0.00042
Harmony	0.999	0.00029
Identical	0.997	0.00144

At the aggregate level, entropy drops to a very low, but nonzero, value. Why not all the way to zero? The agents mostly form acquaintances within their own cells, so the differences are preserved most of the time. Still, in most runs of the model, the homogenization that occurs because of the (infrequent) encounters with agents from neighboring cells is strong enough to overcome the parochialism effect. We have found a few runs in which one cell on the edge of the grid remains distinct on one or more features. This outcome is the result of a "knife edge" balancing act. On the edge, the agents from that cell can encounter only a restricted number of neighbors, so their exposure is limited. Furthermore, by the "luck of the draw," when they encounter outsiders from neighboring cells, they find nothing in common with them. This kind of "diversity" requires that all agents within a cell agree with each other exactly, and they avoid encounters with strangers assiduously.

There is, however, one very interesting property of these multi-agent grid simulations with high parochialism: The individual agents experience a state of harmony throughout the simulation, but aggregate diversity goes from the maximum to zero during the run of the model. Consider the extreme case in which parochialism is set at 0.95. In each cell we create five identical agents, and then we set them encountering one another in random order, once per time step. In Figure 6.3, time paths for

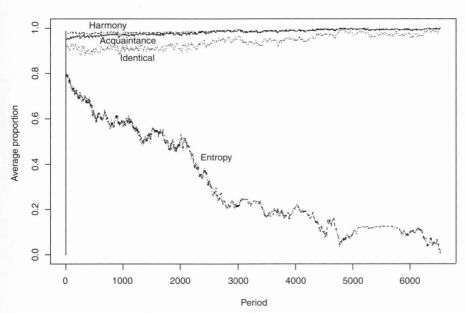

Figure 6.3. Multi-member cells and the impact of parochialism.

indicators from one of the runs of this model are drawn. Note that, when the simulation begins, the level of entropy is in fact high, because opinions are assigned randomly to the cells. Agent experiences of homogeneity are quite high, however, because they typically become acquainted with other agents within their cell, and at the start they are all identical. The measures of acquaintance, harmony, and identicality remain on the high side throughout the simulation. But, as time goes by, entropy goes down. Although the agents do not experience it in any direct or dramatic way, the homogenization process is occurring. If the parochialism coefficient is set at a lower level, the homogenization occurs more quickly, but the agents are more likely to experience diversity as well.

Decreased Levels of Self-Selection

In reviewing the ACM, one might surmise that these simulations tend to homogenize opinion because agents that agree with each other are more likely to become acquainted. The "self-selection" process snowballs to create a situation in which the only agents that become acquainted are totally identical, and it appears to be just a matter of randomness whether or not there will be one homogeneous society or a few homogeneous subgroups. What happens if agents are open to a broader array of interpersonal contacts? Would it be possible to forestall the homogenization by raising the acquaintanceship rate among agents that would not ordinarily interact? On the basis of the agent-based simulations, it turns out the answer is a decisive "no."

Building on the early work of Coleman (1964: Chapter 16), we explored a variant of the model that causes acquaintanceship to occur more often among agents that disagree. As in the original Axelrod model, at each time period one agent encounters another agent, and acquaintanceship occurs with probability proportional to similarity. If the encounter does produce an acquaintance, the search for an interaction partner is complete in that period. Alternatively, if the encounter fails to produce an acquaintance due to similarity, there is some probability that the acquaintance will be initiated anyway. We have called the probability of interaction under these circumstances the "Coleman coefficient." If the interaction does not take place, the individual continues to search up to 10 times until an interaction partner is located.

For those who expect that increased patterns of acquaintance among agents that disagree will preserve diversity, the results of this "Coleman model" will be disappointing.[4] A summary of 100 runs for three values

---

[4] Coleman (1964) would not have been disappointed because this result is entirely consistent with his own analysis. Also see Huckfeldt (1983).

Alterations in the Selection Process

Table 6.3. *Restricted self-selection: The "Coleman" model. Five issues with three opinions per issue.*

| | Summary Statistics for 100 Simulations | | | | | |
| | 0.2 | | 0.5 | | 0.8 | |
Coleman Parameter:	Mean	Standard Deviation	Mean	Standard Deviation	Mean	Standard Deviation
Iterations at end	240.85	79.1	262.92	77.74	272.26	94.58
Variance for each issue:						
Issue 0	0	0	0	0	0	0
Issue 1	0	0	0	0	0	0
Issue 2	0	0	0	0	0	0
Issue 3	0	0	0	0	0	0
Issue 4	0	0	0	0	0	0
Total entropy	0	0	0	0	0	0
Average for all agents across all runs:						
Acquaintance	0.99	0	0.99	0	0.99	0
Harmony	0.99	0	0.99	0	0.99	0
Identical	0.96	0.02	0.96	0.01	0.96	0.02

of the Coleman coefficient is presented in Table 6.3. Compared to the original Axelrod model with one agent per cell (which, implicitly, has the Coleman coefficient equal to 0), the number of iterations that occur before the culture is homogenized is reduced. The conclusion is that the impact of encouraging acquaintance among dissimilar agents is the accelerated elimination of diversity. Or, viewed more positively, the ACM's component of self-selection serves to *sustain* diversity. Agents that *avoid* acquaintance with politically disagreeable others are acting to sustain their own beliefs and, by extension, the beliefs of the other agents in their communication networks. The attenuation of self-selection does not change the fact that, over the long haul, disagreement disappears. But the preservation of these small clusters tends to delay the process of political homogenization.

Neighborhoods and Workplaces

The extensions of the model presented thus far have stayed within the fundamental constraints imposed by the original Axelrod model. The villages (or agents) do not move around – they are never exposed to new context or new information once the local situation stabilizes. Perhaps redesigning the model so that agents can move among diverse contexts will preserve diversity. We strive to create conditions under which agents can experience political communication with a more or less unpredictable set

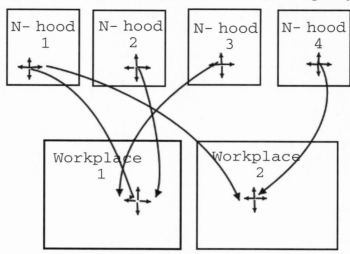

Figure 6.4. Multiple home grids and work grids.

of others in a variety of contexts. We pursue this strategy with the caveat that we do not intend that the agents wander pointlessly seeking political communication partners, but rather they wander with a purpose. Agents have "home" neighborhoods, where they might communicate with family or neighbors, but they also communicate on a systematic basis with agents in other social settings, such as the workplace, church, a labor union meeting, and so forth.

The description of this next step in our modeling exercise requires an explanation of a very significant departure in the design of the simulation model. In Figure 6.4, we present a sketch of the geographical arrangement of the agents and their movement–encounter–acquaintance opportunities. There can be one or more "home grids," which are standard square arrays of agents. There can also be workplaces where agents might have opportunities for encounters and acquaintances. In the home grid, there is some regularity to interaction because the identities of the other agents with which an agent is interacting (if interaction occurs) is relatively predictable. In contrast, interactions in the work grids are less predictable because agents are unevenly distributed across the work grids. Agents from any home grid can be assigned to any of the cells in any of the work grids. Some cells in a work grid can have several agents assigned to them, whereas others might have none. In order to implement this in a meaningful way, it is necessary to redesign the scheduling substructure of the model to allow for movement among these settings, as well as among encounters and acquaintances in the various settings.

Alterations in the Selection Process

This new model requires a more detailed specification with respect to scheduling in order to accommodate the movement between home and work grids. This is a discrete-event simulation, but up to this point we have thought of a time step as a single pass through the list of agents. Now we take the more explicit approach of thinking of time as the passage of days, each of which is made up of a number of small time steps (say, hours). In the simulations described here, we (arbitrarily) set the number of steps per day to 10 and we allow the agents to decide autonomously when to initiate interaction with other agents that happen to be in their vicinity at a given instant.

Each agent begins the day at home, and stays there, on average, for 5 time steps. Some agents spend almost no time at home, whereas others spend all their time at home. When the scheduled time arrives, the agent moves from the home grid and inserts itself into its designated work grid. During the time the agent is moving from one grid to another, it cannot initiate any interactions and none of the other agents find it available for interaction. At the start of each day, each agent randomly selects a time step during which to experience encounters and acquaintances. If the chosen time is before movement into the work grid, then the agent seeks interaction at the home grid.

This design, which allows for both movement and flexible interaction patterns, diverges conceptually from the standard Axelrod model. The re-design creates several changes in the selection of discussants. First, there is the simple fact of mobility – agents move from one context to another, thereby exposing themselves to new opportunities for interaction and communication (Fuchs 1955). Second, the multiple home grids are discrete and separate from one another. Since the residents of different home grids never interact directly with one another, the agents in each home grid might appear, at least on the surface, to be insulated from the homogenizing pressures observed in the other models.

Contrary to these sorts of expectations, the results indicate that homogenization across neighborhoods is still the inevitable outcome. Using the standard Axelrod rules for the selection of discussion partners (modified as above for multiple-occupancy grids) and adjustment of opinion, we find that, over the long run, diversity is eradicated. This is true for any geographical setup which follows the home/work grid dichotomy we have described.

In Table 6.4, we give the summary statistics for a model in which there are five 10 × 10 home grids and three 5 × 5 work grids. One agent is assigned to each position in each home grid (meaning there are 500 agents in all), and agents are assigned positions in the work grids in a random way, meaning that some cells in the work grid are empty whereas others have several occupants. The rules for multi-agent grids described

Table 6.4. *Axelrod agents in a model with five home grids and three workplaces. Five issues with three opinions per issue; parochialism = 0.5.*

	Summary Statistics for 100 Simulations	
	Mean	Standard Deviation
Iterations at end	20286	29.01
Variance for each issue:		
Issue 0	0	0
Issue 1	0	0
Issue 2	0	0
Issue 3	0	0
Issue 4	0	0
Total entropy	0	0
Average for all agents across all runs:		
Acquaintance	0.999	0.002
Harmony	0.998	0.00155
Identical	0.988	0.0077

above were used. The parochialism coefficient has been set to 0.5, meaning that an agent that is in a cell with other agents will pick among those agents with equal likelihood one half of the time, and the rest of the time the agent will pick among agents in one of the four adjoining cells.

How should we interpret this outcome? In the presence of isolated "home grids," the presence of shared "work grids" provides an opportunity for the diffusion of information. This is a primary inexorable consequence of modernity and its accompanying mobility. This mobility has served to eliminate spatially based distinctiveness in a wide variety of settings (see Gamm 1999) by producing bridges that integrate otherwise separate and distinct networks of interaction (Burt 1992).

Selectively Screened Encounters

In the models we have considered thus far, several likely culprits have appeared in our exploration of the model's homogenizing tendency. First, agents are likely to have a basis upon which to form an acquaintance – one or more features in common. Second, the agents interact if they have anything at all in common. If agent A has one out of five features in common with agent B, there is a 20 percent chance they will interact, and A will copy a feature from B. That can happen even if, on the other side of A, there is an agent that agrees with A about everything. Perhaps the shortcoming of this model is that it assumes agents encounter a randomly drawn individual even though more agreeable agents are present in the immediate vicinity.

We now reconceptualize the selection process in the following way. Rather than giving an agent the opportunity to encounter a randomly chosen neighbor, what if we allow agents to search their neighborhoods for encounters with other agents they expect to be the most agreeable? Perhaps doing so will create enough selection bias to create and maintain diversity.[5]

The model is implemented in the following way. Each agent keeps a record regarding each other agent that it has encountered. When the simulation proceeds, the agent searches its neighborhood and draws one possible encounter from each neighboring cell. (If the agent's own cell contains other agents, one of them is selected at random.) This creates a list of possible discussants. From this list of potential encounters, the agent then selects the one that is expected – on the basis of past encounters – to have the most in common with it. If several in the list are equally "appealing," then one is selected at random with equal likelihood.

The only substantive complication is that, at the outset, the agents have no accumulation of records on which to make their decisions. At time 0, there are no acquaintances, and all agents are "strangers." To accomodate this problem, we allow the agents to learn from experience. At the outset, the assumed harmony value for strangers is 0.5. Every time the agent encounters a new agent, that value is adjusted to reflect experience. As a consequence, the agents are able to remember the others they have encountered.

These selective agents can be placed into any of the models, either the original Axelrod grid, the multi-agent grid, or the neighborhood/workplace models. In none of these implementations did we find that heterogeneity was preserved. In Table 6.5, we present two sets of summary statistics for the state of the model when the simulation ends. In Table 6.5a, the results for the standard ACM are shown after encounter-based selectivity is introduced. It is not particularly surprising that the model reaches a steady state in a smaller number of time steps after encounter-based selectivity is introduced. Neither is it a surprise that the agents experience a distribution of encounters in which they are more likely to encounter other agents with which they agree. It is, perhaps, more surprising that the level of entropy is negligible and that the

---

[5] We base this exercise on the following intuition. If you work in a setting with a notorious troglodyte, you may strategically choose patterns of behavior that insure you will never be in the same room at the same time with this individual. Hence, not only are you avoiding an acquaintance with the individual, you are also avoiding encounters.

Table 6.5. *Identity-based selection of discussants. Five issues with three opinions per issue.*

A. Identity-based selection in the standard Axelrod model
(10 × 10 grid)

	Summary Statistics for 100 Simulations	
	Mean	Standard Deviation
Iterations at end	282.03	90.88
Variance for each issue:		
Issue 0	0	0
Issue 1	0	0
Issue 2	0	0
Issue 3	0	0
Issue 4	0	0
Total entropy	0	0
Average for all agents across all runs		
Acquaintance	0.599	0.010
Harmony	0.99	0.0034
Identical	0.958	0.0166

B. Identity-based selection in the five-home grid, three-workplace model

	Summary Statistics for 100 Simulations	
	Mean	Standard Deviation
Iterations at end	10220.6	3588.51
Variance for each issue:		
Issue 0	0	0
Issue 1	0	0
Issue 2	0	0
Issue 3	0	0
Issue 4	0	0
Total entropy	0	0
Average for all agents across all runs:		
Acquaintance	0.599	0.005
Harmony	0.999	0.00181
Identical	0.983	0.009

variance of opinion on each feature is 0. In other words, we do not escape the now familiar outcome in which political disagreement fails to survive, either at the level of individual experience or, perhaps more surprisingly, at the aggregate level of the system as a whole.

The overall implication of these experiments is that the homogenization of public opinion is a pervasive tendency when agents adjust their opinions according to the logic of Axelrod's original culture model.

Conclusion

Tinkering with the structure of the neighborhoods or attempting to place additional conditions on the likelihood of encounters and acquaintances does not preserve self-reinforcing social subgroups or the diversity of opinion. As a result, none of the experiments we have pursued allows an escape from the troubling implication of the model: In order to preserve diversity at the aggregate level, the individual-level experience of diversity must be eliminated by creating homogeneity within groups and an absence of communication between groups. Hence we return to the description of the cross pressured citizen provided by Berelson and colleagues (1954) – individual volatility is the price that must be paid for the integrity of groups in time and space. But this leaves us where we started, with a theoretical implication – the absence of individual level disagreement – that is at odds with the observed empirical reality.

CONCLUSION

We have introduced agent-based modeling as a new departure in our effort to explore the maintenance of diversity within democratic societies. The empirical, survey-based evidence leads to the conclusion that disagreement persists within closely held networks of political communication. Even though citizens depend on one another for political information, and even though this socially communicated information is politically persuasive, the evidence points to the persistence of disagreement among citizens who regularly communicate about politics. At the same time, our empirical analysis is inherently reductionist, with a primary focus on individuals and their interactions at the small scale, micro level. Hence it runs up against the natural and inevitable limitations of any micro-level analysis in its capacity to map out the larger scale, aggregate implications of our hypotheses about individuals and their interactions.

The Axelrod Culture Model provides both a challenge and an inspiration for our efforts to understand the linkage between individual behavior and aggregate outcomes. In general, the ACM points toward the tendency for heterogeneity to give way to homogeneity as the inexorable consequence of social interaction and diffusion among the agents that make up larger population aggregates. In particular, the ACM leads to the contention that aggregate diversity is especially unlikely to survive when the number of alternative opinions being communicated is small. Since many of the important political issues that generate controversy are in fact issues with a small number of options, this becomes a source of serious concern. Moreover, it contradicts our observational record. It suggests political homogeneity and agreement when, in fact, we often observe political heterogeneity.

The problem becomes even more puzzling. Although the ACM predicts that in situations marked by a great variety of opinions on the same issues, aggregate diversity might survive as homogeneous clusters of divergent preferences, none of the ACM results suggests that the experience of disagreement should persist among associated individuals. But this is exactly what our empirical results suggest. That is, the accumulated empirical record shows that real-life citizens regularly and persistently experience disagreement, even within their closely held, self-selected networks of political communication.

In responding to this puzzle, we have made a number of adjustments in the logic through which agents interact and communicate. None of these changes generated a model that preserves the diversity of individual experience. The tendency for repeated social interactions to squeeze out diversity appears to be pervasive across all these adjustments. We might call this phenomenon "cultural drift," an analogy to the homogenization referred to as "genetic drift" in population biology (see Gillespie 1998). As long as the interactions remain strictly dyadic and opinion adjustment reflects only individual level information, we expect to find cultural drift that homogenizes public opinion.

In the next chapter, we propose a reconceptualization of the problem that considers adaptations in the ways that individuals respond to differences of opinion. Although political diversity and disagreement among associated individuals does not survive in all societies at all times, we will argue that the survival of disagreement among associated individuals is a frequently likely outcome, and political homogeneity within communication networks is not the inevitable consequence of political communication among and between citizens. Just as important, we will contend that diversity of experience and opinion, both in the small and in the large, is likely to arise even if no individual actively and intentionally seeks to cultivate diversity. The "magic bullet," as it were, is found in a richer understanding of political communication – an understanding that interprets dyadic effects on individual opinion and judgment in the context of preference distributions that occur within larger networks of political communication.

7

Agent-Based Explanations, Autoregressive Influence, and the Survival of Disagreement

None of the previous chapter's analyses calls into question a theoretical expectation that disagreement will be short-lived among people who communicate on a regular basis. The agent-based models of dyadic, one-on-one interaction clearly lead to a conclusion that time will erase diversity among interacting agents. The present chapter modifies the design of these agent-based models to incorporate the idea that people react to new information only after they compare it against the input they receive from the other agents in their communication networks. Several startling results emerge from this simple premise of autoregressive influence. Self-organized networks develop in which agents experience diversity and respond to it in an understandable way. These networks reflect the micro-level impact of the experience that agents accumulate through a continuing series of dyadic interactions. The agents have no conscious drive to expose themselves to diversity. Rather, they simply adjust to new information in a way that conforms to their experience within networks of acquaintance – to the majority sentiment among other agents with whom they are most familiar. Perhaps surprisingly, diversity is preserved in a system that is often, but not always, stable in its response to exogenous disturbances.

The previous chapter provides scant support to those friends of democratic politics who might hope for the persistent and enduring experience of political disagreement among citizens. In every model, political homogeneity appears to be the long-run stable consequence of interaction among agents. We are inevitably, if reluctantly, led to the conclusion that time and its continuing stream of socially communicated information will eliminate disagreement and diversity among associated citizens. This is a bleak conclusion – bleak because it foretells a style of democratic politics in which individuals fail to benefit from new and diverse information provided by sources with whom they are personally familiar. Not only are the consequences bleak for individual citizens, but they are also bleak for the performance of democratic politics. If individuals fail to encounter disagreement, the system as a whole is inherently limited in its ability to respond to divergent beliefs and interests.

The scientific (as opposed to the normative) problem with these models and their implications is that they are not easily reconciled with the empirical record. As we have seen, the political preferences within citizens' networks of political communication are frequently characterized by remarkably high levels of disagreement and diversity. This is not to suggest either that some citizens are not imbedded within comfortable cocoons of politically compatible associates, or that some political environments are incapable of producing an outcome in which individuals are secluded from the experience of political diversity within their patterns of social interaction. Rather, the empirical record leads us to believe that political homogeneity is not the *inevitably* stable equilibrium outcome within patterns of political communication among and between citizens. Hence, based on empirical results in earlier chapters regarding autoregressive patterns of influence, we pursue the conditions that might give rise to the persistence and durability of political disagreement among citizens.

The focus of our effort is on developing a model of social interaction in which politically diverse individuals communicate with one another and are *sometimes* persuaded by each other. The results of our efforts in the previous chapter indicate that this is a very difficult problem. A variety of extensions to Axelrod's culture model (ACM), which either increase or decrease the exposure of agents to divergent opinions, all lead to the same conclusion: Over the long run, the diversity of opinion is eliminated due to the continuing stream of dyadic interactions.

The model of opinion that we have been discussing shares important logical features in common with models of population genetics (Gillespie 1998). An agent's opinion array, for example $(1,1,2,1,0)$, is scarcely different from a genetic string for an individual. Although interaction in the public opinion model does not entirely parallel genetic reproduction, there are certain similarities. If the loose analogy between the dyadic opinion model and population genetics holds up, we can perhaps gain a deeper insight into the problem that we face. A widely recognized phenomenon in population genetics is known as *genetic drift*, a process in which each generation is less diverse than its predecessor. Genetic drift – the complete takeover of a particular part of the genetic code by one particular trait – occurs over the long run if random interaction occurs among individuals, and if reproduction follows standard genetic laws which randomly mix the traits of two parents. In short, the homogenization predicted by the population geneticist corresponds closely to the pattern of homogenization observed in the models of Chapter 6, and both sets of models share a structural similarity in their focus on dyadic interactions based on random mixing.

Genetic drift is to be expected when interactions occur among paired individuals, and the approaches to the problem of political communication and opinion change considered in the previous chapter all maintained a similar dyadic structure of interaction. Perhaps a more significant conceptual departure is needed if diversity is to be preserved. Hence, we turn our attention to reconsider assumptions regarding the outcomes of the interactions that occur among agents. The analysis of this chapter will show that a relatively minor alteration in the opinion change segment of the model radically alters our expectations regarding the emergent properties of the artificial society. We begin with a discussion of our model building strategy before considering several changes in model design, thereby producing a model in which agents respond to new information through a verification process in which they check new and divergent information against information previously obtained within their networks of acquaintance.

MODEL BUILDING STRATEGY

The alternative model that we present begins as a simple extension of Axelrod's culture model, a model which describes the evolution of culture due to small-scale (localized) social interaction.[1] To review, in Axelrod's model, the agents (or cells in a grid) are described as villages, and each village has a culture, represented by a vector of features. These features are integer-valued, for example, 0, 1, 2. The values of the features are referred to as traits, and are randomly assigned at the outset. In the ACM, a village is randomly selected and can look "up," "down," "left," or "right" to find another village.[2] After a random neighbor is encountered, an acquaintance is formed with probability equal to the similarity in the traits of the two agents. If the acquaintance is formed, then an issue on which the two agents disagree is selected at random and the original agent's opinion on the issue is changed to match that of the acquaintance. Hence, influence automatically follows whenever interaction occurs.

In the previous chapter, we considered the original ACM and several variations in the rules through which agents come into contact with one another. None of the variations served to preserve the agent's experience of diverse opinions over the long run. Regardless of whether agents are more or less likely to encounter and become acquainted with other agents holding divergent preferences, we end up with the same result: Diversity is eliminated. The conclusion seems inescapable – the model produces an inexorable tendency toward the homogeneity of opinion. When diversity *does* survive in the Axelrod model, it is a diversity of the most extreme

---

[1] We should emphasize that none of the analysis in this chapter is intended as a critique of Axelrod or the culture model. Our own efforts are motivated by a dramatically different substantive context, and we depend on the insights of his work.
[2] In other words, the search occurs within a truncated von Neumann neighborhood. For an alternative approach see Epstein and Axtell 1996.

sort. Different cultural islands are completely homogeneous, wholly self-contained, and entirely isolated from one another. When an agent interacts, it interacts with other agents that are wholly identical.

As noted in the previous chapter, two components can be explored within the basic framework of the culture mode. The communication–interaction component, as we argued, does not fundamentally change our expectation regarding the impact of social interaction. As a result, we turn our attention to the second component – the influence component – which describes the manner in which individuals weigh information taken from acquaintances and adjust their opinions accordingly. Because the model is completely general, we can experiment with several different conjectures regarding this component. Further, we can incorporate various ideas about how people change their opinions alongside the various models of communication and interaction that we explore in the previous chapter.

As we have explored various re-designs of this opinion adjustment or influence component, we have sought to keep several general considerations in mind. First, if a society is completely homogeneous, the process of interaction and persuasion should not change that fact, and in this way consensus exerts a powerful self-sustaining influence. This may seem to be a relatively simple assumption, but it carries important implications for what we *cannot* do. For example, we cannot impose random, fickle behavior on a widespread scale. Although widespread and completely unpredictable shifts in opinion would solve the problem of cultural homogenization, they are not consistent with the fact that homogeneity is likely to preserve itself.

Second, we pursue an emergent solution – a solution generated by the logic of interaction and interdependence that is built into the model. In keeping with the insights of biologist Stuart Kauffman (1993, 1995), we seek a system in which diversity arises in a self-organizing way, through an autocatalytic process, a system that transforms a wide range of inputs into a stable pattern of political heterogeneity. To borrow Kauffman's own words, we want diversity "for free" (1995: 71).

Similarly, we seek to avoid a model that requires the careful placement of agents into particular contexts in a way that preserves diversity because the society is designed in a highly contrived manner. If a highly specific set of initial conditions must exist in order for diversity to be sustained, we face the truly daunting problem of explaining how those initial conditions might occur. In contrast, our theoretical goal is to construct a model that preserves diversity across a broad specification of initial conditions. This is not to suggest that the outcome cannot depend on initial conditions. Initial conditions are particularly influential in complex nonlinear systems such as the ones we are studying. Rather, our concern is simply that the outcome of the model not depend on arbitrarily contrived starting points.

Third, and closely related, we are particularly interested in equilibria that are relatively (or locally) stable, in the sense that small mistakes by individuals or changes of opinion due to exogenous shocks do not fundamentally change opinion distributions or undermine the persistence of diversity within communication networks. The more-or-less stable outcome for which we strive is a self-reinforcing system, and hence it is less desirable to find a solution that exists only when exacting conditions are met. Such an outcome, one that is "balanced on a knife edge," can arise in the original ACM. In that model, one can draw initial conditions in which a sharp line exists between two classes of agents with completely different opinions. They will never interact, and in this way the variety of opinion is preserved. In contrast, if some random, exogenous event occurs that produces even a single dyadic communication across this sharp line, then opinion diversity will inevitably be eliminated. Within the context of politics and public opinion, events such as these are inevitable, and hence guarantees of diversity that depend on their absence are, in fact, no guarantees at all.

Our search for a resilient system does not mean that the system needs to be immune from the impact of exogenous shocks. Quite to the contrary, it is entirely possible for an autoregressive system of influence to produce enduring changes in aggregate opinion distributions because of the way that it reinforces politically generated, exogenous shocks. Political communication might maintain the stability of opinion in the face of new inputs, but it might also have the opposite effect of disseminating the impact of inputs. The effect of political perturbations supplied from the external political environment, then, depends on the micro-level interactions among agents. These structured patterns of social interaction and political communication become an indispensable element of the larger political dynamic.

Fourth, we want to confine agent behavior rules to depend only on information that the agents can accumulate through one-on-one interactions. As a result, we do not employ the framework of cellular automata in our study. In contrast, consider the approach of Latané and his colleagues (Nowak, Szamrej, and Latané 1990; Latané, Nowak, and Liu 1994; Nowak and Lewenstein 1996) in the development of their social impact model (SIM). In the SIM, all cells are simultaneously updated against a snapshot of the whole society. Each cell in the grid is acted on by every other cell according to a distance-based law of influence. The mechanism of communication is unspecified, and hence the SIM invokes the sort of "social telepathy" (Erbring and Young 1979) that we seek to avoid (see Chapter 2). Although we take inspiration from the work of Latane and his colleagues, we pursue a model in which agents know about the state of the world only through networks of direct dyadic interactions, and they build up these networks through experimental adjustments in patterns of interaction based on trial and error. Unlike the SIM, which predicts a world in which certain opinions are held in tightly clustered subgroups of homogeneous cells, we strive to understand ways in which diversity can be preserved *within* the immediate experience of individual citizens.

Our modeling strategy is also different from the bounded confidence model proposed by Hegselman and Kraus (2002). In the bounded confidence model, the change formula for a cell takes into account other cells that are similar to the target cell. The cell's behavior thus reflects an average of these similar cells. Within this model, no explanation is offered for the process through which the similar cells become acquainted with one another or for the process through which dissimilar cells are identified and ignored. Likewise, our strategy diverges from that proposed by Shibanai and colleagues (2001). In their model, the agents are given global information about the state of opinion, and they take this information into account when they change opinions. In contrast, we seek to develop a simple process that explains *how* agents learn about the state of opinion and adapt their own opinions accordingly.

In summary, differentiating our research strategy from the cellular automata is the fact that our model is asynchronic and bottom-up. In the cellular automata, each cell is subjected to the simultaneous influence emitted by all cells and the value of the cell is adjusted in light of the values of all cells. As such, they are synchronous models, ones in which a snapshot of the grid is taken and all cells are updated against that snapshot. Instead, in our model, individual updating occurs one at a time, in response to individual interactions. Hence, whereas the motivation that lies behind our effort shares a great deal in common with the motivation that lies behind the social impact model, there are important differences on a number of levels. In particular, we pursue an approach that allows for the formation of endogenous networks of arbitrary size, as individual agents become acquainted and communicate with other individual agents within these networks.

STAUNCHLY HELD OPINIONS

One obvious modification of the earlier models is to introduce resistance to change on the part of individual agents. Since the model assumes that agents exposed to differing opinions automatically change their own opinions in response, many commentators have suggested that we focus on this element of the model. In the ACM, as well as in the variants we have explored, agents exposed to a differing opinion will copy it with certainty. What happens if we instead suppose that opinion change occurs with a lower probability? There is ample empirical justification for the claim that people do not automatically copy features from people with whom they differ. The easiest way to incorporate this observation is to introduce a new parameter for each agent which represents the individual willingness to copy new information. Call this the *flexibility* coefficient, f_i.

In the models we have explored thus far, all agents have flexibility = 1.0. Suppose instead that flexibility coefficients are drawn from an interval, say any number (equally likely) between 0.05 and 0.8. When one agent initiates a contact with another, according to the ACM, they interact with probability equal to their similarity. In the ACM, a feature (or issue) on which they differ is randomly chosen and the agent copies that trait (or opinion) from the other. In this new model, after the issue on which they differ is randomly selected, the opinion is copied with probability f_i.

We have implemented this idea in our computer model, but introducing inflexibility does not prevent the death of diversity, even though it does prolong its life. The summary statistics, displayed in Table 7.1, show an average number of time steps to equilibrium of 1,978 – about four times the number of steps observed in our implementation of the original ACM (Table 6.1). Once the system stabilizes, however, there is no diversity of opinion. The variance of all issues is 0.0, and the experience of the individual agents is perfectly uniform, as must be the case. Levels of harmony average 0.999, and by allowing the model to run 10 more periods, they would equal 1.0. (Agents use a 20-period moving average,

Table 7.1. *Staunchly held opinions in the Axelrod culture model (10 × 10 grid). Five issues with three opinions per issue.*

	Summary Statistics for 100 Simulations	
	Mean	Standard Deviation
Iterations at end	1978.14	826.59
Variance for each issue		
Issue 0	0.0	0.0
Issue 1	0.0	0.0
Issue 2	0.0	0.0
Issue 3	0.0	0.0
Issue 4	0.0	0.0
Total entropy	0.0	0.0
Average for all agents across all runs:		
Acquaintance	0.997	0.0023
Harmony	0.999	0.00096
Identical	0.999	0.0012

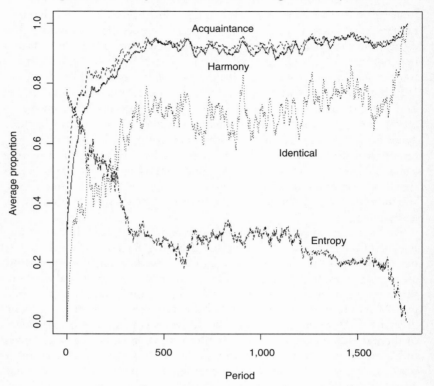

Figure 7.1. The decline of diversity in a model with staunchly held opinions.

but the simulation stops after 10 periods pass without any changes of opinion.)

In Figure 7.1, we selected a representative run from this model to show a particularly important fact. Although it is true that the number of iterations before complete homogenization is increased in the model with staunchly held opinions, it is also true that, even at the early stages, the micro-environments of the agents are quite homogeneous. Notice that within the first 100 time periods, the average level of harmony is above 0.80 and within 500 time periods it is above 0.90. Short of making the agents completely inflexible, the homogenizing tendency of the ACM is not eliminated.

THE INTERESTING CASE OF THE PERVERSE HOLDOUT

An interesting anomaly arises when we introduce the possibility that just one agent is completely resistant to social influence. Consider what happens if one – and only one – agent has $f_i = 0.0$, and all the other agents have $f_i = 1$. In this model, opinion is eventually homogenized, but with a twist: In the end, the opinions held by the one inflexible agent are adopted by all of the others. By the luck of the draw, it might be that the one inflexible agent would never interact with anyone else because it is completely different on all opinions from all neighbors. In such a case, the introduction of an inflexible agent has no effect on the model whatsoever. Such a case is extremely rare, however, and almost all the time, one of the neighbors initiates a contact with the inflexible agent and ends up changing an opinion in response. Hence, if the inflexible agent interacts with anyone, the eventual outcome is that the inflexible agent's opinion is translated through the whole society.

Now, consider what happens if the one inflexible agent has a very small flexibility coefficient of, say, 0.01. In that case, the homogenization still occurs, but given the one-in-one-hundred chance that an inflexible person will change, the society does not necessarily end up as a set of copies of the inflexible agent's original opinions. Because the introduction of completely inflexible agents has this knife-edge property – the difference between 0.0 and 0.01 – it provides an unattractive and less than reasonable solution to the problem.

Not only is it a dubious approach by the modeling criteria that we have set out, it is also dubious on empirical grounds to rely on the introduction of agents for which $f_i = 0.0$. By setting the flexibility coefficient at 0.0, one is supposing that an individual person could in fact withstand the contrary (and unanimous) advice of a million others. Although one might imagine such a personality type,[3] it is probably more realistic to suppose that some people are highly resistant to change, but not completely inflexible.

Perhaps the most important reason to look past the flexibility parameter is theoretical. Introduction of influence-resistant agents constitutes a *deus ex machina* that avoids the more theoretically demanding task – the development of a more intricate understanding of the formation of networks and the formulation of public opinion. If we could explain why some people are in fact highly resistant to new information, whereas others are not, and at the same time develop an explanation for the exposure of agents to diverse information and the survival of heterogeneity, we would be on much better scientific footing. In short, our objective is to see whether diversity might be preserved due to the fundamental logic of social interaction and political communication, absent a reliance on some external and arbitrary condition imposed on the model, such as individualistically defined idiosyncratic resistance.

---

[3] Some of us might even be able to point out meetings where such personality types have been observed to exist.

THE COLLECTIVE IMPACT OF AUTOREGRESSIVE INFLUENCE

In this section, we offer an alternative framework which leads to a set of sufficient conditions for the survival of diversity, within both the aggregated system as a whole and the networks of acquaintance that are experienced by individual agents. Consider the possibility that the models analyzed in Chapter 6 are too abstract and particularistic, creating a world in which individual agents interact in an artificially isolated dyad. The theoretical motivation for our alternative framework is the idea that these dyadic interactions occur in a larger context that serves to moderate the reactions of the individuals within the dyad. This larger context is no silver bullet supplied from some exogenous source. Rather, the context is created through the ongoing interactions of agents within their networks of interaction. Each dyadic interaction is thus interpreted within a larger context created by the ongoing series of all the agent's other dyadic interactions.

Hence, when agents interact within dyadic relationships, they bring a context with them that moderates their reactions to other agents. Agents do not copy opinions from each other in an arbitrary or automatic fashion. Rather, agents change their opinions only when there is sufficient evidence supporting the opinion that has been communicated through the interaction. We assume that such a sufficient reason is found when a majority within the agent's existing network of acquaintances holds the proposed opinion. In this way, the responses within dyads reflect the accumulation of individual experience, and the consequence of this accumulated experience is to create a pattern of autoregressive influence that serves to preserve diversity.

This autoregressive model marks a small but theoretically dramatic departure from the earlier versions of the model we developed in Chapter 6. The solution that we adopt recasts the problem of individual opinion change within networks of political communication. We are primarily concerned with the dynamic consequences of dyads that are dependent, in an autoregressive manner, on preference distributions in the larger network. The empirical evidence (see Chapters 4 and 5) indicates that influence within dyads depends on the larger networks within which individuals are located. We implement the previously demonstrated empirical result that dyadic influence is in fact contingent, in an autoregressive manner, on the presence of various opinions and preferences in the remainder of the network.

Our earlier models in Chapter 6 conflate interaction with persuasion. Whenever an agent communicates with an acquaintance, one opinion is automatically copied from the acquaintance to the agent. In this way, agents are wholly indiscriminate in their adoption of opposing points of view. For many purposes, this is perhaps a wholly adequate model. If you need information regarding web sites for vacation alternatives, you might indeed seek out information from people with travel interests similar to your own and take whatever information they provide.

In contrast, the value of political information taken through social interaction is problematic. Even if you acquire information from a generally trustworthy individual suggesting that George W. Bush is just another rich fraternity kid, you might want to evaluate the worth of that information. The important point is that communicated information does not necessarily translate into influence, and in this sense the influence of even effectively communicated information is quite problematic.

How do people evaluate the worth and credibility of political information? What makes for reliable political information on the part of a communicated opinion or preference? A range of factors could be considered: the clarity with which individuals communicate, the imputed expertise of political discussants, and more. Nevertheless, we have argued that a central part of the explanation lies in the information that is available across the individual's entire network of political communication.

If you think that George W. Bush is high quality presidential material, and one of your friends tells you that George W. Bush is just another rich fraternity kid, how might you respond? According to the models in Chapter 6, you would simply change your opinion. But an alternative strategic response is to contextualize the information obtained from a particular discussant by contrasting it with information provided by other discussants. Hence, if you like Bush but your friend Joe dislikes him, you might take into account the opinions of others regarding his capabilities. If all your other information sources suggest that Bush is an outstanding president, you might downgrade the credibility that you place on Joe's opinion. On the other hand, if all your other information sources agree with Joe, you might reconsider your own opinion on the matter (see McPhee et al. 1963).

In summary, we suggest that people respond by comparing new and divergent opinions against the opinions of others within their communication networks. If an individual is normally Democratic in her political sympathies, and an acquaintance suggests that Bush is an excellent president, then her support for Bush is likely to be contingent on the level of support for Bush in the remainder of her communication network. In this way, any single piece of information is seen within the context of all the information that is available. The social influence of any single interaction ceases to be determinate, and the agent becomes an evaluator of information received through a successive autoregressive process of social interaction.

AUTOREGRESSIVE INFLUENCE AND THE DURABILITY
OF DISAGREEMENT

The incorporation of autoregressive influence within the model requires that current communication and information be evaluated in the context of past communication and information. The simulation model is highly modular, so that the communication–interaction component or module can remain unchanged while exploring changes in the details of the persuasion process. Hence, the communication–interaction process occurs as before, but each agent maintains an ongoing record of past interactions. The agents keep records regarding the other agents with which they have become acquainted, and they employ these records in formulating their responses to new points of view.

We strive to keep our implementation as simple as possible while still incorporating the essential logic of autoregressive influence. Each time one agent encounters another agent, it counts the number of opinions held in common with this other agent, and an acquaintance is formed with probability equal to the proportion of shared opinions. In this way an agent accumulates a set of acquaintances that constitutes a communication network. When a particular acquaintance offers an opinion on a randomly chosen issue, the agent polls the other acquaintances with which agreement has occurred on more than one-half of the issues. If more than one-half of these acquaintances agree with the opinion being considered, it is adopted.

Hence, the autoregressive weighting scheme produces an advantage for opinions that are widely held within the agent's network of acquaintances. At the level of the agent's network, the autoregressive feature of the model rewards majority opinion as it punishes minority opinion. Thus, new opinions or novel preferences should take longer to win acceptance, and individual agents should be less susceptible to persuasion by opinions that constitute a minority position within the network.

Across a series of experiments, using a variety of communication–interaction modules, this autoregressive persuasion model leads to outcomes that are dramatically different from the earlier models in which persuasion is automatic. Diversity of opinion is retained, both within the agents' networks of acquaintance as well as across the aggregated system. Furthermore, the social networks are autocatalytic and robust. No careful orchestration in the initial conditions is required to create these diverse networks. Rather, starting from randomly assigned distributions of individual opinions, the process of dyadic interaction and autoregressive response consistently produces acquaintanceship networks that are characterized by diversity. Finally, these endogenous networks are quite stable and are, in many ways, self-correcting.

Table 7.2. *Autoregressive influence in the Axelrod culture model (10 × 10 grid). Five issues with three opinions per issue.*

	Summary Statistics for 100 Simulations	
	Mean	Standard Deviation
Iterations at end	71.5	13.82
Variance for each issue:		
Issue 0	0.64	0.11
Issue 1	0.64	0.056
Issue 2	0.64	0.061
Issue 3	0.64	0.062
Issue 4	0.63	0.062
Total entropy	0.71	0.016
Average for all agents across all runs:		
Acquaintance	0.44	0.031
Harmony	0.60	0.030
Identical	0.36	0.046

Consider first the example of what happens when we take our implementation of the ACM and impose this new network-oriented model of individual behavior. Recall that the original model has a 10 × 10 grid, discussants are selected at random from the four-sided neighborhood, and interaction occurs with probability equal to the similarity of viewpoint of the agents. For each time step, the list of agents is randomly processed, as each agent encounters a neighbor and the interaction proceeds. The only difference from the original model is that the other agent's opinion is adopted only when it is supported by more than half of the original agent's like-minded acquaintances – acquaintances with which the agent agrees on more than one-half of the issues.

A summary of 100 runs is presented in Table 7.2 The simulation stops after the entire list is processed 10 times without a single change of opinion by any of the agents. In each of the 100 runs of the model, the level of entropy is in the middle ranges when the simulation stops. The variance of the opinions is also far from zero. Furthermore, the experiences of the agents indicate that they are located in diverse acquaintanceship networks. These values can be contrasted against the original ACM findings presented in Chapter 6. Note that the number of iterations is dramatically reduced, and as the records kept by the agents indicate, they are exposed to a substantially greater amount of diversity.

There is not a great deal of variety in the time paths of summary statistics across runs of the model. Consider the example time paths illustrated in Figure 7.2. Note that, because opinions are randomly assigned at the

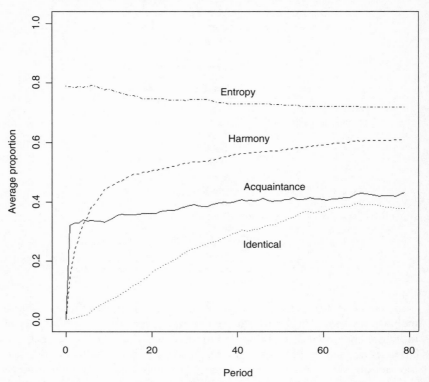

Figure 7.2. Autoregressive networks preserve diversity (one home grid, no work grid).

outset, the entropy level starts at a high value. As the simulation proceeds, the agents accumulate experience with their neighbors. The agents begin to adjust their opinions in response to new input and the stabilizing impact of autoregressive influence is made evident. First, the level of acquaintanceship is lower than in the previous models, reflecting the fact that the opinions of the randomly paired agents are less similar. Encounters still occur, however, because agents frequently have at least one opinion in common. As a result, agents regularly encounter other agents with which they disagree on a randomly chosen issue. Second, only a relatively small proportion of networks are composed of dyads with identical preferences. Finally, the average proportional agreement with any acquaintance (harmony) is only slightly above one-half. That value, which is consistent with earlier empirical results, indicates that there is a considerable level of agreement among the networks, but by no means complete homogeneity.

Autoregressive Influence and Durability of Disagreement

One might argue that the stabilizing influence demonstrated in this figure is a simple artifact of the model's interaction module. Since the agents have, at most, four possible acquaintances (remember: up, down, left, right), the requirement of a majority in favor of the new view really amounts to a requirement of a two-thirds majority in favor of the new view. Such a super-majority may be difficult to find, and hence, instead of demonstrating network-embedded resistance to change, we may be demonstrating the well-known stabilizing impact of a larger-than-bare-majority decision rule.

We address this question by subjecting the autoregressive model to a more challenging test. In order to demonstrate the influence of autoregressive influence on the preservation of diversity within larger networks of communication, we consider the multiple home/work grid model described in Chapter 6. Recall that this model exposes agents to a greater variety of inputs and, as a result, generates larger, more complicated networks. In this model, there are five 10×10 "home" neighborhoods, and each day all the agents spend at least part of their time at home, whereas some agents also go into three 5×5 "work" grids. These agents begin each day at home, but travel to work at some time during the day before returning home. Across these alternative environments, the agents continue to encounter other agents at random, and acquaintances continue to form with probability equal to the proportion of shared opinions. When presented with disagreement on an issue, an agent will adopt the acquaintance's opinion if more than one-half of its agreeable acquaintances[4] support that new opinion instead of the agent's existing opinion. Each "day" – one trip through the list of all agents – requires ten time steps within the simulation.

At the outset, agents have formed few acquaintances and they are simply wandering about, forming acquaintances, accumulating experience, and keeping records. After a few iterations, patterns of influence begin to appear. The averages across 100 runs of the model are presented in Table 7.3 Out of 500 agents, the number of agents persuaded to change in each day is typically less than 10, and that number declines as the networks stabilize. The average duration of the simulation is about 7,871 time steps, or 787.1 "days" (trips through the list of all agents).

The time paths of the measurement variables for one sample run are plotted in Figure 7.3. As in other runs, the diversity measures stabilize after a relatively small number of periods: Agents report neither complete homogeneity nor complete heterogeneity. Note that entropy – indicating diversity – starts at a relatively high level but settles down into a steady

---

[4] An acquaintance is defined to be "agreeable" if the agent has agreed with it in the past on more than one-half of the issues.

Agent-Based Explanations and Autoregressive Influence

Table 7.3. *Autoregressive influence with five home neighborhoods and three workplaces. Five issues with three opinions per issue.*

	Summary Statistics for 100 Simulations	
	Mean	Standard Deviation
Iterations at end	7871.3	29.01
Variance for each issue:		
Issue 0	0.61	0.12
Issue 1	0.64	0.13
Issue 2	0.64	0.12
Issue 3	0.61	0.11
Issue 4	0.61	0.12
Total entropy	0.65	0.054
Average for all agents across all runs:		
Acquaintance	0.49	0.025
Harmony	0.68	0.023
Identical	0.37	0.043

state in the middle range as agent experiences of homogeneity increase. As the harmony measure shows, agents experience agreement with acquaintances about two-thirds of the time, across two-thirds of all issues and with less than one-third of the agents' acquaintances holding identical sets of opinions.

The results of this model address the concern that the stabilizing impact of the autoregressive influence process is an artifact of the small (four acquaintances is the maximum) networks allowed in the earlier design. The average number of other agents encountered by each agent in this revised model is 27, and the average number of acquaintances is 14.[5] These results drive home an important point: diversity is not being preserved by isolating agents from opinions with which they disagree. Rather, diversity is preserved within the networks – both large and small – by providing agents with an autoregressive decision rule for accepting or rejecting the opinion of a discussant.

---

[5] The number of possible agents with whom to form acquaintances and experience encounters is increased not only by creating multiple loci for interaction – home grids and work grids – but also by increasing the number of agents within each cell. The 5 home grids are 10 × 10 and the 3 work grids are 5 × 5, meaning that the 500 agents go to work somewhere in the 75 cells of the work grids. That means each agent at work can "run into" many different discussants.

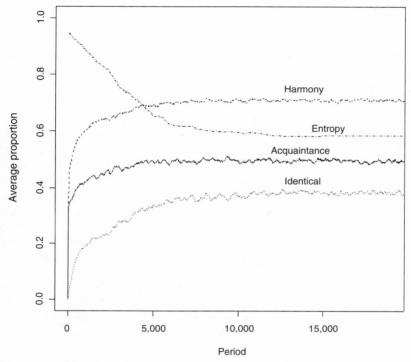

Figure 7.3. Autoregressive networks preserve diversity (five home grids, three work grids).

STABILITY OF NETWORKS DUE TO AUTOREGRESSIVE INFLUENCE

A particularly intriguing aspect of these communication networks is that they are endogenous, self-organizing, and unplanned. They result from the purely individualistic behaviors that we have described – behavior that is interdependent but not explicitly oriented toward the creation of diverse networks. When random input is introduced, more-or-less well-patterned sets of interdependent agents appear as output. Although diverse opinions are present within these networks, there is little motivation for opinion change. We find exposure with the possibility of adjustment, as well as stability.

We hasten to emphasize that no brute force device like the flexibility parameter is involved in this result. Rather, the necessary ingredient for the preservation of diversity is the simple proposition that agents adopt new points of view when a majority of their like-minded acquaintances agree with that new view. No costly or tedious arrangement of individuals into particular patterns is necessary. The only requirement is that individual agents accumulate information from the other agents with which they are acquainted, and that new (or divergent) opinions are judged in the light of the opinions communicated by these other, generally like-minded agents.

In addition to being endogeneous and unplanned (or, like Kauffman, perhaps we should say "free"), the process of autoregressive influence generates networks and opinion distributions that are frequently quite stable. We have considered, for example, what might happen if a random subset of the agents holding one opinion on an issue suddenly change their minds. Alternatively, we have taken all the agents not currently holding a particular opinion and selected a subset to adopt that opinion. By first allowing the model to run until the networks of personal influence have stabilized, and then administering shocks such as these, it becomes clear that many small exogenous shocks are quickly erased by the dynamic processes of social influence. At the same time, other external impacts are not erased, and are indeed magnified as opinion distributions within networks are subsequently transformed, creating a cascading effect across the society.

By way of introduction, consider Figure 7.4, a simulation of the model with 500 agents distributed across five home grids. This figure shows the mean values of opinions on the five issues. Recall that the opinions can be valued 0, 1, or 2, and that the original conditions in the model are

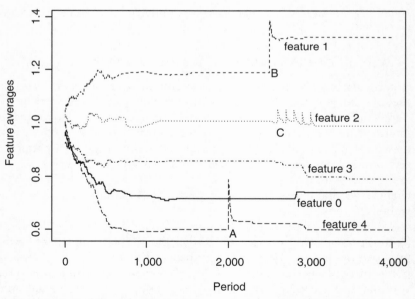

Figure 7.4. Stability of autoregressive networks against exogenous shocks.

randomly assigned, so the average of opinion at the outset is always close to 1.0. After 20,000 time steps we subject the agents to a series of random shocks.

First, at 20,000 time steps we randomly selected 50 agents for which the opinion on issue 4 was 0 and changed their opinion to 2. The pulse effect is labeled "A." Interaction within personal networks quickly erases that intervention.

Second, and in contrast, we selected issue 1 at 25,000 time steps, and changed 50 agent opinions from 0 to 2. That pulse, labeled "B," has a more lasting effect because there was more support for that view in the residual networks.

Finally, consider the small pulses labeled "C." Each small spike in issue 2 represents the fact that we found 25 agents and changed their opinion from 1 to 2 on that issue. It appears that the autoregressive influence in the networks quickly erases each of the five shocks that we applied on issue 2. These small positive shocks are followed by a slight *decline* in the average for that issue.

How should we interpret these shocks? First, they are entirely random and exogenous with respect to the communication process defined by the model. Hence they provide a useful analytic device for considering the consequences of events that occur in the externally defined political environment. When the stock market takes a tumble, or when terrorists attack, or when a president is threatened by impeachment, or when a political candidate makes headlines, individual citizens are encouraged to adopt new opinions or modify existing opinions. These opinion changes initially occur in single file lines – as individualistic responses to the dramas, events, and issues of politics. The question we address is how these individually based responses to the external political environment reverberate through a population that is composed of interdependent citizens.

SERIALIZATION EXPERIMENTS

In order to investigate the impact of these exogenous perturbations more systematically, the computer model is designed to be saved and restarted – a process generally known as *serialization*. For each of the 100 model runs summarized in Table 7.3, the artificial society is saved at the end of the run. (Recall that the model stops when there have been no changes of opinion after 10 complete cycles through the list of agents.) Ten of those preserved societies are then randomly selected to analyze the impact of exogenous shocks more rigorously. These follow-up experiments systematically test the stability of each opinion on each issue by repeatedly applying exogenous shocks to randomly chosen agents. By restarting a saved state

Table 7.4. *Opinion distributions in one run of the autoregressive influence model.*

N of agents	Opinion 0	Opinion 1	Opinion 2
Holding indicated opinion			
Issue 0	110	212	178
Issue 1	130	215	155
Issue 2	185	226	89
Issue 3	186	182	132
Issue 4	213	100	187

20 times, and applying an equivalent series of shocks each time, the stability of these networks can be assessed in a very compelling way. We can examine the stability "within" by restarting the same model over and over, and we can also examine stability "across" by comparing the effects observed with different starting conditions.

As an example of this process, consider in detail the stability analysis of one of these 10 runs of the model. The distribution of opinion in the saved state of this one run is shown in Table 7.4 (The table represents the seventh run, which was chosen for analysis.) One hundred thirty agents held opinion 0 on issue 1 at the time the original simulation model came to a halt. On restarting the model, we randomly selected 5 percent of the agents that did not agree with the chosen opinion – in this case opinion 0 on issue 1 – and set the agents' opinions on issue 1 to value 0. The intervention immediately raised the number of agents with the indicated opinion from 130 to 149. After 1,000 time steps, most of the impact had been erased. The number that held the opinion dropped back to 131. Next, we applied the same kind of exogenous shock again, affecting 5 percent of the agents that did not hold opinion 0 on issue 1. This time, 18 agents (with rounding) are affected. The number of agents holding the opinion in question is raised to 149, but after another 1,000 time steps, it drops back to 134. After three more shocks that affect 5 percent of the agents that hold other opinions (at 1,000 time step intervals), the number holding opinion 0 on issue 1 is 136. The collective impact of five exogenous shocks, then, is a net change of opinion for only 6 agents.

The distribution of opinion is not always this stable. In particular, the impact of these randomly applied events varies across different sets of initial conditions. Moreover, the impact of randomly applied perturbations varies across trials even with *exactly the same* initial conditions. Keep in mind that all the conditions and inputs are exactly the same when a model is restarted – exactly the same kind of perturbation is applied.

Nonetheless, an examination of repeated restarts reveals that a 5 percent perturbation sometimes yields dramatic effects on the distribution of opinion, but sometimes it does not. The variation across restarts is due purely to randomness in the selection of agents for opinion change and the dynamic influences of autoregressive influence in networks. These randomly selected agents are located in a variety of different network settings, and hence the same stimulus produces different results depending on the particular circumstances of the agent. (For an interesting point of comparison regarding the consequences of random samples and stochastic processes, see Granovetter 1978).

The time plots for the 20 restarts of the model that we have been considering in detail (Experiment 7, issue 1, opinion 0) are demonstrated in Figure 7.5. The impact of the exogenous shocks appears to be fairly predictable. Sometimes the impact of the shocks is completely wiped away, whereas most of the time a portion of the impact is translated into a permanent change in the expected direction. After five exogenous shocks, the average number of agents that hold opinion 0 on issue 1 is raised to 142.5. There is substantial variation, however, as the standard deviation across runs is 6.7. Most of the time the impact is positive, and some are larger than others.

Please recall that, in the models we are discussing, there are five issues, three opinions for each issue. Since one can examine the stability of

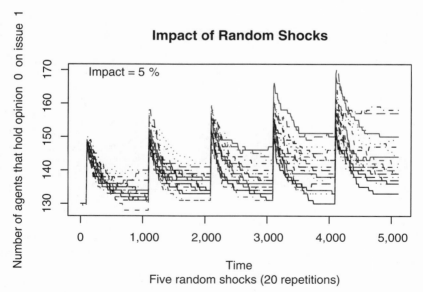

Figure 7.5. Variety observed across 20 restarts of experiment 7.

opinion against interventions for each opinion on each issue, we can conduct 15 batches of restarted simulations for each of the 10 saved models. In
this way, we generated 150 batches of restarts. For each batch, we created
a figure showing the changes in opinion, as well as collecting summary
statistics.

The pattern illustrated in Figure 7.5 is by far the most typical. The social
networks reject much of the impact of interventions, especially when the
number of agents holding a given opinion is small. When an opinion is not
widely held, then random interventions do not have the focused impact
that would be necessary to change the majority view within the networks
of most agents.

On the other hand, when an opinion is already fairly widely held, then
interventions have a more noticeable impact on the distribution of public opinion. The observed patterns fall into two qualitatively different
types, however. First, as shown in Figure 7.6, one can observe that the
repeated perturbations have a significant accumulated effect. This is not
qualitatively different from the previous example, in the sense that the
interventions affect the opinions of some individuals and the process of
social influence tends to mute or resist change. The only difference is in
the magnitude of the change produced, not in the qualitative nature of
opinion dynamics. As we shall see in the next section, positive response
can occur in an altogether different and perhaps more interesting way.

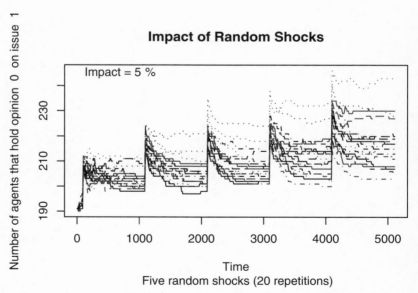

Figure 7.6. Cumulative impact of exogenous shocks in autoregressive networks.

SYSTEMATICALLY UNPREDICTABLE CONSEQUENCES

Do the results of the previous section mean that autoregressive influence necessarily serves as a conservative force that eliminates or moderates external perturbations created by the political environment? Definitely not. In some cases, a qualitatively different pattern emerges. In these cases, one observes opinion networks that not only accept the external input but also exaggerate it. In Figure 7.7, we present two examples of this "multiplier" or "tipping" effect (Schelling 1978; Granovetter 1978). An intervention

a. Short-term effects exceed magnitude of initial shock.

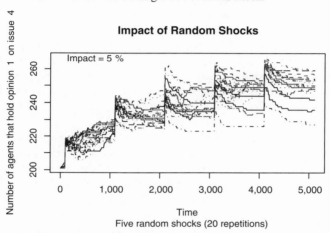

b. Variable presence of tipping points.

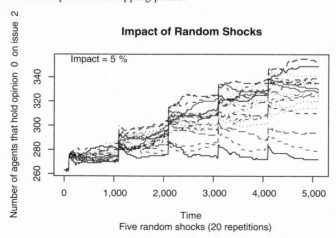

Figure 7.7. Tipping effects in autoregressive networks.

that affects, say 10 agents, might in the short term cause the number of agents that hold a given opinion to rise by more than 10. In Figure 7.7a, the short-term effect of the first random shock is almost always greater than the shock itself. In other batches of re-runs of the model, we find that the tipping effect is frequently observed, but not to the exclusion of other patterns. These batches are the ones in which we observe high levels of variation in the distribution of opinion across models. In Figure 7.7b, one sees that tipping effects occur repeatedly in some of the restarts and not in others, resulting in a wide variety of outcomes across the 20 restarts of the model.

The differences observed across runs of the model point toward the complex nature of the communication networks. As we suggest in Chapter 5, shifts in the distribution of opinion within an individual's communication network carry the potential to magnify rather than extinguish the effect of any particular exogenous shock, but that effect depends on the particular arrangements of agents and opinions. Suppose that a particular agent finds that some other agent holds a discrepant opinion that has been produced by an exogenous perturbation. If the perturbation was large, it may have changed the distribution of opinion within the remainder of the agent's communication network. Hence, when consulting with the other members of the network, the agent may indeed find support for the discrepant opinion. In this way, opinion shifts due to exogenous events in the political environment – media reports, scandals, terrorist attacks, and so on – may be amplified rather than dampened by autoregressive patterns of influence within these exogenous networks. In keeping with the insights of Granovetter (1985) and Boudon (1986), we find the consequences of network communication to be both highly systematic and highly complex, at the same time that they are often highly unpredictable.

The complexity of these social networks can produce other interesting relationships. Thus far, we have seen that social networks might mute or exaggerate the impact of exogenous shocks. They also might *reverse* the impact of perturbations. This can happen because the intervention causes some agents to interact within new contexts. This exposes them to different points of view, possibly changing their sets of trusted discussants. The long-run result can be a "backlash" in which the agents that hold an unpopular opinion no longer resist persuasion against it.

This backlash effect arises in many of the simulations, but it is not the most typical outcome. In only 6 of the 150 batches of simulations do we find that the *net* impact of the perturbation is negative over the long run. Consider the examples shown in Figure 7.8. In Figure 7.8a, we present the most extreme example of backlash observed in all 150 batches. At the outset, 83 agents held opinion 0 on issue 3, and the average reduction in the number of agents holding that opinion was 15.10.

a. Extreme examples of backlash.

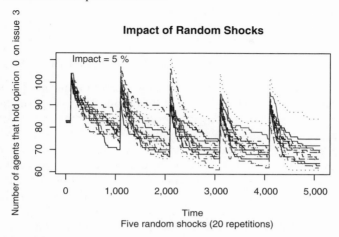

b. Variability in backlash responses.

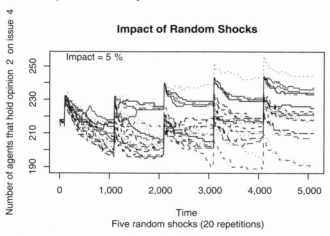

Figure 7.8. Autoregressive networks can exhibit resistance and backlash in the face of exogenous shocks.

The example in Figure 7.8a is intended to highlight the fact that, when an idea is unpopular, a jolt to an opinion in its favor may have an unexpected consequence. One should not conclude, however, that the backlash effect is confined to opinions that are firmly in the minority. Consider Figure 7.8b, which shows a wide variety of possible time paths. In this instance, opinion 2 is the most widely held view – 218 agents hold the opinion. As the figure illustrates, the impact of the intervention is most likely to be small and positive, but there are also more extreme impacts lying in both positive and negative directions.

These simulations demonstrate that the aggregate impacts of identically constructed exogenous shocks vary substantially across experiments. One way to measure the overall consequence of a perturbation is to calculate the average opinion change that results across all opinions on all issues for a given set of simulations. That is to say, we can create a composite index for the impact of perturbations by calculating the average of opinion change across 150 restarts of the model. As it turns out, the distribution of opinion in experiment 7 – the example we considered in detail above – happens to be the most stable distribution. Summarizing all issues and opinions, the composite index of change due to a series of five exogenous shocks is + 9.92. In contrast, the highest composite index for the impact of perturbations was + 20.20.

Not surprisingly, the diversity of opinion, as measured by total entropy, is closely related to the potential for perturbations to cause significant change in the distribution of opinions. Recall that total entropy is an indicator of the variety in opinion profiles across the entire population. If the society could be divided into a small number of blocks of identical agents, then entropy would be a small number. The relationship between entropy and the total impact of perturbations is displayed in Figure 7.9. Clearly, the composite impact of perturbations on an artificial society is highest when the society is most diverse.

The "edge of chaos" is a concept invented by Christopher Langton to describe the particular sensitivity and responsiveness of some systems in certain states (for a history of the term, see: Waldrop 1992: 230–5). Although there is truth in Ray's warning that the term "edge of chaos" might be applied vaguely in many contexts (Ray 1994: 169), it does help to describe the differences we have observed across systems. A system lies in the chaotic region when its response to input is systematic yet un-predictable. The edge of chaos refers to a part of the parameter space in which system response is not entirely unpredictable, but neither is it entirely predictable. Some of the examples we have seen would appear to be located at that edge. If a society has many agents located within heterogeneous communication networks that are evenly balanced on the issues – a situation characterized by a high level of entropy – a set of random opinion changes might have no effect whatsoever, or it might have far-reaching, permanent impacts. In contrast, when most agents are located in homogeneous networks – a situation characterized by low

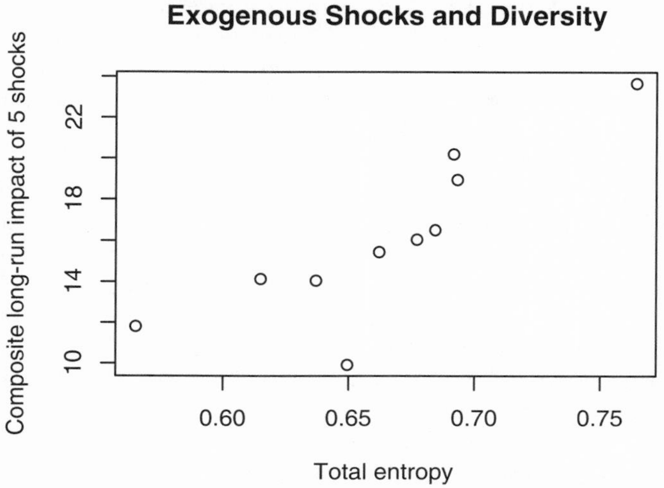

Exogenous Shocks and Diversity

Figure 7.9. Impact of exogenous shocks is greater in systems with higher diversity (entropy).

levels of entropy – these externally stimulated opinion changes are highly unlikely to produce durable change in opinion distributions.

These issues would clearly seem to warrant more attention. Some distributions of opinion would appear to be closer to the edge of chaos than others, but we do not yet have a single numerical measure to indicate where the edge lies or how far a society is from it. Once the edge has been characterized, another set of questions relates to why some distributions move beyond this boundary whereas others do not.

In short, Figure 7.9 brings us full circle back to the argument with which we began. Homogeneous opinion distributions within communication networks (low entropy circumstances) isolate and insulate individuals from the issues, events, and debates of the larger political environment. Heterogeneous opinion distributions within networks (high entropy circumstances) produce an electorate that is more volatile and persuadable, but also more responsive to the compelling issues, events, and debates of the larger political environment.

SUMMARY

A substantial body of evidence has accumulated regarding the distribution of preferences within citizens' networks of political communication. Contrary to a great deal of conventional wisdom, these networks are *not* safe havens from political disagreement. It would appear that most citizens experience disagreement and divergent political preferences within these networks. Moreover, this conclusion is based on the closely held, self-reported relationships of the citizens themselves, and on perhaps the most visible of contemporary political choices, support for a particular presidential candidate. Hence the question becomes, what is the nature of the dynamic process that sustains disagreement among citizens?

As long as persuasion is the inevitable consequence of interaction within discrete dyads, the elimination of political diversity and disagreement over the long haul may be a foregone conclusion. In contrast, a far different outcome emerges when we treat persuasion within dyads as a problematic and less than automatic consequence of interaction across an individual's entire network of acquaintances. Based on earlier empirical results, we conceive the probability of persuasion as a function of an opinion's incidence within an individual's network of relationships. That is, individuals are less likely to be persuaded by opinions that win only limited support within their communication networks. As the analysis shows, the autoregressive model of persuasion serves to maintain diversity and disagreement both in the short run and over the long haul.

In many ways this is a surprising outcome. On the face of it, there does not seem to be any necessary reason why a network-embedded model of dyadic interaction and influence should preserve diversity. After all, the autoregressive model of influence we are describing rewards majority opinion and punishes the political minority, but it produces an aggregate outcome in which the minority does not disappear. This mechanism for maintaining political disagreement defines the influence of majorities and minorities according to the distribution of opinion within closely held micro-environments of political communication. Hence, agents are able to resist divergent viewpoints within their networks because every opinion is filtered through every other opinion.

Furthermore, we acknowledge that it is possible to design starting positions for the simulation that would cause diversity to be eradicated. No doubt carefully crafted chains of networks could be constructed that would fold under the pressure of repeated interaction. The observed political record demonstrates particular circumstances that are likely to eliminate the experience of political diversity among citizens (Huckfeldt and Kohfeld 1989). When preferences are assigned in a random way, however, we have found that network-embedded individuals act in such a way as to preserve diversity both within their immediate spheres and on an aggregate level. The lesson is not that the citizens *always* experience political diversity and disagreement, but rather that political agreement and homogeneity do not constitute a necessary end result in democratic politics.

Conclusion

The ironic aspect of this outcome is that the agents themselves are not seeking diversity in any intentional way. Quite the opposite, they are seeking guidance from the majority of the agents that are most like them. As a consequence, we are inclined to call the resulting diversity an emergent property of the complex system.

Finally, the power of the mechanism we are describing is wholly dependent on the low levels of network density that are built into the model (Granovetter 1973; Burt 1992). If the network densities were high, if networks were wholly self-contained so that all members shared the same interaction partners, then disagreement would disappear even though diverse preferences would be sustained in the larger environment. That is, no one would ever encounter diverse preferences because every particular network would be entirely self-contained and politically homogeneous. In contrast, low network densities, combined with influence that is predicated on the incidence of particular opinions within networks, serve to sustain political diversity in the larger environment as well as the *experience of disagreement* within citizens' closely held networks of political communication.

CONCLUSION

What do these results suggest? First and foremost, they point to the importance of separating the *communication* of information from the *persuasiveness* of information. Even effectively communicated messages may lack influence, and this analysis points to the importance of interdependent citizens as discriminating consumers of political information. Second, these results suggest that political influence is imbedded within an autoregressive process of social influence. People judge new information in the context of old information, and to the extent that new information does not correspond with information they have already collected, it is less likely to be persuasive. Finally, the autoregressive structure that underlies political influence is responsible, perhaps ironically, for sustaining political heterogeneity and diversity within the larger population, as well as for preserving the experience of political disagreement on the part of individual citizens.

8

Heterogeneous Networks and Citizen Capacity: Disagreement, Ambivalence, and Engagement

We have argued that most citizens are not located in politically homogeneous groups, that the experience of disagreement is not a rare event, and hence that political communication among citizens carries the potential for a meaningful process of political deliberation. At the same time, theories of political communication have suggested that disagreement might produce confusion, ambivalence, and political withdrawal. In short, we would appear to be confronted by a democratic predicament: Either citizens are political enthusiasts who are isolated and protected from encounters with divergent perspectives, or they are political refugees who have withdrawn from the uncertainty and discomfort of disagreement. This chapter examines the consequences for political engagement that arise due to patterns of political diversity within the communication networks connecting citizens to one another. How do politically diverse preferences within communication networks affect political opinion, cognition, and levels of ambivalence on the part of individuals within the networks? How are these heterogeneous preference distributions related to levels of political engagement and turnout? We address these questions with data drawn from the 2000 National Election Study.

If communication among citizens is to be politically informative and meaningful, individuals must encounter divergent perspectives and viewpoints. In this sense, disagreement must lie at the core of collective deliberation among citizens in democratic politics. We have argued that political disagreement is both widespread and persistent among citizens who communicate about politics. Most citizens are *not* located in politically homogeneous groups, surrounded by individuals who share their political opinions and attitudes, and hence political disagreement does *not* constitute a rare event. We argue in the last several chapters that disagreement is frequently sustained by the structure of political communication networks. Even if this argument is correct, the implications of political diversity within communication

This chapter is co-authored with Jeanette Morehouse Mendez and Tracy Osborn, based on an effort in Huckfeldt, Morehouse, and Osborn (2004).

networks continue to be problematic. In particular, if political communication networks sustain heterogeneous streams of political information, what are the consequences for the political capacity of citizens and electorates? In this chapter our attention shifts to the implications of disagreement for political communication, ambivalence, and engagement.

Theories of political communication anchored in cognitive dissonance suggest that disagreement produces psychic stress, which in turn leads to confusion, ambivalence, and political withdrawal. Hence, while political communication may be uninformative in the absence of disagreement, the *presence* of disagreement might undermine civic capacity by politically disabling individuals who are exposed to divergent political messages. If people experience disagreement only rarely, then networks of political communication are failing to communicate the substance of politics, and collective deliberation might fail because individuals are not personally engaged with important issues and debates. Alternatively, if political disagreement is a common event that serves to inhibit political engagement, deliberation might fail because disagreement results in decreased levels of political involvement. We would appear to be imbedded in a democratic predicament, forced to accept either of two characterizations of the individual citizens. Either citizens are political enthusiasts who are isolated from the vivid portrayal of alternative political viewpoints, or they are political refugees who have withdrawn from the uncertainty and discomfort of political disagreement.

Within the context of disagreement and ambivalence, this chapter examines the consequences for political engagement that arise due to variability in the structure and content of political communication networks. The analysis addresses several issues and questions regarding these networks of political communication. How does the distribution of preferences within networks affect political opinion and cognition among individuals? How is political diversity within networks related to levels of political ambivalence among citizens? Finally, how are preference distributions within networks related to levels of political engagement and turnout?

The data used in this chapter are drawn from the post-election survey of the 2000 National Election Study. The post-election survey included a battery of questions that asked respondents to supply a range of information regarding their networks of political communication. Respondents supplied the names of not more than four political discussants, as well as a range of information regarding each of the discussants. Hence we are able to address the consequences that arise due to varied levels of agreement and disagreement among citizens within their networks of political communication.

THE CONSEQUENCES OF DISAGREEMENT AMONG CITIZENS

The early and influential work of Lazarsfeld and his colleagues, based on their field work in Elmira and Erie County during the 1940s (Lazarsfeld et al. 1948; Berelson et al. 1954), established the importance of social communication in politics. According to their argument, election campaigns stimulate higher frequencies of political communication, political preferences become socially visible, and hence individuals adopt political preferences that are more frequent within their micro-environmental surroundings. At the same time, they did not suggest, and we should not expect, that a process of group conformity will necessarily eliminate political disagreement within networks of social relations. They recognized the persistence of disagreement among some citizens (Berelson et al. 1954: Chapter 7), and they wrote quite compellingly of the political consequences that arise due to the "cross pressures" created by sustained disagreement among associated individuals – cross pressures that lead to political instability and political ambivalence as a consequence of political uncertainty and mixed political messages.

How important are these cross pressures? Does political disagreement produce politically disabling consequences? These are important questions. If collective deliberation among citizens in a democracy does *not* involve disagreement, its fundamental value is called into question. At the same time, if disagreement produces politically disabling consequences – if individuals withdraw from political life as a consequence of disagreement – then the democratic potential for a shared process of collective deliberation is correspondingly undermined.

This chapter addresses three interrelated problems. The first set of analyses considers the ability of individual citizens to provide justification for their attitudes regarding candidates, within the context of political discussion and heterogeneous political information. A second set of analyses addresses the problem of political ambivalence, considering whether disagreement produces higher levels of ambivalence regarding the candidates. Finally, a third set of analyses examines the consequences of disagreement for political engagement. Taken together, these analyses provide an opportunity to assess the implications of political disagreement for cognitive organization, for conflicting political attitudes, and for political withdrawal.

LIKES, DISLIKES, AND POLITICAL COMMUNICATION

An ongoing element of the National Election Studies' survey content has been the respondents' reported lists of likes and dislikes regarding the presidential candidates – the reasons for their candidate attitudes. In the open-ended formats of these questions, interviewers first ask the respondents what they like and then what they dislike about each of the major candidates.[1] These questions have provided a wealth of data for the analysis of American electoral politics. Based largely on batteries of questions similar to these, the political capacity of the average citizen has been called into question by the relatively low level of conceptual content that appears to be present in their answers (Converse 1964; also see Smith 1980).

Our concern is whether the individual's ability to access likes and dislikes depends on both the characteristics of the incoming stream of political information, and the vehicle through which the information is communicated. And hence the question becomes, what are the conditions under which people have an easier time accessing likes and dislikes as justification for their candidate attitudes?[2] Some individuals are encouraged to provide reasons for their attitudes on a regular and recurrent basis. In this way they might continually rehearse and recall associations in memory between the candidate, the summary attitude, and reasons underlying the summary attitude (see Fazio 1995; Fazio Sanbonmatsu, Powell, and Kardes 1986), thereby enhancing the accessibility of attitude justification.

How should these rehearsal effects occur? One important mechanism is the countless political conversations that occur as part of the larger collective deliberation regarding the choice of candidates in democratic politics. One of the characteristics that distinguish social communication from other forms of information gathering is that it typically involves recurrent two-way social interaction. One can simply absorb the news as provided by the TV news anchor or the newspaper, using the information to update attitudes before setting the information aside, thereby allowing it to languish in long-term memory (Lodge and Steenbergen with Brau 1995; Lodge and Taber 2000). In contrast, a person's status as a (more or less active) participant in casual conversations with coworkers requires one to repeatedly make connections among opinions and the justification for those opinions. This form of active participation may produce more durable associations in memory between an attitude and the reasons and

---

[1] The actual wording of these questions is: "Is there anything in particular about (candidate name) that might make you want to vote for him?" And, "Is there anything in particular about (candidate name) that might make you want to vote against him?"

[2] Political scientists have treated the likes and dislikes both as justifications for candidate attitudes (Lodge, Steenbergen, and Brau 1995) and as the underlying causes of candidate attitudes (Kelly 1983). Also see Rahn, Krosnick, and Breuning (1994).

justification for the attitude, thereby making these reasons more accessible. In other words, if discussion encourages individuals to devote attention and thought to political matters, we might expect individuals who discuss politics to possess more complex cognitive structures regarding political objects (Berent and Krosnick 1995; also see Conover, Searing, and Crewe 2002).

In order to characterize the stream of information to which the individual respondent is exposed, we employ the network battery that was included as part of the post-election survey in the 2000 National Election Study. As described in Chapter 2, each respondent in the post-election survey was asked to provide the first names of the people with whom he or she discusses "government, elections, and politics." After the respondent had provided as many as four names and as few as zero, the interviewer asked the respondent a short series of questions about each discussant, including the respondent's judgment regarding each discussant's vote in the previous election. We use this information to characterize the political composition of the respondents' political communication networks.

The first task is to assess the capacity of citizens to provide reasons for their attitudes regarding the candidates. Rather than focusing on the reasons themselves, we focus on the numbers of reasons offered for liking or disliking each of the candidates, Gore and Bush.[3] In Table 8.1, the numbers of reasons that the respondent offers for liking Gore, liking Bush, disliking Gore, and disliking Bush are each regressed on a series of explanatory variables – individual age, education, political knowledge, and party identification, as well as the number of Gore supporters and Bush supporters in the respondent's network.[4] In each of the regressions,

---

[3] As many as five likes and dislikes were recorded for each candidate, and thus the count varies from 0 to 5 for each of the four likes and dislikes measures. In analyzing these count data, we employ negative binomial regression models in Tables 8.3 and 8.5 (StataCorp, 2001). Because the counts are censored – respondents are unable to offer more than five likes or more than five dislikes – we checked the results with an alternative negative binomial regression model that incorporates an upper limit on the counts (Econometric Software 2002). Taking account of censoring produces no changes in the interpretations offered here.

[4] Age is measured in years. Party identification is measured on the familiar 7-point scale (0 = strong Democrat). Education is measured on a summary scale, where 1 is eight grades of school or less; 2 is nine through 11 grades or 12 grades absent a high school diploma; 3 is a high school diploma or equivalency test; 4 is more than 12 years of schooling; 5 is a junior college degree; 6 is a bachelors degree; and 7 is an advanced degree. Political knowledge is measured as the number of correct answers provided to eight knowledge questions: which parties controlled the House and the Senate before the election; identifications for Trent Lott, William Rehnquist, Tony Blair, and Janet Reno; and the states of residence for George W. Bush and Al Gore.

Table 8.1. *Network effects on number of likes and dislikes regarding the candidates, controlling for individual education, age, and party identification. Negative binomial regressions. Weighted data. (t-values for coefficients are shown in parentheses.)*

	Number of Things That Respondent			
	Likes about:		Dislikes about:	
	Bush	Gore	Bush	Gore
Constant	−1.82	−.36	−.45	−1.69
	(10.44)	(2.09)	(2.66)	(9.60)
Education	.05	.12	.13	.06
	(2.04)	(4.99)	(5.62)	(2.48)
Age	.003	.005	−.002	−.004
	(1.32)	(2.13)	(1.07)	(1.63)
Party identification	.31	−.27	−.26	.23
	(14.25)	(12.79)	(12.57)	(12.69)
RDD sample	−.54	−.08	−.08	−.05
	(.75)	(1.13)	(1.16)	(.79)
Frequency of reading	−.02	−.01	.002	.0004
Newspaper	(1.47)	(1.05)	(.14)	(.03)
Frequency of watching	.04	.04	.02	.002
national news on TV	(3.16)	(3.13)	(1.59)	(.14)
Number of Gore	−.04	.20	.19	.07
supporters in network	(.79)	(6.27)	(6.04)	(1.72)
Number of Bush	.17	−.13	−.05	.19
supporters in network	(5.41)	(3.09)	(1.46)	(6.72)
Political knowledge	.06	.06	.12	.16
	(3.01)	(2.96)	(5.70)	(8.54)
Dispersion parameter (α)	.38	.38	.42	.23
	(s = .07)	(s = .06)	(s = .07)	(s = .06)
LR test for $\alpha = 0$ (df = 1):	63 (p = .00)	80 (p = .00)	79 (p = .00)	37 (p = .00)
N	1495	1493	1490	1497
χ^2, df, p	530, 9, .00	462, 9, .00	494, 9, .00	598, 9, .00
χ^2 (df = 1) for difference	13.44	44.28	32.10	7.10
in effects between Bush	(p = .00)	(p = .00)	(p = .00)	(p = .01)
and Gore supporters				

Source: 2000 National Election Study.

we employ a negative binomial count model (Long 1997; Cameron and Trivedi 1998; Greene 2000).[5]

---

[5] The 2000 National Election Study included two samples – a national random probability sample (unweighted N of 1,006) interviewed primarily in person and a random digit dial sample (unweighted N of 801) interviewed over the phone. In each of the models estimated in the text, a dummy variable is included to indicate the sample for each respondent. In the post-election interview, 168 of the interviews with the national probability sample, as well as all the interviews with the RDD sample,

As Table 8.1 shows, partisan identification is strongly related in expected ways to the respondent's ability to provide reasons for liking or disliking both candidates. Democrats have more reasons for liking Gore and disliking Bush, whereas Republicans have more reasons for liking Bush and disliking Gore. Politically knowledgeable and more highly educated respondents are better able to provide reasons for liking or disliking both candidates (Zaller and Feldman 1992). Respondents who report that they watch the TV news more frequently are, in three out of four cases, able to offer more reasons for liking or disliking the candidates. In contrast, the frequency of newspaper reading fails to produce discernible effects on the numbers of reasons offered for liking or disliking the candidates. Older respondents are better able to provide reasons for liking the candidates, but they are not more likely to provide reasons for disliking them.

The consequences of network political composition are somewhat more complicated. Respondents who have more Gore supporters within their networks are more likely to offer reasons for liking Gore and disliking Bush. At the same time, the number of discussants who support Gore has little or no negative effect on the ability to provide reasons for liking Bush and disliking Gore.[6] Similarly, the presence of more Bush supporters within a network increases the likelihood of providing reasons for liking Bush and disliking Gore, but their presence produces no inhibiting effect on the ability to offer reasons for disliking Bush, and a relatively minor inhibiting effect on the ability to offer reasons for liking Gore. The difference in effects between Gore discussants and Bush discussants is statistically discernible in each of the Table 8.1 regressions. Hence, we see a pattern of pronounced asymmetries: partisan discussants enhance the tendency of the respondent to provide reasons for liking their own candidates and disliking the opposition candidates, but these partisan discussants are less likely to inhibit the respondent from offering reasons for disliking their own candidates and liking the opposition candidates.

The magnitudes of these asymmetries are demonstrated in Table 8.2, where the Table 8.1 count models are used to estimate numbers of reasons for liking or disliking the candidates, across the range of partisan

were completed over the phone. Hence, in a set of analyses not shown here, we replaced the sample dummy variable with a dummy variable that measured whether the post-election interview was conducted over the phone. In addition, explanatory variables in the models were included in multiplicative interaction variables with the dummy variable for survey mode to consider whether effects were contingent on mode of interview. Less than 5 percent of these interaction variables produced discernible effects at the 95 percent confidence level, falling within the neighborhood of our stochastic expectation.

[6] Having more Gore supporters in the network actually increases the ability of the respondent to offer reasons for *dis*liking Gore, but the effect is quite modest.

Table 8.2. *Estimated network effects on likes and dislikes toward candidates.*

A. Estimated number of reasons for liking Bush

		Number of Gore Discussants				
		0	1	2	3	4
Number of Bush Discussants	0	.78	.75	.72	.69	.67
	1	.93	.89	.86	.82	
	2	1.11	1.07	1.04		
	3	1.30	1.25			
	4	1.54				

B. Estimated number of reasons for liking Gore

		Number of Gore Discussants				
		0	1	2	3	4
Number of Bush Discussants	0	.89	1.08	1.32	1.62	1.97
	1	.78	.95	1.16	1.42	
	2	.68	.84	1.02		
	3	.60	.73			
	4	.53				

C. Estimated number of reasons for disliking Bush

		Number of Gore Discussants				
		0	1	2	3	4
Number of Bush Discussants	0	.77	.93	1.13	1.36	1.65
	1	.73	.89	1.07	1.30	
	2	.70	.84	1.02		
	3	.66	.80			
	4	.63				

D. Estimated number of reasons for disliking Gore

		Number of Gore Discussants				
		0	1	2	3	4
Number of Bush Discussants	0	.74	.80	.86	.92	.99
	1	.90	.97	1.04	1.11	
	2	1.07	1.19	1.33		
	3	1.32	1.41			
	4	1.59				

Source: Table 8.1 estimates.

divisions within the networks while other explanatory variables are held constant at typical values.[7] The asymmetries in Table 8.2 are quite pronounced. In Part A of Table 8.2, for example, moving from a respondent with no discussants supporting either candidate to a respondent with four discussants supporting Gore has little or no effect on the number of reasons for liking Bush – the expected number of reasons changes from .78 to .67. In contrast, the expected number of reasons for liking Bush is 1.54 for a respondent with four discussants supporting Bush, a twofold increase over the respondent with no discussants favoring either candidate.[8] What do these asymmetries suggest?

After the respondents' basic partisan orientations are taken into account, the composition of the network has direct and particularized effects on the ability of the respondents to provide reasons for their opinions about the candidates. Thus, it would appear that these effects are distinct from the effects that networks exert on the opinions themselves. It is very important to note that the presence of Bush supporters in the network does *not* dramatically decrease the frequency with which respondents offer reasons for not liking Bush, and that the presence of Gore supporters in the network does *not* dramatically decrease the frequency of reasons for liking Bush. If such effects did arise, it might indicate that the effect of network composition is mediated by the attitude itself. That is, network composition would produce an effect on the attitude toward the candidate, and the attitude would provide an impetus for respondents to generate reasons and justifications.

These results indicate a clearly articulated effect on the capacity of citizens to offer reasons for their candidate attitudes. Respondents surrounded by information with a pro-Gore bias are better able to provide reasons for liking Gore and disliking Bush, but this information has little or no suppressant effect on their ability to provide reasons for disliking Gore or liking Bush. Similarly, respondents surrounded by information with a pro-Bush bias are better able to provide reasons for liking Bush and disliking Gore, but this information has little or no suppressant effect on their ability to provide reasons for disliking Bush or liking Gore.

---

[7] In Table 8.2, party identification is held constant at 3 or independent, education is held constant at 4 or some college, knowledge is held constant at four correct answers out of eight, and age is held constant at 48 years.

[8] How do these discussant effects compare with news media effects? If the number of Bush and Gore discussants is held constant at one of each, reading the paper and watching the news seven days each week (as opposed to zero days) produces combined effects on the number of reasons for liking and disliking the candidates that vary from .04 to .20.

What are the political consequences of these asymmetrical patterns? Most important, network-based informational biases do not provide a direct inoculation against information that is contrary to widely held views within the networks. Your Bush-loving friends may provide reasons for supporting Bush and opposing Gore, but this information offers at most a very weak inoculation against your Gore-loving friends who provide reasons for supporting Gore and opposing Bush.

Theories of motivated reasoning (Kunda 1999) might lead us to expect that these inoculating effects would be present. Why do we fail to find them? At the very least, why do we fail to see inoculating effects that are comparable in magnitude to the more direct effects of political discussion? A full answer to this question lies beyond the boundaries of this project. This does not, however, inhibit us from offering the conjecture that motivated reasoning requires motivated reasoners – individuals who are sufficiently attached to their own preferences and beliefs to resist the illumination that might accompany new information. Hence, at least among many citizens in the context of the 2000 presidential election, such motivation may have been lacking.

Do the effects of these preference distributions within networks depend on the respondent's own partisanship? The results of Table 8.1 demonstrate strong effects of party identification on the likelihood that respondents will provide corresponding likes and dislikes regarding the candidates. Do the network effects depend on partisanship as well? Are Democrats immune to the messages communicated by discussants who support Bush, and are Republicans immune to the messages communicated by discussants who support Gore? In an alternative analysis, we re-estimate, separately for Republican and Democratic partisans, the models in Table 8.1. (See the appendix to this chapter.) The patterns of effects demonstrated in Table 8.1 are sustained in this alternative analysis, and hence it would appear that partisanship does not protect individuals from the need to take disagreeable information into account.

In summary, the presence or absence of particular candidate preferences within networks of political communication helps to explain the ability of individual citizens to offer reasons for their candidate attitudes. The asymmetry of these effects suggests a direct informational effect *without* any substantial inoculating consequences. Having a discussant who favors Bush does not protect individuals from information favoring Gore, and having a discussant who favors Gore does not protect individuals from information favoring Bush. Hence, the stage would appear to be set for the creation of political ambivalence among individuals with politically heterogeneous discussion partners, and this is the question to which we turn.

COMMUNICATION AND THE PRODUCTION OF AMBIVALENCE

Individuals who are politically ambivalent do not have weak attitudes or opinions toward political objects. Rather they are likely to have multiple and strong attitudes about the same object that lie in opposite directions. For example, a voter might be highly ambivalent about Al Gore if she strongly embraces his position on the environment but strongly opposes his policy on abortion.

The implications of ambivalence for political analysis have not been fully realized (but see Lavine 2001; Alvarez and Brehm 2002). As voters move toward the midpoint on a scale favoring a candidate, we typically infer that they are indifferent or disinterested or that they have a weak opinion. In fact, the concept of political ambivalence suggests that the midpoint on a feeling thermometer might reflect multiple, strong, and conflicting attitudes regarding a particular candidate. In this way, independence, indifference, and ambivalence are separate and quite different points of orientation, even though they may be expressed with the same point on a single dimensional scale. Political ambivalence is necessarily multi-dimensional, depending on a larger cognitive map regarding the attitude object and various connecting nodes in memory.

In this section we are particularly concerned with the potential of network-generated information for creating political ambivalence, and our first step is to consider the measurement of ambivalence in the current context. Thompson, Zanna, and Griffin (1995) suggest that the two necessary and sufficient conditions for ambivalence are (1) similarity in magnitude between positive and negative attitude components and (2) positive and negative attitude components that are of at least moderate magnitude. In this context, they consider the following measure:

$$\text{ambivalence} = \text{intensity of components} - \text{polarization of components}$$
$$= (p + n)/2 - |p - n|,$$

where p is the positive or favorable attitude component and n is the negative or unfavorable attitude component. (Both p and n are positively valued.) As the positive and negative components grow larger, the intensity term, $(p + n)/2$, grows larger as well. And as the positive and negative components grow similar in magnitude, the polarization term, $|p - n|$, grows smaller. Hence, the ambivalence measure is *largest* when positive and negative attitude components are large and offsetting, when attitude intensity is high and attitude polarization is low. Correspondingly, the ambivalence measure is *smallest* when the positive (or negative) component is very large and the negative (or positive) component is very small.

How should the positive and negative components be measured? For purposes of this chapter, we employ the number of reasons provided by a respondent for liking and disliking a particular candidate. Hence, we are assuming that respondents who offer five reasons for disliking Al Gore as well as five reasons for liking Al Gore are maximally ambivalent. In contrast, we are assuming that ambivalence is minimized when respondents offer five reasons for liking Gore but no reasons for disliking, or no reasons for liking but five reasons for disliking.[9]

In considering network effects on ambivalence, we begin by considering the intensity of the candidate attitude components separately from their polarization. We employ this strategy because levels of ambivalence are subject to variation in both levels of intensity and levels of polarization. For example, disagreement within discussion networks might increase ambivalence to the extent that levels of polarization are decreased, but decrease ambivalence to the extent that levels of intensity are reduced. Alternatively, disagreement might decrease both intensity and polarization, thereby producing very little net effect on ambivalence. Other patterns of effects are possible as well, and hence we analyze polarization and intensity separately and prior to considering net effects on the combined ambivalence measure.

Network Effects on Intensity. The intensity of the attitude components, considered in Part A of Table 8.3, is measured as the simple sum of reasons for liking and disliking each of the candidates. As the two negative binomial regression models show, the intensity of the Bush attitude is enhanced by both Gore supporters and Bush supporters, and the intensity of the Gore attitude is enhanced by both Gore supporters and Bush supporters.

The magnitudes of the coefficients for Gore supporters and Bush supporters in the first model of Part A are nearly the same. This suggests that a politically heterogeneous network produces as much attitude intensity regarding Bush as a politically homogeneous network, where attitude intensity is measured as the total number of reasons for liking or disliking the candidate. Perhaps more important, an interaction variable measures the presence of both Gore supporters and Bush supporters in the respondent's network, and this variable fails to produce a discernible coefficient, suggesting that intensity is unaffected by the presence of both candidates' supporters. The magnitudes of the network effects on the total count of

---

[9] Thompson (1995) and her colleagues report on research in which subjects are first asked to think about only favorable qualities of an opinion object, and then to rate them on a scale of 1 to 4 which varies from not at all favorable to extremely favorable. The subjects are subsequently asked to consider only the negative qualities of the opinion object, and then to rate them on a scale of 1 to 4 which varies from not at all unfavorable to extremely unfavorable.

Table 8.3. *Network effects on intensity, polarization, and ambivalence.*
Weighted data. Negative binomial regressions.

A. Total number of reasons for liking and disliking Bush and Gore

	Bush Likes and Dislikes		Gore Likes and Dislikes	
	Coefficient	t-value	Coefficient	t-value
Constant	−.34	3.00	−.34	2.91
Education	.08	5.47	.07	4.62
Age	.002	1.16	.002	1.46
Partisan extremity	.03	1.03	.06	2.36
RDD sample	−.05	1.05	−.06	1.40
Frequency of reading newspaper	−.008	.95	−.01	1.19
Frequency of watching national news on TV	.03	3.46	.03	3.09
Number of Gore discussants in network	.12	4.47	.16	6.26
Number of Bush discussants in network	.13	5.50	.06	2.52
Gore discussants X Bush discussants	−.03	1.04	.005	.22
Political knowledge	.10	7.75	.11	8.36
Dispersion parameter (α)	.14	(s = .03)	.13	(s = .03)
LR test for $\alpha = 0$ (df = 1):	33	(p = .00)	40	(p = .00)
N		1483		1491
χ^2, df, p		356, 10, .00		375, 10, .00

B. Polarization: absolute value of "likes" minus "dislikes"

	Bush Polarization		Gore Polarization	
	Coefficient	t-value	Coefficient	t-value
Constant	−.62	5.05	−.65	5.06
Education	.03	1.89	.02	1.32
Age	.005	2.77	.005	3.01
Partisan extremity	.10	3.39	.16	5.93
RDD sample	.02	.30	−.09	1.71
Frequency of reading newspaper	−.01	1.02	−.02	1.66
Frequency of watching national news on TV	.03	3.14	.03	2.82
Number of Gore discussants in network	.15	5.42	.14	5.50
Number of Bush discussants in network	.14	5.43	.10	3.76
Gore discussants X Bush discussants	−.06	2.03	−.05	1.76
Political knowledge	.08	5.72	.08	5.23
Dispersion parameter (α)	.14	(s = .03)	.12	(s = .03)

Table 8.3. *(continued)*

	Bush Polarization		Gore Polarization	
	Coefficient	t-value	Coefficient	t-value
LR test for $\alpha = 0$ (df = 1):	23	(p = .00)	18	(p = .00)
N	1483		1491	
χ^2, df, p:	235, 10, .00		255, 10, .00	

C. Combined effects of networks on ambivalence. Least squares regressions

	Bush Ambivalence		Gore Ambivalence	
	Coefficient	t-value	Coefficient	t-value
Constant	−.003	.03	−.01	.10
Education	.05	2.35	.05	2.21
Age	−.01	2.97	−.01	3.25
Partisan extremity	−.12	4.26	−.20	6.78
RDD sample	−.06	1.14	.08	1.35
Frequency of reading newspaper	.004	.42	.01	1.28
Frequency of watching national news on TV	−.02	1.34	−.02	1.50
Number of Gore discussants in network	−.14	3.53	−.07	1.88
Number of Bush discussants in network	−.11	3.23	−.12	3.58
Gore discussants X Bush discussants	.09	2.10	.12	2.69
Political knowledge	−.03	1.82	−.003	.18
N	1483		1491	
R^2	.07		.08	
SE of estimate	1.00		1.03	

Attitude intensity: total number of likes and dislikes regarding the candidate. *Attitude polarization*: absolute value of the number of likes minus the number of dislikes regarding a candidate. *Attitude ambivalence*: .5 (intensity) − polarization. *Partisan extremity*: varies from 0 (independent) to 3 (strong partisan).
Source: 2000 National Election Study.

reasons for liking or disliking Bush are shown in the left-hand panel of Table 8.4A, where partisan extremity is held constant at 2 or weak partisan, education is held constant at 4 or some college, age is held constant at 48 years, and knowledge is held constant at 4 correct answers.

The same interaction variable also fails to produce a discernible effect on the combined count of reasons for liking or disliking Gore in the second model of Table 8.3A. In contrast to the first model, however, the coefficient for Gore supporters (.16) is substantially larger than the coefficient for Bush supporters (.06). As the right-hand panel of Table 8.4A shows, this produces a higher level of intensity in a four-discussant Gore network than

Table 8.4. *Estimated effects on intensity, polarization, and ambivalence.*

A. Attitude intensity: total number of likes and dislikes

		Bush Attitude Intensity Number of Gore Discussants					Gore Attitude Intensity Number of Gore Discussants				
		0	1	2	3	4	0	1	2	3	4
Number	0	1.83	2.06	2.32	2.62	2.95	1.93	2.26	2.65	3.11	3.65
of Bush	1	2.08	2.34	2.64	2.98		2.05	2.40	2.82	3.31	
Discussants	2	2.37	2.67	3.01			2.17	2.55	2.99		
	3	2.70	3.04				2.31	2.71			
	4	3.07					2.45				

B. Attitude polarization: absolute value of likes minus dislikes

		Bush Attitude Polarization Number of Gore Discussants					Gore Attitude Polarization Number of Gore Discussants				
		0	1	2	3	4	0	1	2	3	4
Number	0	1.38	1.60	1.86	2.16	2.51	1.40	1.62	1.86	2.14	2.46
of Bush	1	1.58	1.73	1.90	2.08		1.55	1.70	1.86	2.03	
Discussants	2	1.82	1.88	1.93			1.72	1.79	1.86		
	3	2.10	2.03				1.90	1.88			
	4	2.41					2.10				

C. Attitude ambivalence: .5 (Intensity) – Polarization
(*Note*: Ambivalence is arbitrarily set to a baseline of 0 for respondents who have neither Gore nor Bush discussants.)

		Bush Attitude Ambivalence Number of Gore Discussants					Gore Attitude Ambivalence Number of Gore Discussants				
		0	1	2	3	4	0	1	2	3	4
Number	0	0	−.14	−.28	−.42	−.56	0	−.07	−.14	−.21	−.28
of Bush	1	−.11	−.16	−.21	−.26		−.12	−.07	−.02	.03	
Discussants	2	−.22	−.18	−.14			−.24	−.07	.10		
	3	−.33	−.20				−.36	−.07			
	4	−.44					−.48				

Source: Table 8.3 estimates.

in either a four-discussant heterogeneous network or in a four-discussant Bush network. And the heterogeneous network produces a higher level of intensity than the homogeneously Bush network.

Recall that the numbers of Gore supporters and Bush supporters vary from 0 to 4, and their sum varies from 0 to 4 as well. Hence, it is entirely possible for a respondent to be without *any* discussants who support *either* candidate. Part A of Table 8.4 shows that, in these circumstances, the predicted levels of attitude intensity are substantially lower. The important point is that attitude intensity tends to be enhanced *either* by homogeneous *or* heterogeneous distributions of partisan discussants, and it is dramatically diminished by reduced numbers of discussants who support a candidate.[10]

Network Effects on Polarization. Network effects on polarization are considered in Part B of Table 8.3 using the negative binomial regression models, where we see that attitude polarization is enhanced by the network presence of either Bush supporters or Gore supporters.[11] In contrast to the regressions of Table 8.3A, these regressions show negative and at least marginally discernible effects for the interactions that measure the network presence of *both* Bush supporters *and* Gore supporters. Thus, polarization is increased by the presence of either Bush supporters or Gore supporters, but is diminished by the presence of both.

These are complicated network effects on polarization, and hence it is particularly helpful to examine the magnitude of effects across various distributions of Gore and Bush supporters within the network. Part B of Table 8.4 displays these network effects on attitude polarization, where a higher number indicates a higher level of attitude polarization toward the particular candidate.

Most important, polarization is minimized in circumstances where none of the discussants supports either Bush or Gore. Polarization generally increases as the number of partisans in the network increases, regardless of the partisan distribution within the network. For example, among respondents with a single Gore-supporting discussant, the polarization of attitudes toward both Gore and Bush increases as the number of Bush-supporting discussants increases. The exceptions to this general pattern occur among individuals with three discussants supporting the same candidate and no discussants supporting the opposite candidate: Attitude polarization decreases very slightly when a discussant who supports the opposite candidate is added to these networks. In addition, Table 8.4B predicts that polarization of the attitude toward Gore stays constant across networks with two Gore discussants, regardless of the number of Bush discussants.

[10] The combined media effects on intensity range from .34 to .37. As Part A of Table 8.4 shows, the effects of 4 partisan discussants versus 0 partisan discussants ranges from .52 to 1.72.

[11] Attitude polarization is measured as the absolute value of the number of reasons for liking a candidate minus the number of reasons for disliking a candidate. This produces a count of the advantage in likes versus dislikes, or dislikes versus likes.

Finally, the potentially inhibiting effects of heterogeneity on polarization can be seen most clearly in networks with four discussants who support one of the major candidates. Reading along the diagonals in Parts C and D of Table 8.4, we see that networks with four discussants supporting the same candidate produce larger polarization effects than networks in which two discussants support one candidate and the other two discussants support the opposite candidate.

Combined Effects on Ambivalence. Partisan diversity within networks has the potential to enhance levels of political ambivalence toward candidates in two interrelated ways. First, the *intensity* of candidate attitudes is enhanced by the presence of discussants who are supporters of either candidate, and this intensity effect is not consistently and discernibly diminished if the discussants hold heterogeneous opinions. Second, the *polarization* of candidate attitudes appears to be modestly diminished by political diversity within networks, particularly in relationship to politically homogeneous networks that are of the same size. Hence, when the number of discussants is held constant, politically diverse communication networks are unlikely to discourage attitude intensity, but they may discourage attitude polarization.

The question thus arises, what are the net, combined effects on ambivalence that are mediated through polarization and intensity? In Part C of Table 8.3 we regress attitude ambivalence toward Bush and Gore on the same sets of explanatory variables employed in Parts A and B. Attitudinal ambivalence is measured in keeping with the procedures outlined by Thompson and colleagues (1995): ambivalence = .5 (intensity) – polarization. The ambivalence measures thus vary from −2.5 to 5 in increments of .5, and we employ a least squares model for the analysis.

As these models show, the coefficients for the numbers of discussants supporting Bush and Gore are both negatively signed for both regressions with very large t-values in three of the four instances ($p < .001$), and a somewhat marginal t-value in the fourth ($p < .10$). The interaction effect is measured with a variable that forms the product of the number of Gore discussants and the number of Bush discussants. In both instances this variable produces a positively signed coefficient and satisfactory t-values ($p < .05$).

Hence, the general pattern of relationships is quite similar for levels of ambivalence regarding both candidates. In order to demonstrate the magnitude of these effects, predicted levels of ambivalence are displayed in Part C of Table 8.4 across the various possible combinations of Bush and Gore discussants. These predicted levels of ambivalence are based on the coefficients of Table 8.3C, but ambivalence levels are arbitrarily set to a baseline of o for main respondents who have neither Bush nor Gore discussants.[12]

Recall that positive values index a higher level of ambivalence. By looking at the diagonals of the two tables in Part C, we focus on changing levels of diversity while holding the size of the network constant. An examination of the diagonals shows that, when the number of discussants is held constant, ambivalence increases as a consequence of increased diversity within networks. In considering ambivalence toward Bush among respondents with four discussants, it becomes clear that ambivalence is at its maximum when the respondent has two discussants who support Bush and two who support Gore. And this same pattern of diagonal variation is present for changing levels of ambivalence toward Gore as well.

Alternatively, by focusing on the rows and columns of the two tables, we are able to assess the consequences of adding or subtracting discussants with particular preferences. Part C shows that ambivalence toward Bush is reduced by increasing the number of discussants beyond one, regardless of the political preferences of particular discussants. In contrast, if a respondent has two or three discussants who uniformly support either Bush or Gore, adding an additional discussant with an opposite preference enhances levels of ambivalence. A somewhat different pattern appears with respect to ambivalence regarding Gore. Among respondents with one Gore discussant, the model predicts that an increased number of Bush discussants has no effect on ambivalence regarding Gore. In every other instance, however, ambivalence toward Gore is enhanced by any increase in the size of a politically homogeneous network that serves to introduce political diversity.

These results lead to the following conclusions. First, increased numbers of partisan discussants produce pronounced effects on attitude intensity. In operational terms, people with more partisan discussants are more likely to have readily accessible lists of reasons for liking or disliking candidates, and these effects are not discernibly diminished by disagreement among discussants. Second, increased numbers of discussants also produce higher levels of attitudinal polarization, but in this context disagreement among discussants produces a relatively modest decrease in levels of polarization. That is, if we hold the number of discussants constant,

[12] This makes for a more straightforward assessment of the marginal effects of preference distributions within networks. Such a procedure is feasible in the current context because, unlike the other models in Table 8.3, the models in Table 8.3C are linear, and hence the marginal effects do not change with the addition of a constant. The adjustment in the first model of Table 8.3C is + .691, and the adjustment in the second model is + .732.

people with heterogeneous networks are more likely to access both likes and dislikes regarding the same candidate.

Finally, in terms of combined effects, heterogeneous networks produce enhanced levels of attitudinal ambivalence regarding candidates, particularly when network size is held constant. These heterogeneity effects become more complex when they are assessed in the context of expanding a politically homogeneous network to include politically divergent discussants, and the results demonstrate both positive and negative effects on ambivalence as a consequence. These complex effects arise due to a pattern of interdependent contingent effects: additional numbers of discussants generally reduce ambivalence whereas increased heterogeneity generally enhances ambivalence. As we have seen, network size and heterogeneity are positively correlated, and hence the combined network effect depends on the relative magnitudes of the particular effects in particular instances.

DIVERSE NETWORKS AND POLITICAL ENGAGEMENT

Now our attention turns to the consequences of network diversity for the political engagement of citizens. Do the same factors stimulating political ambivalence also produce political withdrawal? An earlier literature argued that cross-pressures produced psychic stresses that encouraged individuals to withdraw from politics (Lazarsfeld et al. 1948: 62). In this final section, we address the potential of political disagreement within communication networks for the attenuation of political engagement.

We consider two different forms of engagement – interest in the campaign and the decision to vote. The questions thus become, are people who experience disagreement less likely to profess an interest in politics? Are they less likely to vote? Two different forms of disagreement are considered: (1) dyadic disagreement between the respondent and the discussants within her network and (2) disagreement among the discussants within the network.

The two criterion variables, interest and turnout, are considered with respect to the same set of explanatory variables in Table 8.5.[13] A

---

[13] Interest in the campaign is measured before the election based on three response categories: not much, somewhat, and very much. Twenty-seven percent of the respondents report very much, 49 percent somewhat, and 24 percent not much; and we undertake the analysis of interest using an ordered logit model. Turnout is based on a post-election question asking whether respondents voted in the November election. Seventy-two percent report voting, and we undertake the analysis using a binary logit model.

Table 8.5. *Interest and turnout as a function of political distributions in network. Weighted data.*

	Interest		Turnout	
	Coefficient	t-value	Coefficient	t-value
Constant			−2.57	8.61
Partisan extremity	.55	4.35	.40	2.37
Democrat	−.60	1.93	−.10	.25
Republican	−.52	1.59	−.04	.10
Organizational involvement	.04	.76	.50	4.35
Education	.17	4.25	.33	6.06
Church attendance	.11	2.92	.19	3.67
Frequency of reading newspaper	.06	2.84	.05	1.83
Frequency of watching national news on TV	.24	9.65	.10	3.48
Number of Gore supporters in network	.46	3.64	.68	4.07
Number of Bush supporters in network	.36	3.52	.39	2.95
Democrat X number of Gore supporters	−.07	.45	.18	.63
Democrat X number of Bush supporters	−.03	.22	−.28	1.03
Republican X number of Bush supporters	.05	.37	.14	.71
Republican X number of Gore supporters	−.08	.46	−.39	1.31
Number of Bush supporters X number of Gore supporters	−.16	1.83	−.07	.48
RDD sample	.24	2.11	.31	1.92
Threshold (1)	1.56	s = .23		
Threshold (2)	4.42	s = .26		
N =	1513		1512	
χ^2/df/p =	327/16/.00		219/16/.00	

Note: An ordered logit model is used in the analysis of interest, and a binary logit model is used in the analysis of turnout. Democrat: Dummy coded 1 if respondent identifies as Democrat; 0 otherwise. Republican: Dummy coded 1 if respondent identifies as Republican; 0 otherwise. Church attendance: Frequency of attendance; varies from 0 to 4. Organizational involvement: Number of organizational memberships reported; values above 3 are recoded to 3.
Source: 2000 National Election Study.

respondent's partisanship is measured with three variables. The first variable is a measure of partisan extremity, which varies from o (for an independent) to 3 (for a strong Republican or Democrat). The other two partisanship variables are dummy coded for partisan attachment as a Democrat or a Republican. Several individual level control variables are also included for individual education, organizational involvement, and church attendance.

The composition of the network is measured according to the number of Gore supporters and the number of Bush supporters. In order to consider the consequences of disagreement between the respondent and the discussant, the discussant counts are each multiplied by the two partisanship dummy variables to produce four interaction variables that were also included in the model. These interaction variables allow us to see whether the effects of partisan distributions within networks are contingent on the partisanship of the individual respondent. Finally, an explanatory variable is calculated as the product of the number of Bush discussants multiplied by the number of Gore discussants. This variable allows us to consider whether the disagreement among the discussants creates political withdrawal among respondents.

What do the empirical results indicate? First, a number of the individual level explanatory variables produce discernible coefficients, including individual partisan extremity, organizational involvement, education, and church attendance. More important for our purposes, although the simple counts of Gore and Bush discussants produce statistically discernible coefficients, none of the interactions between the various discussant counts and individual partisanship does the same. This means that disagreement between the *respondent* and the discussants does not serve to attenuate levels of political engagement. In contrast, the table presents some evidence to suggest that disagreement *among discussants*, measured as the number of Gore discussants multiplied by the number of Bush discussants, might serve to diminish levels of respondent engagement. The product of Bush discussants and Gore discussants produces a marginally discernible negative effect on interest, but it does *not* produce a discernible coefficient for turnout.

The relative importance of these network effects can be assessed in terms of the variation in the predicted probabilities of political engagement. The estimates of Table 8.5 are employed in Table 8.6 to calculate the probabilities of being very interested in the campaign and voting across partisan distributions in the communication networks.[14] In Part A of Table 8.6, we see that the probability of being very interested generally increases across the rows or down the columns. Regardless of the discussant's candidate preferences, the addition of a politically engaged discussant does not typically lead to the attenuation of political interest. At the same time, the magnitude of discussant effects is clearly dependent on the partisan distribution within the network. Hence, the probability of being very interested is higher for respondents with four Gore discussants (.45) or four Bush discussants (.36) than it is for respondents with two of each (.26).

In comparison, the interaction between numbers of Gore discussants and numbers of Bush discussants fails to produce a statistically discernible

---

[14] In Table 8.6, partisan extremity is held constant at 2 or weak partisan, church attendance is held constant at 2 or once or twice a month, and education is held constant at 4 or some college.

Diverse Networks and Political Engagement

Table 8.6. *Network effects on political engagement.*

A. Probability of being very interested in the campaign

		Number of Gore Discussants				
		0	1	2	3	4
Number of Bush Discussants	0	.12	.17	.25	.34	.45
	1	.16	.20	.26	.32	
	2	.21	.24	.26		
	3	.28	.27			
	4	.36				

B. Probability of voting in the election

		Number of Gore Discussants				
		0	1	2	3	4
Number of Bush Discussants	0	.62	.76	.86	.93	.96
	1	.70	.82	.90	.95	
	2	.78	.87	.93		
	3	.84	.91			
	4	.88				

Source: Table 8.5 estimates.

coefficient for turnout in Table 8.5, and hence its coefficient is eliminated in the calculation of turnout probabilities in Part B of Table 8.6. As a consequence, the addition of a partisan discussant always produces an enhancement in the turnout probability regardless of the political distribution in the remainder of the network. In other words, turnout is not reduced by political heterogeneity within networks.

In summary, the experience of disagreement within political communication networks does not appear to produce a dramatic retreat from political life. We see, at most, very modest effects on political engagement that arise due to disagreement between respondents and their discussants. And although we do see some evidence of diminished interest levels as a consequence of disagreement among discussants, the same effects are not present in the case of turnout.

In a series of important analyses, Mutz (2002a, 2002b) and Mutz and Martin (2001) have examined the consequences of generalized disagreement for issue opinions and tolerance toward minority viewpoints. How do our results and conclusions differ from these? In general, their analyses are less optimistic regarding the democratic potential of communication across the boundaries of political preference, in part based on the argument that homogeneity is widespread within networks (Mutz and Martin 2001). Whatever differences exist, however, must be seen in the context of the substantive and methodological points of divergence between their studies and ours. First, their research is motivated by questions regarding perceived levels of generalized disagreement. Our own effort is motivated by levels of network heterogeneity regarding a particular political preference – vote choice in a presidential election. Second, Mutz is generally concerned with the consequences of disagreement for issue opinions and tolerance, whereas we are primarily concerned with (1) the comparative informational consequences of agreement and disagreement within networks, (2) the implications of these informational effects for levels of political ambivalence, as well as (3) their implications for levels of political engagement on the part of individual citizens. Given the different focal points of our efforts, the similarities are perhaps as striking as the points of divergence. Most important, both sets of analyses point toward the ambivalence producing consequences of political heterogeneity within patterns of political communication among citizens.

CONCLUSION

Democratic politics is a frequently messy business, filled with contentious issues, perplexing dilemmas, and seemingly irresolvable disputes. This is the way that it must be. If democratic politics is to have substance and meaning, it must repeatedly deal with the most vexing issues that face a society – issues that will inevitably involve deeply felt disagreements. Indeed, the ideal citizens in democratic politics are those individuals who are able to occupy the roles of tolerant gladiators, combatants with the capacity to recognize and respect the rights and responsibilities of their political adversaries (Lipset 1981; also see Gibson 1992).

What do these democratic norms have to do with the roles occupied by individual citizens? Unless citizens come into contact with divergent political viewpoints, collective deliberation among citizens will fail to play a productive role within politics. That is, citizens will fail to grapple with the politically contentious issues that confront the political system. Subject to the structure of political cleavages within a society, it is always possible that social interaction will be insulated from political disagreement. This is most likely to be the case when patterns of social interaction are structured by boundaries that become the basis for political mobilization. The most obvious examples of such situations typically arise when political preference is structured by region, race, and ethnicity (Huckfeldt and Kohfeld 1989).

Moreover, if political disagreement among citizens produces disabling consequences – if citizens are unable to tolerate disagreement except by withdrawing from political life – then the process of collective deliberation within electorates is incapable of playing a meaningful role in the political process. Two patterns widely noted in previous studies appear to produce a combined effect that comes quite close to dismissing the importance of political communication among citizens. On the one hand, disagreement has been treated as a rare event among citizens who inhabit politically cozy networks of like-minded associates. On the other hand, when citizens *are* confronted by political disagreement, they are frequently assumed to grow faint-hearted under the psychic pressure of political disputes.

In contrast to this view, our analysis has shown several things. Perhaps most important, citizens are frequently exposed to political disagreement, and political homogeneity is not the norm among a representative sample of citizens who provided network information during the 2000 election campaign. To restate our earlier results, less than half the respondents report networks of association in which everyone shares their preference. More than one-third of the Gore and Bush supporters point to an associate who supports the opposite candidate. And one-fourth of the respondents identify associates who support Gore and Bush.

Political conversations enhance the capacity of citizens to provide reasons for their support of a particular candidate. Citizens who interact with Bush supporters are better able to provide reasons for liking Bush and reasons for disliking Gore. Conversely, citizens who interact with Gore supporters are better able to provide reasons for liking Gore and disliking Bush. But this means that citizens who interact with Gore supporters *and* Bush supporters are better able to provide reasons for liking *and* disliking Gore, as well as reasons for liking *and* disliking Bush.

As a consequence, political diversity within networks creates the potential for political ambivalence. In comparing citizens who are exposed to heterogeneous and homogeneous messages regarding a candidate, we see little evidence to suggest that those exposed to diverse messages are less likely to demonstrate an intense attitude regarding a candidate. In contrast, citizens exposed to heterogeneous messages *are* less likely to hold a polarized attitude regarding a candidate. In other words, they are more likely to develop an attitude toward the candidate that incorporates positive and negative assessments. Correspondingly, when network size is held constant, individuals imbedded in heterogeneous networks are more likely to hold ambivalent attitudes toward candidates.

Finally, in assessing the potential for political withdrawal, we see that increased levels of political diversity within networks may reduce political interest, but they are less likely to produce an attenuating effect on turnout. In particular, people with four discussants supporting the same candidate do not appear more likely to vote than people with four discussants equally split between the two candidates. In contrast, people with four discussants supporting the same candidate are more likely to express interest in the campaign.

Table 8.7. *Network effects on likes and dislikes regarding the candidates by partisan preference, with controls for education, age, strength of partisanship and political knowledge. Negative binomial regressions. Weighted data.*

A. Number of things that the respondent likes about Bush

	Democratic Partisans		Republican Partisans	
	Coef.	(t-value)	Coef.	(t-value)
Constant	−.72	(1.59)	−.38	(2.06)
Education	.09	(1.21)	.03	(1.27)
Age	.003	(.47)	.003	(1.19)
Partisan strength	−.46	(4.30)	.09	(2.19)
RDD sample	−.11	(.56)	−.012	(.19)
Number of Gore discussants	−.05	(.50)	.03	(.61)
Number of Bush discussants	.32	(2.69)	.13	(4.72)
Frequency read paper	−.04	(.96)	−.02	(1.37)
Frequency watch TV news	.06	(1.65)	.04	(3.01)
Political knowledge	.01	(.18)	.10	(4.86)
Dispersion parameter (α)	3.39	(s = .52)	.02	(s = .03)
LR test for $\alpha = 0$ (df = 1):	174	(p = .00)	0	(p = .00)
N, χ^2, df, p:	739, 39, 9, .00		597, 117, 9, .00	
χ^2 (df = 1) for difference	6.27		2.74	
In effects between Bush and Gore discussants	(p. 01)		(p = .10)	

B. Number of things that the respondent likes about Gore

	Democratic Partisans		Republican Partisans	
	Coef.	(t-value)	Coef.	(t-value)
Constant	−.86	(4.29)	−.95	(2.27)
Education	.08	(3.10)	.23	(3.80)
Age	.01	(2.25)	−.002	(.27)
Partisan strength	.17	(3.75)	−.27	(2.45)
RDD sample	−.14	(1.91)	.02	(.09)
Number of Gore discussants	.17	(5.37)	.36	(3.87)
Number of Bush discussants	−.02	(.45)	−.24	(2.83)
Frequency read paper	−.009	(.66)	.01	(.27)
Frequency watch TV news	.04	(2.86)	−.002	(.05)
Political knowledge	.07	(3.27)	−.05	(.93)
Dispersion parameter (α)	.15	(s = .05)	1.65	(s = .36)
LR test for $\alpha = 0$, df = 1:	8	(p = .00)	105	(p = .00)
N, χ^2, df, p:	738, 179, 9, .00		593, 49, 9, .00	
χ^2 (df = 1) for difference	14.50		25.23	
In effects between Bush and Gore discussants	(p = .00)		(p = .00)	

Table 8.7. *(continued)*

C. Number of things that the respondent dislikes about Bush

	Democratic Partisans		Republican Partisans	
	Coef.	(t-value)	Coef.	(t-value)
Constant	−.89	(4.38)	−1.52	(3.77)
Education	.08	(3.09)	.32	(5.84)
Age	.000	(.05)	−.01	(2.06)
Partisan strength	.15	(2.99)	−.20	(2.03)
RDD sample	−.04	(.45)	−.34	(2.02)
Number of Gore discussants	.19	(5.74)	.27	(2.47)
Number of Bush discussants	.02	(.54)	−.14	(2.08)
Frequency read paper	.01	(.37)	.002	(.08)
Frequency watch TV news	.01	(.87)	−.005	(.17)
Political knowledge	.11	(.02)	.10	(2.02)
Dispersion parameter (α)	.18	(s = .05)	1.39	(s = .27)
LR test for $\alpha = 0$ (df = 1):	12	(p = .00)	78	(p = .00)
N, χ^2, df, p:	737, 181, 9, .00		593, 95, 9, .00	
χ^2 (df = 1) for difference	13.03		10.69	
In effects between Bush and Gore discussants	(p = .00)		(p = .001)	

D. Number of things that the respondent dislikes about Gore

	Democratic Partisans		Republican Partisans	
	Coef.	(t-value)	Coef.	(t-value)
Constant	−.95	(2.43)	−.61	(3.27)
Education	.12	(2.25)	.04	(1.59)
Age	−.005	(.67)	−.003	(1.56)
Partisan strength	−.50	(5.46)	.13	(3.10)
RDD sample	.15	(.96)	−.08	(1.20)
Number of Gore discussants	.13	(1.79)	.007	(.15)
Number of Bush discussants	.32	(4.10)	.16	(5.87)
Frequency read paper	−.04	(1.14)	.008	(.62)
Frequency watch TV news	.004	(.14)	.005	(.41)
Political knowledge	.18	(4.11)	.15	(7.46)
Dispersion parameter (α)	1.32	(s = .25)	.00	(s = .00)
LR test for $\alpha = 0$ (df = 1):	91	(p = .00)	0	(p = .50)
N, χ^2, df, p:	739, 105, 9, .00		594, 198, 9, .00	
χ^2 (df = 1) for difference	3.30		8.94	
In effects between Bush and Gore discussants	(p = .07)		(p = .003)	

Note: Democratic and Republican partisans are those respondents who are strong or weak identifiers, as well as those who are independent but lean toward the party. Partisan strength is coded 3 for strong identifiers, 2 for weak identifiers, and 1 for independents who lean toward the party.
Source: 2000 National Election Study.

What are we to conclude regarding this pattern of effects? Although the experience of political disagreement regarding the candidates may produce less enthusiasm regarding the campaign, it does not encourage people to back away from their commitment as citizens. The same political diversity within networks that creates the potential for political ambivalence and balanced views toward candidates may also serve to mute political enthusiasms. In the context of the American founding, and particularly in the context of Madison's unwillingness in the *Federalist 10* to place ultimate trust in wise leaders, balanced views and political ambivalence may be highly representative of a skeptical tradition in American political history. What are the costs? Perhaps politics becomes less enjoyable for those who experience ambivalence-producing diversity, but it is much less clear that political disagreement compromises their ability to function as citizens.

APPENDIX TO CHAPTER 8

Table 8.7 extends the earlier analysis of Table 8.1 by estimating the models separately for Democratic and Republican partisans in order to evaluate whether the discussant effects are contingent on individual partisanship. Democratic partisans are defined as strong and weak identifiers, as well as independents who lean toward the Democratic party. Similarly, Republican partisans are defined as strong and weak identifiers, as well as independents who lean toward the Republicans. A measure is also included in each of the models to assess strength of partisanship, where 1 is an independent leaner, 2 is a weak identifier, and 3 is a strong identifier. We consider the effects separately for Democrats and Republicans because the interaction variables between partisanship and the numbers of Bush and Gore supporting discussants, in combination with the simple measures of partisanship and discussant counts, produce excessive collinearity in the original Table 8.1 models. The analysis sustains the general pattern of discussant effects shown in Table 8.1, but it also shows that the aberrant and previously demonstrated negative effect of Bush discussants on reasons for liking Gore is isolated among Republican partisans, and a negative effect of Bush discussants on reasons for disliking Bush is similarly isolated among Republican partisans. Hence, to the extent that we see these negative inoculation effects, they only exist among Republican partisans.

9

Summary, Implications, and Conclusion

Not only is political disagreement widespread within the communication networks of ordinary citizens, but political diversity within these networks is entirely consistent with a theory of democratic politics built on the importance of individual interdependence. Contrary to commonly held theoretical expectations, the persistence of political diversity and disagreement does not mean that interdependence is absent among citizens or that political influence is lacking. Indeed, our analysis ratifies the theoretical vantage point from which we began. Democratic electorates are composed of individually interdependent citizens who depend on one another for political information and guidance, and political communication and persuasion are thus central to citizenship and democratic politics. Political heterogeneity within communication networks is not simply the error term within an explanation for individual opinion and preference that is built on patterns of communication and influence among citizens. The important point is that diversity is frequently produced as the systematic byproduct of political interdependence among citizens. Hence, both agreement and disagreement can be understood within the context of interdependent citizens who are connected through complex networks of political communication.

None of this is intended to suggest that disagreement and political diversity are always or only the consequence of interdependence. Levels of political interdependence depend on the frequency of communication; communication frequency depends on levels of political activation and attentiveness; and hence political interdependence is relaxed under conditions of political quiescence. In terms of the Columbia studies, as the frequency of political communication declines, political preferences and opinions become increasingly idiosyncratic and individually independent (Berelson et al. 1954: Chapter 7). In short, disagreement and diversity are not always produced by complex patterns of political interdependence, but neither does the presence of diversity and disagreement constitute evidence of political independence.

Moreover, we are not suggesting that political heterogeneity and disagreement inevitably survive within communication networks. It is not difficult to document important failures in the preservation of political heterogeneity – circumstances in which diversity is eliminated and individual citizens fail to encounter dissenting voices (Huckfeldt and Kohfeld 1989). One can certainly locate instances of political homogenization, but it is perhaps more interesting, both scientifically and substantively, to ask why homogenization is the exception rather than the rule. The compelling question thus becomes, what are the circumstances that sustain political diversity, even in politically high stimulus environments when individuals are attentive to politics and the frequency of communication among citizens is correspondingly high?

LOW DENSITY NETWORKS AND AUTOREGRESSIVE INFLUENCE

Our argument is that political disagreement and diversity are better able to survive in circumstances characterized by the joint presence of two conditions: lower density communication networks where the influence of particular opinions is autogressively weighted by the frequency of the opinions within the network. First, in terms of low density networks, patterns of communication among citizens must involve the absence as well as the presence of connecting ties among individuals – a form of social organization that is at variance with the conception of highly cohesive, self-contained social groups. Second, in terms of autoregressive weights on communication and influence, patterns of communication must exist in which the effectiveness of communication and the flow of influence within dyads depend on the distribution of opinions and preferences within larger networks of communication. Both sets of circumstances are well documented in the evidence we have presented.

Low Density Networks. Low network densities are characterized by the absence as well as the presence of connecting ties among individuals. This produces a situation in which the communication networks among associated individuals are overlapping but less likely to be identical. Our analyses show a multiplicity of gaps and holes in the construction of communication networks, with documentation of these missing links in two separate forms.

First, high proportions of the respondents to the 1996 Indianapolis–St. Louis study report that their discussion partners do not interact with one another on a frequent basis and often do not know one another. This produces a particularly important implication for our purposes. Even though two individuals discuss politics with one another on a frequent and recurrent basis, they may still be located in communication networks that are quite distinct. In this way, it becomes entirely possible that the two associates might be imbedded in politically divergent networks of political communication – in informational contexts that are characterized by dramatically different distributions of political opinion and preference. Hence, the odds of socially sustained political disagreement are enhanced. The likelihood increases that two associates will persistently *disagree* because the remainders of their communication networks point in politically opposite directions.

Second, the Indianapolis–St. Louis Study adds to earlier evidence (Huckfeldt and Sprague 1995) documenting low levels of reciprocity within networks. This situation arises when discussants named by main respondents do not in turn identify the main respondents as their own discussants. In other words, networks of political communication often incorporate asymmetrical communication links. This raises an obvious question: How can political discussion occur on only one side of a dyad?

The role of these asymmetries is more readily understood if we treat political discussion as an instance of information transmission. When two individuals interact, the flow of information may sometimes be unidirectional, and the value of the information that is transmitted may vary between the two participants. Hence, discussants may usefully be conceived as informants, and discussion networks as webs of both reciprocal and non-reciprocal informant relationships. As before, we are pushed away from a conception of communication networks as highly cohesive groups that sustain high rates of interaction within self-contained social cells and low rates of interaction beyond these cells. Once again, even though two people communicate on a frequent and recurrent basis, they might be located in highly divergent informational contexts.

Autoregressive Influence. Autoregressive patterns of influence occur when the effectiveness with which an opinion is communicated, or the influence of the communicated opinion on others, depends on the incidence of the opinion in the larger network of communication. Analyses of both the Indianapolis–St. Louis Study and the 2000 National Election Study document a process of autoregressive influence (also see Ikeda and Huckfeldt 2001, and Huckfeldt et al. 1998a). The effectiveness and persuasiveness of the communication that occurs within a particular dyad is conditional on an individual's full range of informational contacts, on the entire distribution of preferences within an individual's network of communication. In this way, the social communication process tends to sustain majority preferences within communication networks. Hence, the importance of any particular information source is weighted by the extent to which it corresponds to the distribution of remaining information sources.

The agent-based modeling simulations in Chapter 7 demonstrate that the combination of these two circumstances – autoregressive influence within the context of lower density networks – serves to sustain political diversity within communication networks. In contrast, within *high* density networks, a process of autoregressive influence would serve to reinforce the closed, impermeable boundaries on self-contained social groups. And *absent* a process of autoregressive influence, individuals would indiscriminately tend to adopt whatever preference or opinion happens to be communicated through a dyadic connection. As Axelrod (1997a) demonstrates, the end result of indiscriminate influence within dyads is the elimination of disagreement and diversity across an individual agent's range of contacts.

In this way, autoregressive influence and lower density networks lie at the core of our argument. The maintenance of political diversity and the persistence of disagreement do not run counter to processes of political communication and influence among citizens. Disagreement and diversity are not simply the stuff of rugged individualists, but rather the end result of complex networks of relationships among citizens, coupled with a process in which these citizens evaluate each information source in the context of every other information source.

POLITICAL IMPLICATIONS FOR GROUPS AND INDIVIDUALS

Complex, low density communication networks, coupled with autoregressive patterns of influence, yield a number of political consequences. In particular, citizens possess the capacity to cope with political disagreement, and they are frequently located within politically diverse communication networks. This leads, in turn, to a number of important implications for our understanding of individual citizens, the groups to which they belong, and the patterns of communication that connect groups and individuals within the political process.

Persistent Disagreement Frequently Occurs within Communication Networks

Political diversity often survives, even within recurrent patterns of political communication. As we have documented, a lack of political consensus regarding presidential vote choice tends to be the modal condition within networks of communication during presidential elections. Diversity persists even though people frequently communicate their opinions and preferences to each other in an effective manner, and even though they

Political Implications for Groups and Individuals

frequently depend on one another for political guidance. The persistence of diversity is a direct consequence of the factors we have identified – low density (and hence complex) networks of political communication coupled with autoregressive patterns of influence within networks.

Disagreement Is More Likely within Extensive Communication Networks

Diversity is most likely to persist among those individuals who communicate the most, who are located in the most extensive networks of political communication. The importance of network size makes itself felt in two separate ways. First, people located within larger networks confront a higher likelihood of disagreement due to the combinatorial mathematics of probability theory. The odds increase exponentially that they will regularly encounter divergent preferences. Second, larger networks are more likely to be lower density networks (Baybeck and Huckfeldt 2002), and lower density networks increase the likelihood that people will communicate with others who are located in politically divergent communication networks.

Which citizens are most likely to encounter disagreement? Who are the individuals located in these larger, less dense networks? The primary correlates of network size tend also to be important correlates of citizenship capacity and engagement – education and organizational involvement (Baybeck and Huckfeldt 2002). Hence better educated and organizationally involved individuals are more likely to be located in larger, lower density networks, and these are the individuals who are also likely to be located in politically diverse communication networks.

Ambivalence Is a Consequence of Disagreement

The analysis in Chapter 8 demonstrates higher levels of ambivalence among individuals who encounter diverse political messages through their networks of political communication. Regardless of whether the discussants agree or disagree, an increase in the number of discussants who support a presidential candidate enhances the level of attitude intensity regarding the presidential candidates. It increases the capacity of citizens to offer more reasons for liking or disliking the presidential candidates. In contrast, increased levels of diversity within the networks produce lower levels of attitude polarization – individuals in politically diverse networks are likely to produce balanced views that include reasons for both liking and disliking particular candidates. Conversely, homogeneous networks produce higher levels of attitude polarization – individuals who only offer reasons for either liking or disliking a particular candidate, but not both.

Summary, Implications, and Conclusion

Disagreement and Ambivalence Yield Balanced, Less Polarized Opinions

Taken together, this would seem to imply that citizens who encounter politically diverse messages are more likely to hold intense but balanced (or ambivalent) views regarding politics and political candidates, and they are less likely to hold intense and polarized (or partisan) views. For these purposes we can think in terms of three ideal types – the disengaged citizens who are unable to provide justification for their attitudes regarding the candidates; the intense and polarized citizens (the partisans) who are only able to provide reasons for liking one candidate and disliking the other; and the intense and balanced citizens (the ambivalent citizens) who are able to provide both likes and dislikes regarding the candidates. Small and politically sparse networks of communication are likely to yield the low intensity citizen; large homogeneous networks are likely to yield the intensely partisan citizen; and large diverse networks are likely to yield the intensely ambivalent citizen.

Ambivalence Is Not Simply the Antithesis of Political Engagement

Although citizens who experience disagreement report less interest in the campaign, they do not demonstrate a decreased likelihood of voting. In the words of Berelson and colleagues (1954: 27), "Since partisanship increases political interest, anything that weakens partisan feelings decreases interest. Such is the effect of attitudinal 'cross-pressures.'" In the context of the disagreement effects on political ambivalence, it is thus not surprising to find disagreement effects on interest as well. At the same time, it would be a mistake to connect ambivalence too closely to a lack of political engagement.

Ambivalence is defined by higher levels of attitude intensity coupled with lower levels of attitude polarization. To the extent that particular forms of engagement depend on intensity, we should not expect to see disagreement effects on engagement. In contrast, to the extent that other forms of engagement depend on attitude polarization, we should expect to see attenuating effects that arise due to disagreement. In general, we might expect to see partisan engagement decrease as a consequence of disagreement and ambivalence, whereas non-partisan forms of engagement should be more resilient. Moreover, to the extent that the levels of political diversity within communication networks have increased in the modern era, we might expect that they will be directly related to, and perhaps responsible for, correspondingly lower levels of partisan loyalty and partisan behavior within electorates (Dalton, Flanagan, and Beck 1984).

Political Implications for Groups and Individuals

The Effects of Social Capital Depend on Network Structure and Composition

Putnam's work (1993, 2000) on social capital formation productively focuses attention on the involvement of citizens within formal organizations – choirs, bowling leagues, and so on. And as his early work emphasizes (1993), the importance of these organizational involvements lies in creating horizontal networks of social interaction. At the same time, to specify the consequences of such networks more fully, it becomes crucial to address their structure and composition. Within the context of organizational involvement, this means an understanding of the likely consequences that arise due to various types of organizations, as well as the structure and partisan composition of the networks that they generate and sustain. One might expect that some forms of organizational engagement – perhaps church groups and recreational groups – would be more likely to generate partisan homogeneity within networks. Other types of organizations – particularly the workplace – might generate networks that are politically diverse as well as being spatially dispersed and of lower density (Mondak and Mutz 2001; Baybeck and Huckfeldt 2002). In short, the form and content of social capital are complex and variegated, with important consequences for its utilization within political and civic life (Granovetter 1985; Coleman 1988).

Heterogeneous Networks May Be a Product of the Modern Era

What are the factors responsible for creating the large heterogeneous networks that create intensely ambivalent citizens versus large homogeneous networks that create the intensely partisan citizens? In an earlier era in American politics, when (1) an individual's location in social structure was dictated by religious and European ethnic group membership and (2) group membership was strongly correlated with political preference, individuals were more likely to be located in politically homogeneous networks (Levine, Carmines, and Huckfeldt 1997). In the modern era, as these conditions have become progressively attenuated, many people are more likely to be located in politically heterogeneous networks.

As an example of this process, consider the emigration of Catholic ethnics out of American cities into the suburbs, as well as their emigration out of the working class and into higher education and middle class status. At the culmination of this process, social location and political preference were much less closely correlated with membership in a religious–ethnic group. And as a consequence, Catholics became more likely to encounter politically diverse opinions within their networks of political communication. Gamm's (1999) analysis of the resilience of Irish Catholic communities in South Boston offers a substantive example to the contrary, but an example that coincides with the underlying theoretical point. To the extent that individuals are unwilling or unable to sever their ties to the group, and to the extent that the group maintains distinctive political loyalties, this process can be arrested. As a consequence, political homogeneity within networks might be maintained.

Disagreement Is Related to the Decline of Partisanship

The implication of this argument for the decline of partisanship becomes quite clear. One of the most important trends across the past century, and particularly during the post–World War II period, was a suburbanization process that undermined the spatial integrity of earlier social and political groups (Warner 1978; 1968). These groups were dislodged from both urban neighborhoods and farm communities, and relocated in suburban locales that were likely to produce mixed patterns of settlement, exposing the new suburbanites to a politically heterogeneous population mix with inevitable consequences for the composition of social networks.

The role of politically diverse networks in the decline of partisanship extends beyond a residential sorting and mixing process. The modern era is characterized by an increasingly complicated spatial organization of individual involvements. The typical American lives in one place, works in another, and bowls (or plays tennis) somewhere else (Brady and Huckfeldt 2002). Each of these locales provides opportunities for recurring social interactions – for the construction of complex, low density, and often heterogeneous communication networks. Hence, if measures were available – they are not – we would expect to see a dramatic increase in the complexity and political diversity of communication networks over the past one hundred years, and we would also expect to see a close relationship between increased heterogeneity within networks and the decline of partisanship within the population.

Political Homogeneity Persists within Networks under Particular Circumstances

The most notable examples of persistent homogeneity within communication networks are related to the politics of race and ethnicity. In documenting the suburban migration of Jews from Boston and the unwillingness of the Irish to leave, Gamm (1999) demonstrates the importance of spatial organization for the vitality of social and political groups, and presumably for the maintenance of interaction patterns within the groups. Some groups are more effective than others at restricting interaction beyond the group and hence at creating and maintaining communication networks that are more likely to be politically homogeneous. The Boston Irish provide an historical illustration of an introverted group, and even though the maintenance of politically homogeneous communication networks has had little to do with their unwillingness to leave the city, it is an inevitable if unintended consequence.

In contrast, African Americans illustrate a very different set of circumstances – a group whose members have been denied full entry into the surrounding society. Nearly 150 years after the end of slavery, and 50 years after *Brown* v. *the Board of Education* provided a constitutional prohibition of de jure segregation, various manifestations of racial separateness continue to persist. In particular, communication networks that include both whites and blacks are relatively rare phenomena.

When politics is organized by race, as it frequently continues to be, we can expect to see the maintenance of homogeneity within networks of political communication. In the Mississippi presidential election of 1984, more than 90 percent of blacks supported Walter Mondale and more than 80 percent of whites supported Ronald Reagan. In the Chicago mayoral election of 1983, more than 90 percent of blacks supported Harold Washington and more than 90 percent of whites supported Bernie Epton. In the 1995 O. J. Simpson trial, substantial majorities of whites believed that Simpson was guilty, and substantial majorities of blacks believed he was innocent. Given the low rates of interaction and communication across racial lines, it becomes mathematically inevitable that very few whites or blacks will encounter disagreement over racially structured opinions and preferences.

Diversity Produces Important Implications for Political Dynamics

The presence or absence of widespread disagreement within communication networks generates important consequences for the dynamics of individual preference formation and for the convergence of aggregate opinion. Rather than insulating individuals from the external political environment, social communication carries with it the potential to magnify the consequences of the external environment by exposing individuals to nonredundant, politically disparate information. In particular, our argument points to the important dynamic implications of autoregressive influence within the context of low density networks – networks characterized by individuals who serve as bridges of communication between and among otherwise disconnected individuals. Within the autoregressive influence process we have specified, the conversion of any single individual to a particular opinion or preference carries the potential to enhance or impede the influence of dyadic information flows throughout the networks of relationships within which the individual is located, most particularly within dyads that do not include this individual as a participant.

It is important to reiterate that our argument does not suggest a determinate outcome to the political communication process that occurs through networks of interdependent citizens. Citizens are continually exposed to exogenous political events, not only through the print and electronic news media, but also through the receipt of network mediated information. These exogenous, real-world events produce individual opinion changes that generate ripple effects throughout these networks of political communication. And as the distribution of opinion changes within communication networks, the influence of information communicated through particular dyads changes as well.

The mix of information to which many citizens are exposed is heterogeneous, unstable, and subject to the impact of events in the political environment. Rather than simply serving as a buffer, networks of political communication also serve to transmit this information in a way that connects individuals to the political process. This process is not politically neutral – it is an important element of an inherently political process. The flow of information that occurs among and between citizens is best seen within the context of the opinion distributions that exist in these larger communication networks. In some contexts, autoregressive influence and low density communication networks serve to minimize the impact of external events, but in others they draw the attention of citizens to these events, as well as magnifying the consequences of these events for individual opinion.

CONCLUSION

The argument that motivates this book implies several observational challenges for political scientists and others who would understand democratic politics. First and foremost, politics cannot be understood wholly in terms of aggregate groups of citizens any more than it can be understood wholly in terms of individuals. An analysis that focuses on individual citizens in isolation from one another is politically and scientifically incomplete. And analyses are similarly compromised if they focus entirely on aggregates – states, counties, precincts – without taking into account the patterns of interdependence that exist among and between the individuals who populate these aggregate units. The moral is that politics, at both micro and macro levels, revolves around interdependent citizens, and unless this interdependence is taken into account, we run the risk of ignoring a fundamental aspect of politics.

A primary challenge of political analysis is to specify the nature of this interdependence. Who depends on whom, or what? What are the circumstances that create this interdependence? What are the consequences of interdependence, both for individuals and for politically relevant aggregates and groups? In the words of Erbring and Young (1979), the goal is to move beyond simple contextual explanations that depend on "social telepathy" – unspecified connections between individuals and their surroundings.

In general, the theoretical and observational consequences produced by these systems of communication and influence among citizens are often underestimated. The nonlinear, stochastic complexity of the underlying mechanisms renders any direct translation into simple causal models a relatively futile undertaking. Endogeneity problems are endemic: People impose their preferences on their own patterns of interaction, but they also respond to the content of those interactions (Achen and Shively 1995). And even when the endogeneity problems are addressed, other problems and consequences of nonlinear interdependence remain to be tackled.

None of these observational complexities should be allowed to truncate theoretical development. The solution to the problem is neither to minimize nor to ignore the methodological and theoretical challenges. This effort has employed survey research, social network name generators, snowball surveys, and agent-based simulations, but there is no single solution to these issues. Only an eclectic blend of innovative methodologies and approaches is likely to generate progress in our basic understanding of the political consequences that arise due to patterns of interdependence among citizens in democratic politics.

Our hope is that we have persuaded the reader that agreement and homogeneity are not the determinate outcomes of communication and influence among citizens, just as disagreement and diversity do not constitute evidence of individual independence. Dynamically complex patterns of communication and influence yield outcomes that are far more compelling – outcomes in which agreement as well as disagreement might be socially sustained, and in which deliberation as well as diversity might jointly persist within the communication networks that connect the ordinary citizens of democratic politics.

Appendix A

The Indianapolis–St. Louis Study

The Sample

The main respondent sample (n = 2,174) for the Indianapolis–St. Louis Study was drawn from lists of registered voters in St. Louis City and County and Marion County (Indianapolis). The response rate was 58 percent, calculated as the ratio of completions to the sum of completions, refusals, partials, and identified respondents who were persistently unavailable to complete the interview. The response rate drops to 53 percent if we add to the base those respondents in households where no one ever answered the phone after repeated call backs. The cooperation rate – completions to the base of completions, refusals, and partials – is 64 percent. Comparable rates for the discussant sample (n = 1,475) were 59 percent, 56 percent, and 72 percent.

The weekly pre-election interview target was 20 main respondents and 15 respondents at each of the two study sites, and discussant interviews were completed within three weeks of the relevant main respondent interview. After the election, interviews were completed as rapidly as possible without weekly targets, and the time spacing of main respondent and discussant interviews was not controlled. On this basis, 612 main respondents and 452 discussants were interviewed from March through June; 732 main respondents and 384 discussants were interviewed from July through the election; and 830 main respondents and 639 discussants were interviewed after the election through early January.

Eighty percent of the 2,174 main respondents responded to the request for first names of discussants. Of those who provided this social network information, 60.8 percent agreed to provide additional contact information (surnames, phone numbers, and so forth) on individuals in the network, 25.7 percent refused, and the remainder agreed to a call back to collect the information. Ultimately, at least one discussant was interviewed for 872 main respondents, or 40 percent of the entire main respondent sample of 2,174.

In order to establish a *post hoc* baseline sample for the study of campaign effects on political activation (see Chapter 5), we returned to the field in October and November of 1997 using the same questionnaire and sampling design. During this period we completed 438 interviews with main respondents and 265 interviews with their discussants.

Timing Responses

Response times for questions were measured by the interviewers using activated timers which recorded the time elapsed between the end of the question and the beginning of the respondent's answer. In addition, latent timers recorded the time elapsed between the answers to two sequenced questions, and these latent timers are used in data verification procedures.

Several problems may occur in the use of activated timers. First, respondents sometimes answer a question before the question is completely read. In such an instance, the interviewer was instructed to record the response time as being simultaneous by instantaneously turning the activated timer on and off. Second, after stopping the activated timer and recording the respondent's answer to the question, the interviewers are asked whether the timing was successful, and thus we are able to redefine unsuccessful timings as missing data. The primary reason for an unsuccessful timing is a "trigger happy" interviewer who stops the timer too quickly. Third, respondents sometimes ask for clarification about a question. Interviewers were instructed to let the activated timer run during these questions, adding to a highly skewed distribution of response times. Hence, the activated timing is set to missing when the recorded time lies more than three standard deviations above the sample mean. Finally, interviewers occasionally and inadvertently erased valid timings by using a skip command to return to an earlier question at the respondent's request. In these cases, the recorded times are artificially low – faster than the time that is actually required to turn the timer on and off – due to the interviewer's action in returning to the original place in the interview. Interviewers were instructed to reset such activated timers to missing, but we are also able to validate the activated timings by comparing them with the elapsed time between the answers to sequenced questions. If the latter is too short to allow a question to be read (one second), the time measurement is set to missing.

Measuring Preferences and Judgments across the Campaign

Candidate evaluations in election campaigns are moving targets, even in the 1996 campaign, which seemingly lacked the volatility of more dramatic contests. When we began interviewing early in March, a long list of Republican candidates were in the race, and no one knew what role Ross Perot would play. By early in the summer, however, the major party candidates had been determined, even if the intentions of Mr. Perot were still ambiguous. Thus, we adopted several different questions to ascertain the voting intentions of the main respondents, as well as to ascertain the main respondents' judgments regarding their discussants' political preferences.

Before the campaign had identified the candidates with some certainty, defined as the period prior to the first week of July, we used an open-ended question for the respondent's own intention: "If the election was held today, whom would you like to be elected?" We used a closed-choice question for the respondent's perception of the discussant: "As things currently stand, do you think [name] will vote for the Democratic candidate, the Republican candidate, an independent candidate, or do you think [name] probably won't vote?"

Beginning the first week of July, after the major party nominees were clarified, we asked: "Thinking about the presidential election, will you vote for Bill Clinton, Bob Dole, some other candidate, or haven't you decided?" And: "As things currently stand, do you think [name] will vote for Bill Clinton, Bob Dole, some other candidate, or do you think [she/he] probably won't vote?"

After the election, the questions became: "Thinking about the presidential election, did you vote for Bill Clinton, Bob Dole, or did you vote for some other candidate?" And: "Do you think [name] voted for Bill Clinton, Bob Dole, some other candidate, or do you think [she/he] didn't vote?"

Before the major party candidates were clarified, only trivial numbers of respondents reported supporting an independent candidate other than Perot, but significant numbers of respondents reported supporting some other Democrat or Republican, and thus in the first wave of the study – when we used the first open-ended version of the question regarding respondent vote choice – we distinguished between support for Democratic candidates, Republican candidates, and Perot. After the major party candidates were clarified, only a very insignificant number of respondents named a candidate other than Dole, Clinton, or Perot, and thus we set these other candidates to missing.

Network Name Generators

Respondents were randomly assigned one of two social network name generators in soliciting the first names of those individuals with whom they communicated. The text for these questions is shown below. One of the questions – based on discussions of "important matters" – is built on the name generator used in the General Social Survey during the 1980s (Burt 1986). The other – based on explicitly political discussion – is based on the experience of the 1984 South Bend Study (Huckfeldt and Sprague 1995). The texts of these questions, which are designed to be parallel in construction, are as follows:

Important matters. From time to time, people discuss important matters with other people. Looking back over the last few months, I'd like to know the people you talked with about matters that are important to you. These people might or might not be relatives. Can you think of anyone?

Politics. From time to time, people discuss government, elections and politics with other people. I'd like to know the people you talk with about these matters. These people might or might not be relatives. Can you think of anyone?

Appendix B

The Opinion Simulation Software

By referring to the Opinion Simulation as an agent-based model, we intend to convey the idea that the individuals are represented as separate, self-contained computer objects and that those objects carry out actions according to information that they collect and maintain on their own. An agent-based model generates "bottom-up" results because the agents are highly individualized, and their behavior is not dictated by a high level entity. Beyond the agents, where our analytical focus resides, other types of objects exist as well – objects that represent the environment and objects that collect data and show it on the screen. The environment in the Opinion model is rather like a series of chess boards, where agents are able to position themselves within any particular board or move from one board to another.

About the Code

The Opinion model is written in Objective-C and makes liberal use of the Swarm Simulation libraries. Objective-C, a language invented by Brad Cox, was chosen for Swarm because it is a simple extension of the C language that incorporates concepts from object-oriented programming. Objective-C is not so well known as C++, another object-oriented extension of C, but it has many of the same advantages. Programs written in Objective-C are reasonably fast, and the language is quite easy to learn if one has experience in C or Java. Programs that access the Swarm libraries can be written in other languages as well. After Objective-C, the next most frequently used language is Java. The Swarm libraries also have built-in support for javascript and C++, but these require advanced understanding of DCOM and are thus not widely used.

The Swarm program that was used to generate the results described in Chapters 6 and 7 is available without charge. The web address for materials related to this project is: http://lark.cc.ku.edu/~pauljohn/Swarm/

The Opinion Simulation Software

MySwarmCode/OpinionFormation. The code is available in a gzipped tar archive called Opinion-2.0.tar.gz. That software is made available under the greater GNU Public License, and we offer no warranty of any kind. We are not assuming any responsibility for your inconvenience or for any damage that you might cause using this program, but we have no reason to expect that any damage or inconvenience will occur. The Opinion program is not a "free standing" piece of software. Instead, it liberally draws on the Swarm Simulation libraries, and thus the Swarm libraries must be available on your computer.

If you do not have the Swarm libraries in your computer system, we encourage you first to browse through the information in this appendix and then consider installing Swarm. Swarm is developed primarily on Unix or Unix-like platforms, such as GNU/Linux or Sun Solaris, but it can be run under Mac OSX and newer versions of Microsoft Windows if you are willing to install the required supporting libraries. You can find out more about how to download and install the Swarm libraries at the website of the Swarm Development Group: http://www.swarm.org.

A detailed description of how to build or install Swarm lies beyond the scope of this book. These tasks are accomplished with a standard set of GNU tools, including the GNU compiler collection, libtool, and the auto tools (automake, autoconf, autoheader). Those who have experience working in the GNU framework, which is part of the Free Software Foundation, will find this to be familiar. For those who have no experience of that kind, there are pre-built ("binary") distributions available for most systems.

If Swarm Simulation System (version 2.1.121 or newer) is installed on your system, compiling and running a Swarm program like Opinion should be straightforward. Make sure that you have properly installed Swarm and can run the sample Swarm applications (such as Heatbugs). Then proceed as follows. Untar the archive file (Opinion-2.0.tar.gz) by entering the following statement at the terminal:

tar xzvf Opinion-2.0.tar.gz

This creates a directory called "Opinion-2.0," and a number of files will be located in that directory. In Table B.1, we categorize the files by function. Some files make up the program itself and control the way it is compiled and initialized. In addition, a subdirectory named "doc" contains HTML-formatted documentation. That documentation is generated by a program called autogsdoc. Within the code itself, we have embedded a large number of descriptions and comments, and the autogsdoc program scans through the code and creates a set of HTML files. One set of the documentation is available online in case you want to examine it without downloading the archive: http://lark.cc.ku.edu/~pauljohn/Swarm/MySwarmCode/OpinionFormation/Opinion-Doc.

Table B.1. *Classes and files in Opinion-2.0.*

These are the most important classes in Opinion-2.0. The code that contains a class is separated into two parts. There is a "header" file with the extension "h" and an "implementation" file that has the extension "m."

A. Classes that initiate, administer, and oversee the simulation

ObserverSwarm (ObserverSwarm.h, ObserverSwarm.m): The top level swarm in a run that uses the graphical interface. This controls images on the screen and triggers the actions of lower level swarms.

ModelSwarm (ModelSwarm.h, ModelSwarm.m): An intermediate level swarm that causes the creation of all the substantively important objects in the simulation, including agents and the environment.

AgentSwarm (ModelSwarm.h, ModelSwarm.m): An intermediate level swarm that is used to group together the elements needed to schedule agent actions.

Parameters (Parameters.h, Parameters.m, paramIvars.h): A high level object that collects input parameters and makes them available to any other object that needs to know their values.

B. Classes used to create agents and control their actions

Citizen (Citizen.h, Citizen.m): Features common to all citizens.

Axelrod (Axelrod.h, Axelrod.m): Agents for the Axelrod culture model, subclassed from Citizen.

Coleman (Coleman.h, Coleman.m): Agents for the Coleman model, subclassed from Axelrod.

SelectiveCitizen (SelectiveCitizen.h, SelectiveCitizen.m): Agents who are able to remember the identities of other agents and selectively interact with them, subclassed from Axelrod.

HJCitizen (HJCitizen.h, HJCitizen.m): Agents for the network model of autoregressive influence, subclassed from SelectiveCitizen.

C. Classes that agents and the observer use to keep records

Position (Position.h, Position.m): An object that an agent uses to remember its location within a particular environment.

MovingAverage (MovingAverage.h, MovingAverage.m): Agents use moving averages to summarize their experience.

Attribute (Attribute.h, Attribute.m): An attribute is a "memory object" that an agent can use to remember the specific qualities that are observed in another agent.

Table B.1. *(continued)*

D. Classes used to create the environment in which agents exist and move about

MultiGrid2d (MultiGrid2d.h, MultiGrid2d.m): A two-dimensional grid of cells that allows many agents to inhabit the same cell.

MultiGridCell (MultiGridCell.h, MultiGridCell.m): A general purpose class that can be used for the cells in a MultiGrid2d. This is typically subclassed to make specific applications.

AppSpecificCell (AppSpecificCell.h, AppSpecificCell.m): A subclass of MultiGridCell that includes the specific details of the Opinion model.

AVLSet.h (AVLSet.h, AVLSet.m): A Swarm-style collection that is backed by an AVL tree (binary search tree).

E. Classes used to run simulations in batch mode

BatchSwarm (BatchSwarm.h, BatchSwarm.m): A nongraphical replacement for ObserverSwarm.

BatchColormap (BatchColormap.h, BatchColormap.m, colors.m): Handles colors for usage in the BatchRaster object.

BatchRaster (BatchRaster.h, BatchRaster.m): A class that can write a file in the "ppm" format to record the raster on which agent opinions are displayed.

MyArguments (MyArguments.h, MyArguments.m, paramIvars.h): Handles command line arguments when the program is run.

Why Are There So Many Files?

Newcomers are often bewildered by the large number of different files that make up the program. Generally speaking, the different kinds of objects that will exist in the model are represented by separate files. The subdivision of different elements is justified on both practical and theoretical grounds. The practical side is obvious: By keeping code in small, separate, easy to understand sections, the danger of coding mistakes is reduced. Another practical benefit is that work on separate small bits of a project is more likely to be reusable for other purposes if it is cleanly separated.

The practical justification is important, but it is dwarfed by the theoretical justification for this model building strategy. This framework builds useful programs because one strives to separate and compartmentalize different elements in a way that reflects the substantive considerations at hand. This is one of the most important justifications for object-oriented programming. By far the most important concept in object-oriented programming is *class*. A class consists of a set of variables and methods (actions that can be carried out, messages that can be understood by members of the class). To a social scientist, the idea of a class will be very similar to an "ideal type." When a program runs, a class is used to create generic objects, which inherit the properties (variables and methods) from the class. One can create hundreds or thousands of instances from a class, and then assign individualized properties to them by setting the values of their individual (instance) variables. A program can be written so that many different types of agents (agents created as instances of many classes) are active at the same time.

Another important concept in object-oriented programming is inheritance. Classes can be created in a hierarchy. A class can inherit properties from its *superclasses*, which are in turn inherited by its *subclasses*. For example, in Opinion-2.0, the top-level class for the agents is called Citizen. A Citizen has variables that are common to all agents we might ever want to use. The Citizen class, however, is an abstract, general purpose class.

The substantively important elements in the model are controlled by the subclasses of the Citizen class. The Citizen class has the fundamental ability to keep track of an agent's position and to schedule the agent's movement. The Citizen class does not have the ability to interact with other agents. That is a specialized action that must be carried out by subclasses. The customization of the Citizen class occurs in the way that the agents choose other agents for interactions and then respond to the input they receive. The Axelrod class inherits from Citizen, and it can be used to create instances that behave in the way Axelrod's Culture Model stipulates. The other classes that we offer, most important, Coleman and HJCitizen, are subclasses that override the substantive details – the ways in which agents find each other for interactions and adjust their opinions.

Running the Model

In order to compile the program, open a terminal and change into the directory where Opinion-2.0 is stored. Type the command "make". The "make" program is able to read the Makefile from the directory, which controls how the compiler turns the code into an executable program. As long as the system's Swarm setup is sound, then one should see a lot of output written in the terminal as the object files that represent the individual classes are created and the executable program "opinion" is created by linking them together. Then the program can be run by typing the command:

```
./opinion
```

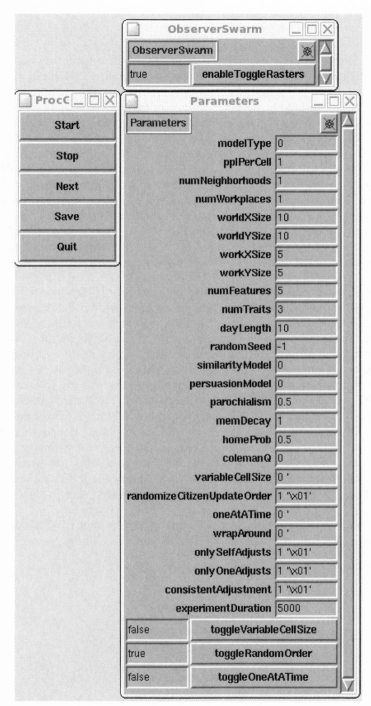

Figure B.1. The graphical interface.

When the program starts, three windows should appear on the screen. A snapshot of these windows is displayed in Figure B.1. On the left side is the Swarm control panel, which can start and stop the simulation. On the bottom right, is the display of the Parameters class. These values can be selected to determine the kinds of agents that are created, the number of issues (or "features"), the number of opinions per issue ("traits"), the number and size of home neighborhoods and workplaces for these agents, and many other parameters. These parameters are described in detail within the source code for the program and its documentation.

The third window at start time is a probe display for the Observer Swarm. Only one option appears in that window: enableToggleRasters is going to control how many "zoom raster" pictures are shown for each home neighborhood after the model is started. (A "raster" is a rectangular array of colors, called zoom rasters because they can be resized by the user.) If enableToggleRasters is "false," then the screen will show one colored raster picture for each issue in the model. If there are five home neighborhoods, and five issues, that means there will be 25 raster pictures to summarize the state of affairs. Since that clutters the screen, the option is available to condense the screen output. If enableToggleRasters is set equal to "true," it means that one raster is shown for each neighborhood, and the user can use the left mouse button to click on the raster and cycle through the different issues used in the model.

After the start button is pressed, the parameter values are put to use, the model objects are created, and the simulation begins. Three different kinds of windows should appear on the screen. First, the zoom rasters appear. They use colors to display the state of opinion within each cell of each home neighborhood. In Figure B.2, we display just one raster, because the parameters that are shown in Figure B.1 indicate that there is only one home grid and we have set enableToggleRasters to "true." So this raster is showing the state of opinion on one issue.

Second, as illustrated in Figure B.3, four graphs appear which display the time lines of several variables. The "Perceived Similarity" graph shows

Figure B.2. A raster represents one home grid.

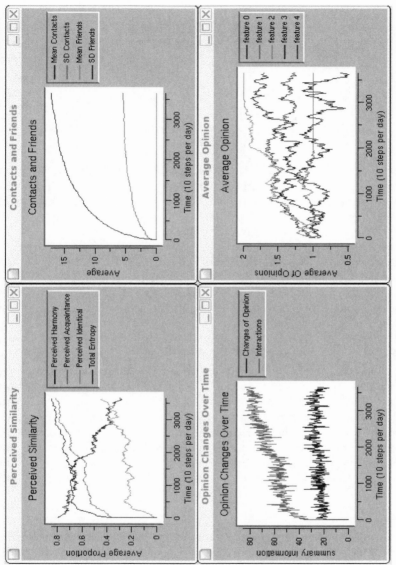

Figure B.3. Graphs summarize the state of key variables.

229

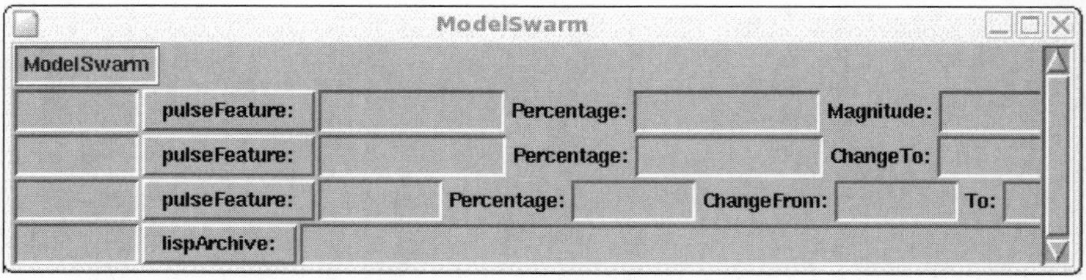

Figure B.4. Interaction with the model through the graphical interface.

averages of the experiences of the agents. The graph entitled "Opinion Changes Over Time" records the number of agents that have had interactions during the most recent "day" and it also shows the number that have changed their minds. The "Average Opinion" graph simply shows an average of agent opinions. Although the average in itself is not inherently meaningful, it is a useful way to track swings and stabilization in public opinion. Finally, "Contacts and Friends" shows data about the number of other agents that have been contacted and the number that are considered to be trusted discussants (or "friends" for short). A trusted discussant is one with whom the agent agrees on more than one-half of the issues.

Third, a window called "Model Swarm" appears. This window, shown in Figure B.4, allows the user to interact with the simulation in a few ways. The first three items represent different kinds of exogenous shocks that can be applied to the model. One can take a randomly selected set of agents who hold opinion 1 on issue 2 and change their opinion to the value 2, for example. These "shock" methods were the last major item introduced into the code of Opinion-2.0. The last item in the Model Swarm window allows the user to enter a file name and save the exact state of the simulation into a file.

About Days and Schedules

We divide time into units called "days" or "periods" in order to schedule agent actions. In the Parameters class, there is a variable called dayLength, which represents the number of Swarm time steps that make up a day in the Opinion simulation. At the outset of each day, each agent is sent a signal to "wake up" and plan its activities. The agent will remain at home for a randomly chosen number of time steps, and then will go to work. At some time during the day (a randomly chosen time), the agent will initiate an interaction with another agent chosen from the agent's current context. If no other agents are nearby, then the agent cannot have a political interaction and that agent does nothing. At the end of the day, each agent returns to its home position. The cycle repeats indefinitely, with the agents being woken up in random order and scheduling their movements and interactions according to the logic we have specified.

The Opinion-2.0 model has several important features that might interest Swarm programmers. First, it is an implementation of dynamic scheduling. The actions of the agents are determined by evolving, individual level processes in which agents decide what to do. Second, there are different fine-grained approaches to coding a model with dynamic scheduling. The essence of these alternative approaches is as follows.

One approach is to use a single "master schedule" and have the agents plan their actions and then place them onto the master schedule. The master schedule then accumulates many actions that are supposed to happen at a given time step, and when that time step arrives, all the concurrent actions are processed according to one of several rules. The agent actions might be processed in a first-come, first-serve method, or the agents might be randomized and their actions carried out.

The alternative approach is to have no master schedule to carry the actions of the agents. Instead, treat each agent as if it were a Swarm in and of itself. That means it has the ability to create a Schedule object and place actions onto it. This approach is conceptually closer to the philosophy of agent-based modeling. The central Swarm schedule then ticks through time and triggers actions in all lower level schedules that are set for that time step. We are happy to report that we have implemented these various detailed scheduling regimes and the results of the simulation are not affected. The user can replicate these differences by using C preprocessor flags that are described in the documentation.

Serialization

A unique and important feature of the Opinion-2.0 code is that it implements serialization. Serialization refers to the ability to save the simulation at a particular time, and then later restart the simulation at that point. We have used the Swarm tools that use the Scheme language (a Lisp variant) to store the state of the simulation. It is a rather elaborate process to make sure that the state of the simulation is saved in its entirety. Not only must one save the parameters, but one must also save the agents, the precise state of all their instance variables, and all the objects that the individual agents are using to record their experiences. In the stability analysis of Chapter 7, we demonstrate the value of serialization by restarting models and subjecting them to random shocks.

Appendix B
Batch Mode

The graphical interface is especially useful for interacting with a model and debugging it. After the code stabilizes, one wants to run the model over and over again, changing the random seed that starts the random number generators, and changing the parameters. In Opinion-2.0, we recommend that the command line interface be used to conduct batch runs.

In the terminal, if one types:

./opinion –b

the model will run in batch mode according to the default parameters. All the important parameters can be adjusted from the command line, however. If one types this:

./opinion –help

one will see the following output which describes all the variables that can be controlled from the command line:

Usage: opinion [OPTION ...]

-s, – varyseed	Select random number seed from current time
-S, – seed=INTEGER	Specify seed for random numbers
-b, – batch	Run in batch mode
-m, – mode=MODE	Specify mode of use (for archiving)
-h, – numNhoods=numNhoods	N of Neighborhoods
-t, – show-current-time	Show current time in control panel
–no-init-file	Inhibit loading of ~/.swarmArchiver
-W, – numWorkpl=numWorkPlaces	N of workplaces
-n, – pplPerCell=N	Set pplPerCell
-v, – verbose	Activate verbose messages
-I, – inputfile=filename	set fn
-R, – run=RunNumber	Run is ...
–seed=SeedNumber	Seed
-p, – parochialism=Parochialism	Parochialism
-w, – worldsize=WorldSize	Dimension w and h
-T, – numTraits=numTraits	N of Opinions (traits)
-F, – numFeatures=numFeatures	N of Issues (Features)
-M, – modelType=modelType	Model Type, 0 ... x
-c, – variableCellSize=VCS	VariableCellSize
-H, – homeProb=homeProb	Probability of being home

The Opinion Simulation Software

-d, – dayLength=dayLength	Time steps per day
-e, – onlySelfAdjusts=0 or 1	Only self may adjust opinion
-o, – onlyOneAdjusts=0 or 1	Only one may adjust opinion
-a, – consistentAdjustment=0 or 1	
-q, – colemanQ=colemanQ	Coleman Q
-r, – wrap=0 or 1	wrapping neighborhoods
-E, – experimentDuration=integer	experiment duration
-f, – input=input useless	Does nothing
-u, – distFeature=disturbedFeat	Disturbed feature
-g, – magDisturb=mag	Disturbance Magnitude/Value (model dependent)
-P, – pctDisturb=disturbPct	Disturbed Percentage
-?, – help	Give this help list
– usage	Give a short usage message
-V, – version	Print program version

The command line options can be either the short form, using one dash and no equal sign, or two dashes as well as an equal sign. These two commands are the same:

./opinion –b –T3 –F5 –w10 –n1 –h5 –W3

./ opinion -b – numTraits3 – numFeatures=5 – worldsize=10 – pplPerCell=1 – numHoods=5 – numWorkpl=3

Either of these will initiate a batch run of the model, with five issues (features) and three opinions on each issue (traits). There will be five home neighborhoods, and the size of each home grid will be 10 cells square. There will be one agent created per cell in the home grids. There will be three separate workplace grids. Any parameters that are not set in the command line will assume default values.

References

Abelson, Robert P. 1995. Attitude Extremity. In *Attitude Strength: Antecedents and Consequences*, eds. Richard E. Petty and John A. Krosnick. Mahwah, New Jersey: Erlbaum, 25–41.

Abelson, Robert P. 1964. Mathematical Models of the Distribution of Attributes Under Controversy. In Norman Fredriksen and Harold Gulliksen, eds. *Contributions to Mathematical Psychology*. New York: Holt, Rinehart, and Winston, 142–60.

Abelson, Robert P. 1979. Social Clusters and Opinion Clusters. In Paul W. Holland and Samuel Leinhardt, eds., *Perspectives on Social Network Research*. New York: Academic Press, 239–56.

Achen, Christopher H. and W. Phillips Shively. 1995. *Cross-Level Inference*. Chicago: University of Chicago Press.

Alvarez, Michael and John Brehm. 2002. *Hard Choices, Easy Answers: Values, Information, and American Public Opinion*. Princeton, NJ: Princeton University Press.

Anselin, Luc. 1988. *Spatial Econometrics: Methods and Models*. Boston: Kluwer.

Apple Computer, Inc. 2002. *The Objective-C Programming Language*. Apple Computer, Inc. http://developer.apple.com/techpubs/macosx/ Cocoa/Objective C/index.html.

Asch, Solomon E. 1955. Opinions and Social Pressure. *Scientific American* 193: 31–5.

Asch, Solomon E. 1963. Effects of Group Pressure Upon the Modification and Distortion of Judgments. In *Groups, Leadership and Men: Research in Human Relations*, ed., Harold Guetzkow. New York: Russell and Russell, 177–90. Originally published by Carnegie Press, 1951.

Axelrod, Robert, 1997a. The Dissemination of Culture: A Model with Local Convergence and Global Polarization. *Journal of Conflict Resolution* 41: 203–26.

Axelrod, Robert. 1997b. *The Complexity of Cooperation: Agent-Based Models of Competition and Collaboration*. Princeton, NJ: Princeton University Press.

Axtell, Robert, Robert Axelrod, Joshua M. Epstein, and Michael D. Cohen. 1996. Aligning Simulation Models: A Case Study and Results. *Computational and Mathematical Organization Theory* 1: 123–41.

Balch, Tucker. 2000. Hierarchical Social Entropy: An Information Theoretic Measure of Robot Team Diversity. *Autonomous Robots* 8: 209–37.

References

Barabasi, Albert-Laszlo. 2002. *Linked: The New Science of Networks*. Cambridge, MA: Perseus.

Barber, Benjamin. 1984. *Strong Democracy: Participatory Politics for a New Age*. Berkeley, CA: University of California Press.

Bassili, John N. 1993. Response Latency versus Certainty As Indexes of the Strength of Voting Intentions in a CATI Survey. *Public Opinion Quarterly* 57: 54–61.

Bassili, John N. 1995. Response Latency and the Accessibility of Voting Intentions: What Contributes to Accessibility and How it Affects Vote Choice. *Personality and Social Psychology Bulletin* 21: 686–95.

Bassili, John N. 1996. Meta-Judgmental versus Operative Indexes of Psychological Attributes: The Case of Measures of Attitude Strength. *Journal of Personality and Social Psychology* 71: 637–53.

Baybeck, Brady and Robert Huckfeldt. 2002a. Urban Contexts, Spatially Dispersed Networks, and the Diffusion of Political Information. *Political Geography* 21: 195–220.

Baybeck, Brady and Robert Huckfeldt. 2002b. Spatially Dispersed Ties Among Interdependent Citizens: Connecting Individuals and Aggregates. *Political Analysis* 10: 261–75.

Berelson, Bernard R., Paul F. Lazarsfeld, and William N. McPhee. 1954. *Voting: A Study of Opinion Formation in a Presidential Election*. Chicago: University of Chicago Press.

Berent, Matthew K. and Jon A. Krosnick. 1995. The Relation between Political Attitude Importance and Knowledge Structure. In Milton Lodge and Kathleen M. McGraw, eds., *Political Judgment: Structure and Process*. Ann Arbor, MI: University of Michigan Press, 91–109.

Besag, J. E. 1974. Spatial Interaction and the Statistical Analysis of Lattice Systems. *Journal of the Royal Statistical Society, Series B* 36: 192–236.

Besag, J. E. and C. Kooperberg. 1995. On Conditional and Intrinsic Autoregressions. *Biometrika* 82: 733–46.

Blau, Peter M. 1960. Structural Effects. *American Sociological Review* 25: 178–93.

Books, John W. and Charles L. Prysby. 1991. *Political Behavior and the Local Context*. New York: Praeger.

Boudon, Raymond. 1986. *Theories of Social Change*. Berkeley, CA: University of California Press.

Boyd, Lawrence H. and Gudmund R. Iversen. 1979. *Contextual Analysis: Concepts and Statistical Techniques*. Belmont, CA: Wadsworth.

Bryk, Anthony S. and Stephen W. Raudenbush. 1992. *Hierarchical Linear Models: Applications and Data Analysis Methods*. Newbury Park, CA: Sage.

Burt, Ronald S. 1986. A Note on Sociometric Order in the General Social Survey Network Data. *Social Networks* 8: 149–74.

Burt, Ronald S. 1992. *Structural Holes*. Cambridge, MA: Harvard University Press.

Calvert, Randall L. 1985. The Value of Biased Information: A Rational Choice Model of Political Advice. *Journal of Politics* 47: 530–55.

Cameron, A. Colin and Pravin K. Trivedi. 1998. *Regression Analysis of Count Data*. New York: Cambridge University Press.

Carley, Kathleen. 1993. A Theory of Group Stability. *American Sociological Review* 56: 331–54.

References

Carmines, Edward G. and James A. Stimson. 1989. *Issue Evolution: Race and the Transformation of American Politics*. Princeton, NJ: Princeton University Press.

Coleman, James S. 1988. Social Capital in the Creation of Human Capital. *American Journal of Sociology* 94: S95–S120.

Coleman, James S. 1957. *Community Conflict*. New York: Free Press.

Coleman, James S. 1964. *Introduction to Mathematical Sociology*. New York: Free Press of Glencoe.

Congdon, Peter. 2001. *Bayesian Statistical Modeling*. West Sussex, England: Wiley.

Congdon, Peter. 2003. *Applied Bayesian Modeling*. West Sussex, England: Wiley.

Conover, Pamela Johnston, Donald D. Searing, and Ivor M. Crewe. 2002. The Deliberative Potential of Political Discussion. *British Journal of Political Science* 32: 21–62.

Converse, Philip E. 1995. Foreword. In Richard E. Petty and Jon A. Krosnick, eds., *Attitude Strength: Antecedents and Consequences*. Mahwah, NJ: Erlbaum, xi–xvii.

Converse, Philip E. 1964. The Nature of Belief Systems in Mass Publics. In D. E. Apter, ed., *Ideology and Discontent*. New York: Free Press, 206–61.

Cox, Brad and Andrew J. Novobliski. 1986. *Object-Oriented Programming: An Evolutionary Approach*, Second edition. Addison Wesley Publishing Company.

Dalton, Russell, Scott Flanagan, and Paul Beck, eds. 1984. *Electoral Change in Advanced Industrial Democracies*. Princeton, NJ: Princeton University Press.

Davis, James A., Joe L. Spaeth, and Carolyn Huson. 1961. Analyzing Effects of Group Composition. *American Sociological Review* 26: 215–25.

DeAngelis, Donald L. and Louis J. Gross, eds. 1992. *Individual-Based Models and Approaches in Ecology: Populations, Communities, and Ecosystems*. New York: Chapman and Hall.

Delli Carpini, Michael X. and Scott Keeter. 1993. Measuring Political Knowledge: Putting First Things First. *American Journal of Political Science* 37: 1179–206.

Delli Carpini, Michael X. and Scott Keeter. 1996. *What Americans Know about Politics and Why It Matters*. New Haven, CT: Yale University Press.

Denton, Robert. 1994. *The 1992 Presidential Campaign: A Communication Perspective*. Westport, CT: Praeger.

Downs, Anthony. 1957. *An Economic Theory of Democracy*. New York: Harper and Row.

Druckman, James N. and Kjersten R. Nelson. 2003. Framing and Deliberation: How Citizens' Conversations Limit Elite Influence. *American Journal of Political Science* 47: 728–44.

Durkheim, Emile. [1897] 1951. *Suicide*. Translated by John A. Spaulding and George Simpson. New York: Free Press.

Eckel, Bruce. 2000. *Thinking in Java, 2nd ed*. Upper Saddle River, NJ: Prentice Hall.

Econometric Software. 2002. *LIMDEP: Version 8*. Bellport, NY: Econometric Software, Inc.

Epstein, Joshua M. and Robert Axtell. 1996. *Growing Artificial Societies: Social Science from the Bottom Up*. Washington, DC: Brookings Institution Press.

Erbring, Lutz and Alice A. Young. 1979. Individuals and Social Structure: Contextual Effects As Endogenous Feedback. *Sociological Methods and Research* 7: 396–430.

Eulau, Heinz. 1963. *The Behavioral Persuasion in Politics*. New York: Random House.

References

Eulau, Heinz. 1986. *Politics, Self, and Society: A Theme and Variations*. Cambridge, MA: Harvard University Press.

Fabrigar, Leandre R. and Jon A. Krosnick. 1995. Attitude Importance and the False Consensus Effect. *Personality and Social Psychology Bulletin* 21: 468–79.

Fazio, Russell H. 1990. A Practical Guide to the Use of Response Latency in Social Psychological Research. In Clyde Hendrick and Margaret S. Clark, eds., *Research Methods in Personality and Social Psychology*. Newbury Park, CA: Sage Publications, 74–97.

Fazio, Russell H. 1995. Attitudes as Object-Evaluation Associations: Determinants, Consequences, and Correlates of Attitude Accessibility. In R. E. Petty and J. A. Krosnick, eds. *Attitude Strength: Antecedents and Consequences*. Mahwah, NJ: Erlbaum, 247–82.

Fazio, Russell H. and Carol J. Williams. 1986. Attitude Accessibility as a Moderator of the Attitude-Perception and Attitude-Behavior Relations: An Investigation of the 1984 Presidential Election. *Journal of Personality and Social Psychology* 51: 505–14.

Fazio, Russell H., Jeaw-Mei Chen, Elizabeth C. McDonel, and Steven J. Sherman. 1982. Attitude Accessibility, Attitude-Behavior Consistency, and the Strength of the Object-Evaluation Association. *Journal of Experimental and Social Psychology* 18: 339–57.

Fazio, Russell H., D. M. Sanbonmatsu, M. C. Powell, and F. R. Kardes. 1986. On the Automatic Activation of Attitudes. *Journal of Personality and Social Psychology* 50: 229–38.

Festinger, Leon. 1957. *A Theory of Cognitive Dissonance*. Palo Alto, CA: Stanford University Press.

Festinger, Leon, Stanley Schachter, and Kurt Back. 1950. *Social Pressures in Informal Groups: A Study of Human Factors in Housing*. Palo Alto, CA: Stanford University Press.

Festinger, Leon, Kurt Back, Stanley Schachter, Harold H. Kelley, and John Thibaut. 1950. *Theory and Experiment in Social Communication*. Ann Arbor, MI: Research Center for Dynamics, Institute for Social Research, University of Michigan.

Finifter, Ada. 1974. The Friendship Group as a Protective Environment for Political Deviants. *American Political Science Review* 68: 607–25.

Fiorina, Morris P. 1981. *Retrospective Voting in American National Elections*. New Haven, CT: Yale University Press.

Fishkin, James S. 1991. *Democracy and Deliberation: New Directions for Democratic Reform*. New Haven, CT: Yale University Press.

Fishkin, James S. 1995. *The Voice of the People: Public Opinion and Democracy*. New Haven, CT: Yale University Press.

Fiske, Susan T. and Shelley E. Taylor. 1991. *Social Cognition*. 2nd ed. New York: McGraw-Hill.

French, John R. P. Jr. 1956. A Formal Theory of Social Power. *The Psychological Review* 63: 181–94.

Friedkin, Noah E. 1986. A Formal Theory of Social Power. *Journal of Mathematical Sociology* 12: 103–26.

Friedkin, Noah E. 1998. *A Structural Theory of Social Influence*. New York: Cambridge University Press.

Friedkin, Noah E. and Eugene C. Johnsen. 1990. Social Influence and Opinions. *Journal of Mathematical Sociology* 15: 193–205.

References

Fuchs, Lawrence H. 1955. American Jews and the Presidential Vote. *American Political Science Review* 49: 385–401.

Fuchs, Lawrence H. 1956. *The Political Behavior of American Jews*. Glencoe, IL: Free Press.

Gamm, Gerald H. 1999. *Urban Exodus: Why the Jews left Boston and the Catholics Stayed*. Cambridge, MA: Harvard University Press.

Gelman, Andrew, John B. Carlin, Hal S. Stern, and Donald B. Rubin. 1995. *Bayesian Data Analysis*. London: Chapman and Hall.

Gelman, Andrew and Gary King. 1993. Why Are American Presidential Election Campaign Polls So Variable When Votes Are So Predictable? *British Journal of Political Science* 23: 409–51.

Gibson, James L. 2001. Social Networks, Civil Society, and the Prospects for Consolidating Russia's Democratic Transition. *American Journal of Political Science* 45: 51–69.

Gibson, James L. 1992. The Political Consequences of Intolerance: Cultural Conformity and Political Freedom. *American Political Science Review* 86: 338–56.

Gill, Jeff. 2002. *Bayesian Methods: A Social and Behavioral Sciences Approach*. Boca Raton, FL: Chapman and Hall.

Gillespie, John H. 1998. *Population Genetics*. Baltimore, MD: Johns Hopkins University Press.

Granberg, Donald. 1987. Candidate Preference, Membership Group, and Estimates of Voting Behavior. *Social Cognition* 5: 323–35.

Granberg, Donald and Edward Brent. 1983. When Prophecy Bends: The Preference-Expectation Link in U.S. Presidential Elections. *Journal of Personality and Social Psychology* 45: 477–91.

Granovetter, Mark. 1973. The Strength of Weak Ties. *American Journal of Sociology* 78: 1360–80.

Granovetter, Mark. 1978. Threshold Models of Collective Behavior. *American Journal of Sociology* 83: 1420–43.

Granovetter, Mark. 1985. Economic Action and Social Structure: The Problem of Embeddedness. *American Journal of Sociology* 91: 481–510.

Greene, William H. 2000. *Econometric Analysis, 4th ed*. Upper Saddle River, NJ: Prentice Hall.

Greig, J. Michael. 2002. The End of Geography? Globalization, Communications, and Culture in the International System. *Journal of Conflict Resolution* 46: 225–43.

Gutmann, Amy and Dennis Thompson. 1996. *Democracy and Disagreement*. Cambridge MA: Belknap.

Harary, Frank. 1959. A Criterion for Unanimity in French's Theory of Social Power. In *Studies in Social Power*, ed., Dorwin Cartwright. Ann Arbor, MI: Institute for Social Research, 168–82.

Hegselmann, Rainer, Andreas Flache, and Volker Moller. 1999. Cellular Automata Models of Solidarity and Opinion Formation: Sensitivity Analysis. In *Social Science Microsimulation: Tools for Modeling, Parameter Optimization, and Sensitivity Analysis*, eds., Ramzi Suleiman, Klaus G. Troitzsch, and Nigel Gilbert. Heidelberg, Germany: Springer, 151–78.

Hegselmann, Rainer and Ulrich Krause. 2002. Opinion Dynamics and Bounded Confidence: Models, Analysis, and Simulation. *Journal of Artificial Societies and Social Simulation* 5(3), http://jasss.soc.surrey.ac.uk/5/3/2.html.

References

Homans, George C. 1950. *The Human Group.* New York: Harcourt, Brace and Company.

Huckfeldt, Robert. 1983. Social Contexts, Social Networks, and Urban Neighborhoods: Environmental Constraints upon Friendship Choice. *American Journal of Sociology* (November): 651–69.

Huckfeldt, Robert. 1986. *Politics in Context.* New York: Agathon.

Huckfeldt, Robert. 1990. Structure, Indeterminacy, and Chaos: A Case for Sociological Law. *Journal of Theoretical Politics,* 2: 413–33.

Huckfeldt, Robert. 2001. The Social Communication of Political Expertise. *American Journal of Political Science* 45: 425–38.

Huckfeldt, Robert, Paul A. Beck, R. Dalton, and Jeffrey Levine. 1995. Political Environments, Cohesive Social Groups, and the Communication of Public Opinion. *American Journal of Political Science* 39: 1025–54.

Huckfeldt, Robert, Paul Allen Beck, Russell J. Dalton, Jeffrey Levine, and William Morgan. 1998. Ambiguity, Distorted Messages, and Nested Environmental Effects on Political Communication. *Journal of Politics* 60: 996–1030.

Huckfeldt, Robert, Ken'ichi Ikeda, and Franz Urban Pappi. 2003. Agreement and Disagreement in Democratic Politics: Deliberation Among Citizens in Germany, Japan, and the United States. Prepared for delivery at the annual meeting of the American Political Science Association, Philadelphia, August, 2003.

Huckfeldt, Robert, Paul E. Johnson, and John Sprague. 2002. Political Environments, Political Dynamics, and the Survival of Disagreement. *Journal of Politics* 64: 1–21.

Huckfeldt, Robert and Carol Weitzel Kohfeld. 1989. *Race and the Decline of Class in American Politics.* Urbana, IL: University of Illinois Press.

Huckfeldt, Robert, Jeffrey Levine, William Morgan, and John Sprague. 1998. Election Campaigns, Social Communication, and the Accessibility of Perceived Discussant Preference. *Political Behavior* 20: 263–94.

Huckfeldt, Robert, Jeanette Morehouse Mendez, and Tracy Osborn. 2004. Disagreement, Ambivalence, and Engagement: The Political Consequences of Heterogeneous Networks. *Political Psychology* 25: 65–96.

Huckfeldt, Robert, Eric Plutzer, and John Sprague. 1993. Alternative Contexts of Political Behavior: Churches, Neighborhoods, and Individuals. *Journal of Politics* 55: 365–81.

Huckfeldt, Robert and John Sprague. 1995. *Citizens, Politics, and Social Communication.* New York: Cambridge University Press.

Huckfeldt, Robert and John Sprague. 1987. Networks in Context: The Social Flow of Political Information. *American Political Science Review* 81:1197–216.

Huckfeldt, Robert, John Sprague, and Jeffrey Levine. 2000. The Dynamics of Collective Deliberation in the 1996 Election: Campaign Effects on Accessibility, Certainty, and Accuracy. *American Political Science Review* 94: 641–51.

Ikeda, Ken'ichi and Robert Huckfeldt. 2001. Political Communication and Disagreement among Citizens in Japan and the United States. *Political Behavior* 23: 23–52.

Johnson, Paul E. 1996. Unraveling in a Variety of Institutional Settings. *Journal of Theoretical Politics* 8: 299–330.

Johnson, Paul E. 1999. Simulation Modeling in Political Science. *American Behavioral Scientist* 42: 1509–30.

Johnson, Paul E. 2002. Agent-Based Modeling: What I Learned From the Artificial Stock Market. *Social Science Computer Review* 20: 174–86.

References

Johnson, Paul E. and Alex Lancaster. 2000. *Swarm User Guide*. Santa Fe, NM: Swarm Development Group. http://www.swarm.org/swarmdocs/userbook/userbook.html.

Joslyn, Mark R. 1998. Opinion Change After the Election. Paper delivered at the annual meeting of the American Political Science Association, Boston, September.

Kahneman, Daniel and Amos Tversky. 1973. On the Psychology of Prediction. *Psychological Review* 80: 237–51.

Katz, Elihu. 1957. The Two-Step Flow of Communication: An Up-to-Date Report on a Hypothesis. *Public Opinion Quarterly* 21: 61–78.

Katz, Elihu and Paul F. Lazarsfeld. 1955. *Personal Influence: The Part Played by People in the Flow of Mass Communications*. Glencoe, IL: Free Press.

Kauffman, Stuart. 1993. *Origins of Order: Self-Organization and Selection in Evolution*. New York: Oxford University Press.

Kauffman, Stuart. 1995. *At Home in the Universe: The Search for the Laws of Self-Organization and Complexity*. New York: Oxford University Press.

Kelley, Stanley. 1983. *Interpreting Elections*. Princeton, NJ: Princeton University Press.

Kessell, John. 1988. *Presidential Campaign Politics: Coalition Strategies and Citizen Response*. Chicago, IL: Dorsey.

King, Gary. 1997. *A Solution to the Ecological Inference Problem*. Princeton, NJ: Princeton University Press.

Knoke, David. 1990. *Political Networks: The Structural Perspective*. New York: Cambridge University Press.

Krosnick, Jon A. and Richard E. Petty. 1995. Attitude Strength: An Overview. In Richard E. Petty and Jon A. Krosnick, eds. *Attitude Strength: Antecedents and Consequences*. Mahwah, NJ: Erlbaum, 1–24.

Krueger, Joachim and Russell W. Clement. 1994. The Truly False Consensus Effect: An Ineradicable and Egocentric Bias in Social Perception. *Journal of Personality and Social Psychology* 67: 596–610.

Krueger, Joachim and Joanna S. Ziegler. 1993. Social Categorization and the Truly False Consensus Effect. *Journal of Personality and Social Psychology* 65 (4): 670–80.

Kunda, Ziva. 1999. *Social Cognition*. Cambridge, MA: MIT Press.

Langton, Kenneth P. and Ronald Rapoport. 1975. Social Structure, Social Context, and Partisan Mobilization: Urban Workers in Chile. *Comparative Political Studies* 8: 318–44.

Latané, Bibb. 1981. The Psychology of Social Impact. *American Psychologist* 36: 343–56.

Latané, Bibb and Hiroaki Morio. 2000. Maintaining Diversity: Simulating the Role of Nonliniarity and Discreteness in Dynamic Social Impact. In *Social Science Microsimulation: Tools for Modeling, Parameter Optimization, and Sensitivity Analysis*, eds., Ramzi Suleiman, Klaus G. Troitzsch, Nigel Gilbert. Heidelberg, Germany: Springer, 196–217.

Latané, Bibb, Andrzej Nowak, and James H. Liu. 1994. Measuring Emergent Social Phenomena: Dynamism, Polarization, and Clustering as Order Parameters of Dynamic Social Systems. *Behavioral Science* 39:1–24.

Latané, Bibb and Andrzej Nowak. 1997. Self-Organizing Social Systems: Necessary and Sufficient Conditions for the Emergence of Clustering, Consolidation, and Continuing Diversity. In *Progress in Communication Science, Volume 13*, eds., George Barnet and Franklin J. Boster. Westport, CT: Ablex, 43–74.

References

Laumann, Edward O. and Franz Urban Pappi. 1976. *Networks of Collective Action: A Perspective on Community Influence Systems*. New York: Academic Press.

Lavine, Howard. 2001. The Electoral Consequences of Ambivalence Toward Presidential Candidates. *American Journal of Political Science* 45: 915–29.

Lazarsfeld, Paul, Bernard Berelson, and Hazel Gaudet. 1948. *The People's Choice*. New York: Columbia University Press.

Levine, Jeffrey, Edward C. Carmines, and Robert Huckfeldt. 1997. The Rise of Ideology in the Post-New Deal Party System, 1972–92. *American Politics Quarterly* 25: 19–34.

Lichbach, Mark I. and Alan S. Zuckerman. eds. 1997. *Comparative Politics: Rationality, Culture and Structure*. New York: Cambridge University Press.

Lipset, Seymour Martin. 1981. *Political Man. Expanded edition*. Baltimore, MD: Johns Hopkins University Press.

Lodge, Milton. 1995. Toward a Procedural Model of Candidate Evaluation. In *Political Judgment: Structure and Process*, eds., Milton Lodge and Kathleen M. McGraw. Ann Arbor, MI: University of Michigan Press, 111–40.

Lodge, Milton and Marco Steenbergen with Shawn Brau. 1995. The Responsive Voter: Campaign Information and the Dynamics of Candidate Evaluation. *American Political Science Review* 89: 309–26.

Lodge, Milton and Charles Taber. 2000. Three Steps Toward a Theory of Motivated Political Reasoning. In Anthony Lupia, Mathew D. McCubbins, and Samuel L. Popkin, eds. *Elements of Reason: Cognition, Choice, and the Bounds of Rationality*. New York: Cambridge University Press.

Long, J. Scott. 1997. *Regression Models for Categorical and Limited Dependent Variables*. Thousand Oaks, CA: Sage.

Lupia, Arthur and Mathew D. McCubbins. 1998. *The Democratic Dilemma*. New York: Cambridge University Press.

MacKuen, Michael B. 1990. Speaking of Politics: Individual Conversational Choice, Public Opinion, and the Prospects for Deliberative Democracy. In John A. Ferejohn and James H. Kuklinski, eds. *Information and Democratic Processes*. Urbana, IL: University of Illinois Press, 59–99.

Marsden, Peter V. and Noah E. Friedkin. 1994. Network Studies of Social Influence. In Stanley Wasserman and Joseph Galaskiewicz, eds. *Advances in Social Network Analysis*. Thousand Oaks, CA: Sage 3–25.

Marsden, Peter V. 1981. Introducing Influence Processes into a System of Collective Decisions. *American Journal of Sociology* 86: 1203–35.

May, Robert M. 1973. *Stability and Complexity in Model Ecosystems*. Princeton, NJ: Princeton University Press.

McPhee, William N. with Robert B. Smith and Jack Ferguson. 1963. A Theory of Informal Social Influence. In William N. McPhee, *Formal Theories of Mass Behavior*. New York: Free Press.

Mendelberg, Tali. 2002. The Deliberative Citizen: Theory and Evidence. In Michael Delli Carpini, Leonie Huddy, and Robert Y. Shapiro, eds., *Political Decision-Making, Deliberation and Participation: Research in Micropolitics*, Vol. 6. Greenwich, CT: JAI Press, 151–93.

Miller, Warren. 1956. One Party Politics and the Voter. *American Political Science Review* 50: 707–25.

Minar, Nelson, Roger Burkhart, Chris Langton, and Manor Askenazi. 1996. *The Swarm Simulation System: A Toolkit for Building Multi-Agent Simulations*. Santa Fe, NM: Santa Fe Institute Technical Report 96-04-2.

References

Mollié, A. 1996. Bayesian Mapping of Disease. In W. R. Gilks, S. Richardson, and D. J. Spiegelhalter, eds. *Markov Chain Monte Carlo in Practice*. London: Chapman and Hall, 359–79.

Mondak, Jaffery J. and Diana C. Mutz. 2001. Involuntary Association: How the Workplace Contributes to American Civic Life. Presented at the Annual Meeting of the Midwest Political Science Association.

Moscovici, Serge, Angelica Mucchi-Faina, and Anne Maas, eds. 1994. *Minority Influence*. Chicago, IL: Nelson Hall.

Mutz, Diana. 2002a. Cross-Cutting Social Networks: Testing Democratic Theory in Practice. *American Political Science Review* 96: 111–26.

Mutz, Diana. 2002b. The Consequences of Cross-Cutting Networks for Political Participation. *American Journal of Political Science* 46: 838–55.

Mutz, Diana C. and Paul S. Martin. 2001. Facilitating Communication across Lines of Political Difference: The Role of Mass Media. *American Political Science Review* 95: 97–114.

Nowak, Andrzej, and Maciej Lewenstein. 1996. Modeling Social Change with Cellular Automata. In Ranier Hegselmann, Ulrich Mueller, and Klaus Troitzsch, eds., *Modeling and Simulation in the Social Sciences from a Philosophy of Science Point of View*. Amsterdam, Netherlands: Kluwer, 249–85.

Nowak, Andrzej, Jacek Szamrej, and Bibb Latané. 1990. From Private Attitude to Public Opinion: A Dynamic Theory of Social Impact. *Psychological Review* 97: 362–76.

Page, Benjamin I. and Robert Y. Shapiro. 1992. *The Rational Public*. Chicago, IL: University of Chicago Press.

Pappi, Franz Urban. 2001. Soziale Netzwerke. In Bernhard Schäfers and Wolfgang Zapf, eds. *Handwörterbuch zur Gesellschaft Deutschlands*. Opladen, Germany: Leske and Budrich, 605–16.

Parunak, V., R. Savit, and R. Riolo. 1998. Agent-Based Modeling vs. Equation-Based Modeling: A Case Study and Users Guide. *Proceedings of Workshop on Multi-agent systems and Agent-based Simulation (MABS'98)*, Heidelberg, Germany: Springer. Center for Electronic Commerce Paper CEC-0 115.

Przeworski, Adam. 1974. Contextual Models of Political Behavior. *Political Methodology* 1: 27–61.

Przeworski, Adam and John Sprague. 1986. *Paper Stones: A History of Electoral Socialism*. Chicago: University of Chicago Press.

Putnam, Robert D. 1966. Political Attitudes and the Local Community. *American Political Science Review* 60: 640–54.

Putnam, Robert D. 2000. *Bowling Alone: The Collapse and Revival of American Community*. New York: Simon and Schuster.

Putnam, Robert D. with Robert Lenardi and Raffaella Y. Nanetti. 1993. *Making Democracy Work: Civic Traditions in Modern Italy*. Princeton, NJ: Princeton University Press.

Rahn, Wendy M., Jon A. Krosnick, and Marijke Breuning. 1994. Rationalization and Derivation Processes in Survey Studies of Candidate Evaluation. *American Journal of Political Science* 38: 582–600.

Rawls, John. 1996. *Political Liberalism*. New York: Columbia University Press.

Ray, Thomas. 1994. Evolution and Complexity. In George A. Cowan, David Pines, and David Meltzer, eds. *Complexity: Metaphors, Models, and Reality*. Reading, MA: Addison-Wesley, 161–76.

Rogers, William. 1993. Regression Standard Errors in Clustered Samples. *Stata Technical Bulletin* 13: 19–23.

References

Ross, Lee. 1990. Recognizing the Role of Construal Processes. In *The Legacy of Solomon Asch: Essays in Cognition and Social Psychology*, ed., Irvin Rock. Hillsdale, NJ: Lawrence Erlbaum Associates, 77–96.

Ross, Lee, Gunter Bierbrauer, and Susan Hoffman. 1976. The Role of Attribution Processes in Conformity and Dissent. *American Psychologist* 31: 148–57.

Schelling, Thomas C. 1978. *Micromotives and Macrobehavior*. New York: Norton.

Schmitt-Beck, Rüdiger. 2003. Mass Communication, Personal Communication and Vote Choice: The Filter Hypothesis of Media Influence in Comparative Perspective. *British Journal of Political Science* 33: 233–59.

Shannon. C. E. 1949. *The Mathematical Theory of Communication*. Champaign-Urbana, IL: University of Illinois Press.

Shibanai, Yasufumi, Satoko Yasuno, Itaru Ishiguro. 2001. Effects of Global Information Feedback on Diversity. *Journal of Conflict Resolution* 45: 80–96.

Simon, Herbert A. 1985. Human Nature in Politics: The Dialogue of Psychology with Political Science. *American Political Science Review* 79: 293–304.

Smith, Eric R. A. N. 1980. The Levels of Conceptualization: False Measures of Ideological Sophistication. *The American Political Science Review* 74: 685–96.

Smith, John Maynard. 1974. *Models in Ecology*. Cambridge, England: Cambridge University Press.

Smith, John Maynard. 1982. *Evolution and the Theory of Games*. Cambridge, England: Cambridge University Press.

Sniderman, Paul M. 1993. The New Look in Public Opinion Research. In A. W. Finifter, ed., *Political Science: The State of the Discipline II*. Washington, D.C.: American Political Science Association, 281–303.

Sniderman, Paul M., Richard A. Brody, and Philip E. Tetlock. 1991. *Reasoning and Choice: Explorations in Political Psychology*. New York: Cambridge University Press.

Sprague, John. 1976. Estimating a Boudon Type Contextual Model: Some Practical and Theoretical Problems of Measurement. *Political Methodology* 3: 333–53.

StataCorp. 2001. *Stata Statistical Sofware: Release 7.0*. College Station, TX: Stata Corporation.

Sullivan, John L., James Piereson, and George E. Marcus. 1982. *Political Tolerance and American Democracy*. Chicago, IL: University of Chicago Press.

Thompson, Megan M., Mark P. Zanna, and Dale W. Griffin. 1995. Let's Not Be Indifferent About (Attitudinal) Ambivalence. In Richard E. Petty and Jon A. Krosnick, eds., *Attitude Strength: Antecedents and Consequences*. Mahwah, NJ: Erlbaum, 361–86.

Tversky, Amos and Daniel Kahneman. 1974. Judgment Under Uncertainty: Heuristics and Biases. *Science* 185: 1124–31.

Visser, Penny S. and Robert R. Mirabile. 2002. *Attitudes in the Social Context: The Impact of Network Composition on Individual-Level Attitude Strength*. Chicago, IL: University of Chicago. Unpublished manuscript.

Wakefield, J. C., N. G. Best, and L. A. Waller. 2000. Bayesian Approaches to Disease Mapping. In P. Elliott, J. C. Wakefield, N. G. Best, and D. J. Briggs, eds., *Spatial Epidemiology: Methods and Applications*. Oxford: Oxford University Press, 104–27.

Waldrop, M. Mitchell. 1992. *Complexity: The Emerging Science at the Edge of Order and Chaos*. New York: Simon and Schuster.

Warner, Sam Bass. 1968. *The Private City: Philadelphia in Three Periods of Its Growth*. Philadelphia, PA: University of Pennsylvania Press.

References

Warner, Sam Bass. 1978. *Streetcar Suburbs: The Process of Growth in Boston, 1870–1900*. Cambridge, MA: Harvard University Press.

Watts, Duncan J. 1999. *Small Worlds: The Dynamics of Networks between Order and Randomness*. Princeton, NJ: Princeton University Press.

Watts, Duncan J. and Steven H. Strogatz. 1998. Collective Dynamics of "Small World" Networks. *Nature* 393: 440–2.

Weber, Max. 1966. On the Concept of Sociology and the Meaning of Social Conduct. In *Basic Concepts in Sociology*, translated by H. P. Secher. New York: Citadel Press, 29–58. Originally published posthumously in 1926 as Chapter 1 of *Wirtschaft und Gessellschaft*.

Weisberg, Herbert F. 1980. A Multidimensional Conceptualization of Party Identification. *Political Behavior* 2: 33–60.

White, Harrison. 1970. *Chains of Opportunity: System Models of Mobility in Organizations*. Cambridge, MA: Harvard University Press.

Zaller, John R. 1992. *The Nature and Origins of Mass Opinion*. New York: Cambridge University Press.

Zaller, John R. and Stanley Feldman. 1992. A Simple Theory of the Survey Response: Answering Questions versus Revealing Preferences. *American Journal of Political Science* 36: 579–616.

Index

Index

Books in the Series